POST-COMMUNIST DEMOCRATIZATION

Democracy is not just a matter of constitutions, parliaments, elections, parties, and the rule of law. In order to see if or how democracy works, we must attend to what people make of it, and what they think they are doing as they engage with politics, or as politics engages them. This book examines the way democracy and democratization are thought about and lived by people in China, Russia, and eleven other countries in the post-communist world. It shows how democratic politics (and sometimes authoritarian politics) works in these countries, and generates insights into the prospects for different kinds of political development. The authors explore the implications for what is probable and possible in terms of trajectories of political reform, and examine four roads to democratization: liberal, republican, participatory, and statist. The book will be of interest to students and scholars of comparative politics, political theory, and post-communist studies.

JOHN S. DRYZEK is Professor of Social and Political Theory in the Research School of Social Sciences at the Australian National University. He has also taught at the Universities of Oregon and Melbourne. He is the author of a number of books on environmental politics and democracy, most recently *Deliberative Democracy and Beyond* (2000), and *Democracy in Capitalist Times* (1996).

LESLIE TEMPLEMAN HOLMES is Professor of Political Science at the University of Melbourne. His recent books are *Post-Communism* (1997) and *The End of Communist Power* (1993). In August 2000, he was elected President of the International Council for Central and East European Studies (ICCEES) for a five-year term.

Series Editor
Robert E. Goodin
Research School of Social Sciences
Australian National University

Advisory Editors
Brian Barry, Russell Hardin, Carole Pateman, Barry Weingast, Stephen Elkin, Claus Offe, Susan Rose-Ackerman

Social scientists have rediscovered institutions. They have been increasingly concerned with the myriad ways in which social and political institutions shape the patterns of individual interactions which produce social phenomena. They are equally concerned with the ways in which those institutions emerge from such interactions.

This series is devoted to the exploration of the more normative aspects of these issues. What makes one set of institutions better than another? How, if at all, might we move from the less desirable set of institutions to a more desirable set? Alongside the questions of what institutions we would design, if we were designing them afresh, are pragmatic questions of how we can best get from here to there: from our present institutions to new revitalized ones.

Theories of institutional design is insistently multidisciplinary and interdisciplinary, both in the institutions on which it focuses, and in the methodologies used to study them. There are interesting sociological questions to be asked about legal institutions, interesting legal questions to be asked about economic institutions, and interesting social, economic, and legal questions to be asked about political institutions. By juxtaposing these approaches in print, this series aims to enrich normative discourse surrounding important issues of designing and redesigning, shaping and reshaping the social, political, and economic institutions of contemporary society.

Other books in this series
Robert E. Goodin (editor), *The Theory of Institutional Design*
Brent Fisse and John Braithwaite, *Corporations, Crime, and Accountability*
Itai Sened, *The Political Institution of Private Property*
Bo Rothstein, *Just Institutions Matter*
Jon Elster, Claus Offe, and Ulrich Preuss, *Institutional Design in Post-Communist Societies: Rebuilding the Ship at Sea*
Mark Bovens, *The Quest for Responsibility*
Geoffrey Brennan and Alan Hamlin, *Democratic Devices and Desires*
Adrienne Heritier, *Policy-Making and Diversity in Europe: Escape from Deadlock*
Eric Patashnik, *Putting Trust in the US Budget: Federal Trust Funds and the Politics of Commitment*

POST-COMMUNIST DEMOCRATIZATION

Political discourses across thirteen countries

JOHN S. DRYZEK
Australian National University

and

LESLIE TEMPLEMAN HOLMES
University of Melbourne

CAMBRIDGE
UNIVERSITY PRESS

PUBLISHED BY THE PRESS SYNDICATE OF THE UNIVERSITY OF CAMBRIDGE
The Pitt Building, Trumpington Street, Cambridge CB2 1RP, United Kingdom

CAMBRIDGE UNIVERSITY PRESS
The Edinburgh Building, Cambridge, CB2 2RU, UK
40 West 20th Street, New York, NY 10011-4211, USA
477 Williamstown Road, Port Melbourne, VIC 3207, Australia
Ruiz de Alacón 13, 28014 Madrid, Spain
Dock House, The Waterfront, Cape Town 8001, South Africa

http://www.cambridge.org

First published 2002

Printed in the United Kingdom at the University Press, Cambridge

Typeface Minion 10.5/12 pt.   *System* LATEX 2_ε [TB]

A catalogue record for this book is available from the British Library

Library of Congress Cataloguing-in-Publication Data
Dryzek, John S., 1953–
Post-communist democratization: political discourses across thirteen countries / John S.
Dryzek and Leslie Templeman Holmes.
     p.   cm. – (Theories of institutional design)
Includes bibliographical references and index.
ISBN 0 521 80664 X – ISBN 0 521 00138 2 (pb.)
1. Europe, Eastern – Politics and government – 1989–   2. Post-communism – Europe, Eastern.
3. Democratization – Europe, Eastern.   I. Holmes, Leslie Templeman.   II. Title.   III. Series.
JN96.A58 D79   2002
320.947 – dc21   2001043249

ISBN 0 521 80664 X hardback
ISBN 0 521 00138 2 paperback

Contents

Illustrations

Preface

If we want to know what democracy means in practice, then we must look at what people make of it, in new, old, and proto-democracies alike. This study maps the way democracy and democratization are thought about and lived by people in the post-communist world – including the people for whom the idea of democracy has negative associations. We seek not just to understand how democratic politics is or is not conceptualized and practiced in these countries, but also to generate insights into the prospects for democratic development and institutional change. Thus we relate an account of the discursive field of democracy in each society to its histories and contexts (up to and including late 2000, when the final version of the typescript was completed), and explore the implications for what is probable and possible when it comes to trajectories of political reform. Political development and discourses of democracy (and authoritarianism) interact: discourses help determine what is possible and likely in political development, which in turn can change the terms of discourse.

In these pages we develop and test no general theory of democratization – such a theory is probably as elusive as Macintyre's (1973) general theory of holes. We are interested in explanation, and are happy both to deploy and to develop theory in its service. But we are also interested in interpretation and reconstruction. We believe that there is such a thing as human agency in institutional redesign, which means rejecting any kind of determinism, be it the cultural determinism of a country's past or the theoretical determinism of law-like generalizations about democratic development. The discourses of democracy we identify in each country constitute both constraints upon and resources for those interested in different kinds of political reform. They contain interpretations of the past, and possibilities for the future.

This project was anticipated in 1989 by John Dryzek as he observed the "Autumn of the People" in Central and Eastern Europe at the same time as he was developing the basic methodology in a study of the United States (Dryzek and Berejikian, 1993). A move to the University of Melbourne in 1995 facilitated cooperation with post-communist specialist Leslie Holmes, and funding was soon secured. The project began in earnest in Budapest in September 1996 with the recruitment of project assistants for the various countries we wanted to cover – and more! We thank the Political Science Department of the Central European University for hosting that first meeting, and also for facilitating subsequent meetings of project participants. At CEU, Gabor Toka smoothed our path initially, and Zsolt Enyedi was invaluable in helping us recruit participants and giving them a sense of what this sort of empirical research entailed. In October 1998 we gathered all our Europe- and North America-based participants in a workshop at the Robert Schuman Centre at the European University Institute in Florence. We thank the Schuman Centre for its hospitality, and especially Monique Cavallari for helping to organize the Florence workshop.

All the fieldwork was carried out by our project assistants: Tigran Melkonian and Arseny Saporov for Armenia; Igor Severine for Belarus; Gallina Andronova, Antoaneta Dimitrova, and Maria Spirova for Bulgaria; Stanislava Benesova for Czechia; Otar Kipshidze and Giorgi Papuashvili for Georgia; Calin Goina for Moldova; Anna Giedryś and Piotr Kazmierkiewicz for Poland; Zoltan Szasz Alpar, Bogdan Chiritoiu, Bogdan Nica, and Mihály Szilágyi-Gal for Romania; Pavel Ananienko, Nikolai Chelestov, Tatiana Rogovskaia, and Alexander Vistgoff for Russia; Stefan Auer for Slovakia; Victor Hohots and Kyrylo Loukerenko for Ukraine; Siniša Nikolin and Vladislav Sotirović for Yugoslavia. The obstacles to the field research were sometimes quite challenging, and we thank all our assistants for their persistence and skill in bringing the fieldwork to a successful conclusion.

Beyond the individuals we have already mentioned, we thank Jeffrey Berejikian, Steven Brown, Graeme Gill, Robert Goodin, Åse Grødland, Bruce Headey, Claus Offe, Tony Phillips, Denise Powers, Richard Rose, and Janos Simon for advice and support. We also thank the four anonymous reviewers selected by Cambridge University Press. The book is better for their advice. The research was supported by Australian Research Council large grant number A79601177. The logistics of organizing a thirteen-country study at very long distance were formidable. The project was made possible by e-mail links to all the countries in this study, and John Dryzek spent many hours in front of a computer in the middle of the night, occasionally getting a sense of what life must have been like for a Cold War spymaster as he pondered cryptic communications from distant places. But his family could hardly tell any difference. In Melbourne, Wendy Ruffles was always helpful and cheerful in organizing financial transactions to far-flung places.

Aside from the Florence workshop, portions of the research were presented at the International Conference on Communist and Post-Communist Studies at the University of Melbourne in 1998, the Politics Department at Monash University, the Political Science Department at the University of Minnesota, the Political Science Program in the Research School of Social Sciences at the Australian National University, and the School of Public and International Affairs at Virginia Polytechnic Institute and State University.

A note on authorship credit

The research assistants who helped to draft chapters are listed as full co-authors for the appropriate country chapter. In addition, for useful inputs during the course of our writing we would like to thank Vladislav Sotirović for the Yugoslavia chapter, Gallina Andronova for the Bulgaria chapter, and Piotr Kazmierkiewicz for the Poland chapter. The Chinese study had a history somewhat different from the other chapters, in that it was designed and executed by Yali Peng (with advice from John Dryzek). The China chapter was first published under Yali's name in *Modern China* (Peng, 1998); the version that appears here was revised by John Dryzek and Leslie Holmes to make it consistent with the approach of this volume.

PART I

Introduction

1

The discourses of democratic transition

In 1989, the "Autumn of the People" ushered in high hopes concerning the possibilities for democratic transformation in the countries of the soon-to-be-post-communist world. Suddenly the Soviet bloc was no more – and within two years the Soviet Union itself would be gone too. While the revolution took different forms in different countries, in many ways 1989 was the hour of those who had labored in oppositional civil society, often underground, sometimes in prison. Suddenly they were joined on the streets by many others. This fine democratic hour seemed to hold lessons even for the more established liberal democracies in the West, which featured at that time a much less heroic kind of democratic politics, beholden to routine, ambition, material interest, and money. For a moment, democracy in its most inspirational form seemed to be found in the East rather than in the West.

Many of these high hopes have now withered. It is one thing to overthrow an exhausted system (or even just to walk into the vacuum left by its collapse), quite another to deal on a day-to-day basis with ethnic tensions, the legacy of economic stagnation, a global capitalist political economy that soon turns out to be ungenerous and unforgiving, severe environmental pollution, and inherited creaking state bureaucracies. Simultaneous negotiation of institutional, economic, and attitudinal transition has often proven extraordinarily difficult, especially in the presence of ethnic conflicts and controversies over borders and boundaries.[1] Moreover, each of these three

---

[1] For an argument that simultaneity can actually facilitate transition by focusing reformers' attention on everything that needs to be done and how different aspects can and should be interrelated, see Di Palma, 1993. For a counterargument, see Binder, *et al.*, 1971 (we were led to these sources by Ramet, 1997).

dimensions of transition has several aspects. Institutional transition refers to legal, social, and educational institutions, as well as governmental ones. Attitudinal transition covers attitudes not only toward new institutions and laws, but also toward changing class structures, identities, and international allegiances. Since 1989 the post-communist world has witnessed plenty in the way of economic catastrophe, ethnic warfare, civil conflict, political instability, and lingering and sometimes resurgent authoritarianism. Of course, some countries have fared much better than others on the various dimensions of transition; but whether or not there is light at the end of them, many tunnels have had to be negotiated, and remain to be negotiated.

By now there exists a number of studies of the experience of political and economic transition in post-communist societies. So why add another at this juncture, more than a decade after those heady days of 1989? We believe we do have something different, novel, and important to offer. We present here a study that is based on the way democracy and democratization are conceptualized and lived by ordinary people and political activists in the post-communist world – including those for whom democracy is a negative symbol – for democracy is not just, or perhaps even mainly, a matter of introducing institutions such as a constitution, parliament, elections, a party system, and a legal system. Such institutional hardware is vital, but so too is the institutional software. That is, to understand if or how democracy works, we must attend to what people *make* of it, and what they think they are doing as they engage politics, or politics engages them. Here, a glance at a different time and place is instructive. Attempts to parachute Westminster-style institutions into ex-British colonies in Africa in the 1950s and 1960s produced only parodies of the original, mainly because those involved with these institutions had little or no exposure to the habits, traditions, and dispositions necessary to make these particular institutions function.

What people make of democratic institutions matters precisely because what is at issue is democracy, unique among the political forms in human history. Such a question is much less pressing for political systems in which what the people think as they engage or are engaged by politics is mostly irrelevant.

It is common to begin books about democracy with the observation that democracy as a concept today meets something approaching universal approval – provided that one does not inquire too closely into what democracy actually means to all those who applaud it, for democracy is a contested concept, especially in societies in the process of transition from an authoritarian or totalitarian political economy. Political actors in these societies often justify their projects and preferred political orders in the language of democracy – even when these projects are directly opposed to one another, as in the case of the violent confrontation between president and parliament in

Russia in 1993. But widespread appeal to the symbols of democracy should not necessarily lead to cynicism about the language of democracy. Rather, it suggests that we should pay close attention to the variety of meanings that can be embedded in this language by political actors and ordinary people. It is these meanings we propose to study, for they reveal what people can and do make of democracy, and of the institutions with which they are confronted.

We show that in post-communist societies there prove to be many varied interpretations of what constitutes the essence of democracy – though probably no more varied than within the more established liberal democracies.[2] In addition, as we shall see in this study, the generalization about universal approval of the concept of – the very word – democracy no longer holds. Within some (but not all) of these societies, there are indeed those who ascribe negative connotations to the term itself. We intend to explain the variety of positive and negative interpretations and accounts of democracy through reference to the histories – both recent and more distant – and contexts of each society, and examine their consequences for what is found and what is possible in the way of political models and reform trajectories.

We shall develop an account of the discourses of democracy prevailing in the mid- to late 1990s in Armenia, Belarus, Bulgaria, China, Czechia, Georgia, Moldova, Poland, Romania, Russia, Slovakia, Ukraine, and Yugoslavia (Serbia and Montenegro).[3] For each country, this account resembles what Bourdieu (1990, 1993) calls a "discursive field," constituted by the positions that actors, often opposing one another, can occupy. The structure of the field constrains what positions can be taken, but is itself determined by the actions, interactions, and contestations of those taking positions (for a good application of this idea to Soviet and Russian politics, see Urban, 1997). In developing this account for each country, we deploy methods that give full rein to individuals to express their own subjective conceptualizations of what democracy and democratization mean. These results are, then, firmly grounded in the way people think and so act politically; it is these subjective dispositions and capabilities that we seek to reconstruct. Of course, we cannot remove our own vantage point entirely: we do not offer unmediated views from inside post-communist countries.[4]

---

[2] The relative *proportions* of the various interpretations might well differ between these two kinds of society. However, even this should not be assumed, and requires empirical testing. Individual countries in both groups might be closer to individual countries in the other group than to their group's norm.

[3] We tried to include Hungary in our analysis, but a severe glitch late in the project meant that this aspiration was frustrated. Hungary's absence does not affect our basic argument.

[4] Cumings (1999, p. 4) speaks of a "parallax view" that looks at both sides (in his case, the United States and East Asia) from a point that is in neither, but rather "off center," such that *both* sides are problematized.

But we do not intend simply to report on the discursive field of democ-racy for each society. As just mentioned, we shall seek to explain the content and pattern of the discourses that we find through reference to both the deeper history and the contemporary circumstances of each country. This does not mean that we should expect to find simple congruence between these circumstances and prevailing discourses. Dissonance is also possible. For example, if there is little or no congruence between public policy on fun-damental matters and popular discourses, then there is a risk of instability, protest, perhaps even violence. At any rate, whether it is stability, instabil-ity, breakdown, or reform that is at issue in a particular case, the extant discourses can shed explanatory light on political-economic situations and how they change.

We conceptualize the relationship between political development and discourses in interactive terms: discourses help condition what is possible and likely in terms of political development, while political development can change the terms of discourses. However, we believe discourses can be relatively stable over time, though dramatic events such as the revolutions of 1989 might occasionally change their configuration quite radically. We cannot *prove* this stability, because our empirical work was carried out at one time in the late 1990s. However, in drawing out connections between discourses and historical legacies, we try to render plausible the idea that dis-courses can endure over years, decades, possibly even (in Poland and China) centuries. Though their historical reach is quite variable, the discourses we identify represent more than passing reactions to events.

In addition, we will explore connections and conflicts between these dis-courses and particular models of democracy and democratization, for all democratic theories, be they liberal, participatory, republican, feminist, plu-ralist, or elitist, make claims about the capabilities and dispositions of indi-viduals who compose any actual or potential political order. Our method-ology can test such claims for particular times and places, and so illuminate the possibilities for congruence and dissonance between the various models of democracy and the particular cases to which they might apply.

Discourses and models of democracy

Among those who make it their business to study post-communist political transformations, there have, we think, been rather too many for whom an adequate model of democracy remains a minimalist or electoralist one. This model takes its bearings from Joseph Schumpeter's (1942) depiction of real-istic democracy as the electoral struggle between competing elites. Ordinary citizens have an occasional voter's role in this model, but they are treated in general as uninformed and apathetic, and so incapable of exercising effective control over the content of public policy. This model fell from favor long ago among democratic theorists, but remains popular among transitologists (see, for example, Di Palma, 1990; Huntington, 1991; Mueller, 1996), most of whom have no interest in the efforts of democratic theorists.[5] Contrasting the fortunes of democratic theorists' ambitious models with what happens in the real world, Sartori (1991, p. 437) declares that "the winner is an entirely liberal democracy, not only popularly elected government, but also, and indivisibly, constitutional government; that is, the hitherto much belittled 'formal model of democracy' that controls the exercise of power."

On the minimalist account, we should stop worrying about political transition or transformation once competitive elections have occurred. As John Mueller puts it,

> most of the postcommunist countries of central and eastern Europe have essentially completed their transition to democracy . . . what they now have is, pretty much, it. They are already full-fledged democracies if we use as models real Western countries (as opposed to some sort of vaporous ideal) . . . In consequence, it may be sensible now to decrease the talk of "transition" and to put a quiet, dignified end to the new field of transitology. (Mueller, 1996, pp. 102–3)

Following this advice, once we stop worrying about transition, we can start to worry about consolidation, conceptualized simply as stabilization of regular competitive elections (Schedler, 1998). Here it may be especially important for both old (ex-communist) and new (nationalist) "counter-elites" to accept the electoral order (Kopecky and Mudde, 2000, p. 524). Huntington's (1991, p. 267) two-election test (requiring a freely elected government to cede power after a subsequent electoral defeat) can be applied as an empirical indicator of (minimalist) consolidation.[6]

---

[5] One of the anonymous reviewers of our typescript suggested that we were setting up a straw man by stressing the influence of Huntington in this field. But corroborating our assessment, M. Steven Fish recently concluded that "Huntington-type views" predominate in the literature on post-communist transition and have been of "immense global influence" (Fish, 1999, pp. 796 and 821).

[6] Beyond these brief comments, we do not consider it necessary for our purposes to enter the heated and sometimes precious debate concerning the appropriateness of the terms "transition," "transformation," and "consolidation." For what it is worth, we see the whole stage between the collapse of one system and the crystallization and stabilization of another as transition. Typically, in the early stages, the transitional society is coming to terms with its past (the legacy); this stage can be called the transformation phase (Bryant and Mokrzycki, 1994; for a reversal of this understanding of transition and transformation, see Schneider, 1997, p. 17). Later, the focus is more on perfecting the new institutions and practices through trial and error. This is the consolidation phase. Defining the point at which the consolidation stage has been completed (i.e., the new system is consolidated) is notoriously difficult (for a useful analysis, see the review article by Encarnación, 2000). Roughly, we

On the face of it, the minimalist model seems to imply that it hardly matters what people *think* about what they are doing as they participate (or indeed, choose not to participate) in democratic institutions. Yet closer examination reveals that even the minimalist model of democracy demands certain qualities in the political dispositions and capabilities of the masses, and somewhat different ones for elites. For the masses, the model requires a widespread attitude toward electoral politics that is apathetic yet supportive, accepting voting as the limit of participation. This attitude means leaving all important decision-making to be unquestioned, the preserve of elected elites (Zakaria, 1997 criticizes this minimalist approach as "illiberal democracy"). On this account, what O'Donnell describes and criticizes as "delegative democracy," emerging in some countries in Latin America and the post-communist world, passes the minimalist test. Under delegative democracy, "whoever wins election to the presidency is thereby entitled to govern as he or she sees fit, constrained only by the hard facts of existing power relations and by a constitutionally limited term of office" (O'Donnell, 1994, p. 57). To O'Donnell, this situation is not representative democracy because there is no accountability, no need for election promises to be remembered (for questioning of whether such an arrangement should even be called democracy, see A. Brown, 1999, especially p. 6).

The minimalist model does not require much in the way of political literacy or toleration of those with different points of view. Political literacy and

would argue that it has been reached when most members of the polity have accepted that the broad parameters of the system are settled – when, to paraphrase Offe, there are no longer major debates *about* the basic rules, but only *under* them (or, in Przeworski's [1991] terms, the new system has become "the only game in town"). One way to test this empirically would be to survey people on whether or not they believe that the basic *system* – as distinct from a particular *regime* (a leadership team) – will still be in place a decade hence. Of course, as Russia in the late 1990s warned us, the wording of the questionnaire would have to distinguish between normative acceptance of a system and a feeling that everything is likely to be basically the same – chaotic! – ten years hence. Clear explanation of what is understood as a system should largely overcome this problem. For us, however, the problem would remain that we see democracy as an ongoing interactive process, rather than some clearly defined end goal. In this sense, it is impossible to be entirely satisfied with the very concept of "consolidated," which implies completion as a form of closure. Yet we want to be able to continue with our argument without being accused of being unaware of a very important theoretical debate that others might believe we should engage. To return to the opening point of this footnote, we are not interested in becoming embroiled in an argument we believe can only go around in circles. For one of the most heated debates on "transition" and "consolidation," which considers the appropriateness of comparing different macro-regions of the world as well as these concepts, see (in this order) Schmitter and Karl, 1994; Bunce, 1995b; Karl and Schmitter, 1995; and Bunce, 1995a. For an early, rather cantankerous rejection of the notion of transition, see Jowitt, 1992, who believes that transition necessarily implies transition to democracy. His belief that the prospects for this in many countries of the region were slim explains his rejection of the term.

tolerance can be treated as the preserve of, and protected by, elites. However, proponents of the minimalist model must require acceptance on the part of ordinary people of the rules of the electoral game, and of the legitimacy of the political system to which elections are central (Plasser, Ulram, and Waldrauch, 1998). Without a supportive discourse, such acceptance can rest only on pragmatic compliance contingent on economic performance, or on habituation (Powers, 1998), or even on coercion. All three of these latter alternatives provide weak defenses for democracy, especially if economic crisis arrives. There needs to be something more robust, a normative commitment. In short, democracy needs popular *legitimacy*. Thus intelligent minimalists should attend to democracy's discourses.

Among liberal constitutionalists, there is in fact some recognition of the need for institutional transformation to be accompanied by a supportive civil society and political culture, and so (in our terms) discourses of democracy. However, such recognition is apt to treat civil society's discourse in one-dimensional terms, according to how well this discourse measures up to the requirements of liberal institutions.

There is no denying the analytical purchase that the minimalist model supplies when it comes to comparisons across time and space. With a little stretching, it can underwrite a temporal scale (in years) for rating the degree to which a democracy is consolidated (e.g., Lijphart's [1984, p. 38] "30–35" years of continuous existence before a new democracy can be considered consolidated). But this undoubted convenience for the analyst is, we believe, bought at the unacceptable price of insensitivity to the variety of forms that democratic political development can take, and to variations in the quality of democracy in systems that both pass and fail minimalist tests.

Other models of democracy can be both more demanding and more nuanced in terms of what they seek in the capabilities and dispositions of masses and elites alike. The methods we deploy do in fact enable us to investigate discourses in fine detail, rather than just array them crudely on a supportive/not supportive dimension. We will reveal a rich variety of parallels and conflicts between particular models of democracy and post-communist political discourses. This juxtaposition yields insights into just what kinds of democracy may be possible or impossible in different places, and how the ideals of democratic theorists and reformers (or, for that matter, reactionaries) might connect to political practice. We should emphasize that our interest is quite different from those consolidation scholars who eschew a minimalist model in favor of a more demanding set of tests that more countries fail (for example, Green and Skalnik Leff, 1997). We are interested in understanding, not condemnation.

Once we acknowledge that there is more to democratic life than a universally applicable, one-size-fits-all, minimalist model of democracy, a range of possibilities opens up. This opening enables some fruitful connections to theories of democracy, as well as more nuanced interpretation of the paths that democratization can take. Such possibilities can be arrayed along the following dimensions, among others.[7]

Social democracy to libertarianism. Social democrats, in whose ranks may now be found a fair number of reformed communists, believe in substantial state intervention in the market economy along with governmental provision of welfare programs. Thus a democratic system should do more than allow citizens to make demands and representations (inputs); it should also ensure that citizens' needs are met (outputs). In contrast, libertarians believe that civil society and the economy can and should assume many of the tasks social democrats assign to the state. Libertarians believe in a small state and maximal scope for the market. True libertarians believe this arrangement is appropriate anywhere and at any time. Advocates of "shock therapy," applied most famously in Poland after 1989,[8] borrow some libertarian prescriptions for a limited transition period, but also require a very interventionist state to design the new market order.

Authoritarianism to open society. Authoritarianism can be exercised in the service of either a planned or market economy. One school of thought argues that effective marketization cannot proceed under democratic auspices. For example, Przeworski (1991, p. 183) argues that market-oriented reforms "are based on a model of economic efficiency that is highly technical. They involve choices that are not easy to explain to the general public and decisions that do not always make sense to popular opinion." Thus "A reform policy is not one that emerges from broad participation, from a consensus among all the affected interests, from compromises" (Brucan, 1992, p. 24; for a more comparative argument that too much democracy in developing and underdeveloped economies causes poor economic performance, see Gasiorowski, 2000). In contrast, advocates of the open society believe that political and economic liberalization can and should proceed hand in hand, for only an experimental, trial-and-error approach enables mistakes to be recognized and corrected, a process impossible under authoritarianism (Pickel, 1993).

Civil society to a strong state. Civil society conceived of in terms of political association not encompassed by the state or the economy played a large

---

[7] For a simpler but useful typology of kinds of democracy in the post-communist world, see Commisso, 1997, esp. pp. 1–15.

[8] Though Murrell (1993) has persuasively challenged the notion that it was implemented very extensively in Poland.

part in the revolutions of 1989. Many commentators were quick to write off civil society in this heroic guise, and some lament the persistence of the attitudes associated with it (Linz and Stepan, 1996), but it has its advocates as a continuing inspiration for post-communist societies (for example, Arato, 1993). A different, more prosaic version of the civil society model emphasizes the organization of interests, especially those with economic roots such as businesses and unions. Along these lines, Ost (1993) laments the weakness of civil society organizations in post-communist Eastern Europe, which leaves the field clear for a politics of identity that emphasizes religion and nationalism, together with a strong state (for further discussion of the weakness of post-communist civil society, see Bernhard, 1996; Pickvance, 1999). But a strong state may be a necessity where civil society is weak, and it does not have to be tied to the politics of identity. While it might at first sight seem paradoxical to argue that the consolidation of democracy requires firm central leadership, post-communist societies often lack not only the civil society (in the prosaic sense) but also the institutions, civic traditions, and culture of compromise that can make liberal democracy work, and can avoid a slide into political chaos and/or dictatorship. In this light, the key to democratic consolidation is effective state leadership committed to democratic and constitutionalist principles. Here, a strong state is one with the capacity to establish frameworks and laws, implement policies, and keep political development on a democratic course until civil society can assume more political responsibilities (L. Holmes, 1998). Of course, strong states can be put to very different uses by those not committed to such principles. Authoritarian states can be strong states, especially in the sense of being intrusive into citizens' lives and possessing large coercive apparatuses. Here we consider only the case for the strong state *within a democratic context*. This state is a capable state, which can establish effective democratic institutions and legal frameworks in the early post-authoritarian era and promote democratic political culture. It is strong enough to collect the taxes to fund democratization,[9] and capable of resisting both authoritarianism and anarchy. It does not have to be large; the Russian state machinery under Yeltsin was large but not very capable, hence not strong in this sense.

Pluralism to republicanism. Pluralists, indeed most liberals, believe that politics is properly about the reconciliation and aggregation of partial

---

[9] This problem of adequate funding of democracy is not confined to transition countries. Much of the recent political corruption in Western Europe – notably Germany – relates to inadequate legitimate funding of political parties. In today's world, there is no such thing as a free lunch, and no cost-free democracy.

interests, mostly material ones. Republicans, in contrast, believe in a more unitary notion of the public interest, and political argument that is geared toward the creation or discovery of this interest. Republicans allow that there may be different points of view about what is in the public interest, but they are reluctant to recognize the legitimacy of merely material and partial interests in political debate, such as those of particular economic sectors or classes.

Elitism to participation. Proponents of participatory democracy, and populism in a non-pejorative sense, believe that as many citizens as possible should join in effective exercise of political power. Participatory democrats distrust any elite domination of democracy. Others believe even democratic politics is inevitably, and perhaps properly, for elites. The elite in question might be a republican elite committed to citizen virtue, it might be an elite committed to democratic guidance, or it could be a plural elite, composed for example of the leaders of different parties.

Nationalism to cosmopolitanism. One of the uglier aspects of some – but not most – of the countries we study is resurgent ethnic nationalism that in some cases has meant violence, even ethnic cleansing and genocide. Of course, nationalism comes in many variations, some of which abhor violence. What all nationalisms share is the belief that full membership in the political community is reserved for people with particular characteristics, and this principle can apply to democratic community too. Thus it is possible to be both a nationalist and a democrat. Auer (2000) argues that nationalism can sometimes promote liberal democratization in contemporary Central and Eastern Europe. This argument is consistent with deeper European history, where nationalism and democracy have occasionally reinforced each other – especially when nation could be defined in opposition to empire. National governments could be more responsive than imperial ones.[10] Cosmopolitans are those who deny the importance of ethnicity and nationality in establishing claims to full citizenship. Real cosmopolitans have little use for national boundaries. An intermediate position on the nationalism–cosmopolitan continuum would emphasize state citizenship, and so state boundaries, but interpret citizenship in constitutional terms, for which anyone living within the boundaries of the state is fully eligible.

---

[10] Integrationist and civic forms of nationalism are in the longer term more compatible with liberal democratization than are ethnic and divisive forms. But the former must be sensitive to ethnic difference where it exists, promoting dialogue between the two or more groups. This dialogue itself can be seen as integral to democracy.

These dimensions identify particular kinds of models or programs for politics. The discourses that we find can act as both constraints and resources for those interested in advancing or conserving such models and programs. They act as constraints when reformers can find little resonance for their model in any of the discourses present in a society. They act as resources when points of connection can be found. There will rarely be a point-by-point similarity between a model of political development and a discourse – though as our discussions of Poland and Czechia will show, this can sometimes happen. More important is the creative tension that can exist between the proposals of theorists and reformers on the one hand, and the capabilities and dispositions of citizens on the other.

In the apt metaphor developed by Elster, Offe, and Preuss (1998), processes of post-communist political and economic transformation take the form of "rebuilding the ship while at sea." The builders have to work with the ship as it is (there is no *tabula rasa*), rather than how blueprints say it should be. Contrary to what economists such as Jeffrey Sachs and David Lipton (the foremost advocates of shock therapy) used to maintain, it is not clear that there *are* any blueprints (in the sense of appropriate prior examples of such transition from which to learn). Part of the character of the ship is given by its economic structure and formal political institutions; but a big part of its character is given by the discourses that prevail on board. Rebuilders must live with, work within, and draw upon these discourses. While we certainly do not suggest that formal institutional and structural factors are unimportant, we would expect discourses to be especially important in coordinating action and determining outcomes where the institutional hardware is weak or underdeveloped – which is generally the case in post-communist societies.

Our implicit commitment is to the idea of democracy as an open-ended conversation, to which political leaders and activists, ordinary people, social scientists, and political theorists alike can contribute. Thus there is no single, fully specified destination called "democracy" to which all societies are heading – or indeed which some may be prevented from reaching (see Hughes, 2000 for a critique of this tendency among transitologists). There are many routes that can be followed, and many ways in which they can be blocked. Charles Tilly (1993, p. 17) points out that it is important not to read history backwards – that one should not (say) interpret the whole sweep of eighteenth-century French history as preparations for the revolution of 1789. That the revolution happened does not mean it always had to happen, or that there was one path leading to it. The same can be said for the history of the present in post-communist societies, which should not be read backwards in terms of movement toward (or indeed away from) one particular democratic destination.

Throughout, we will follow a comparative approach: we are interested not just in discourses, events, and possibilities within each country, but also in what can be learned by examining crosspolity patterns. We will even make comparisons with more established liberal democracies at some points.

Each of the substantive chapters will report results for a particular country, relating these results to the political-economic experience of that country, with the emphasis on the period since 1989. We seek to develop an analysis of what transition has *meant* in terms of the lived experience of people in the country in question. We will build to crossnational comparisons and generalizations about the problems and prospects associated with post-communist democratization.

Freedom and necessity in democratization

We intend, then, to explore the variety of meanings of democracy and democratization – more precisely, the discourses of democracy – that can be found in the post-communist world. We approach this issue as social scientists, and will deploy some social scientific tools in our mapping of discourses of democracy. But we care about this issue because we are democrats. We are democrats not just in the bland sense in which just about anyone can so categorize themselves, but in a commitment to democracy as a project that must itself be pursued through democratic means. Some of the main resources for (as well as constraints upon) this project can be found in the discourses about democracy that are found in particular societies. This commitment sets us apart from those minimalists who believe that democracy is something that is either absent or present, rather than a matter of degree and variety.

In further contrast to minimalists, we care a great deal about the degree to which democratic control is authentic as distinct from symbolic, and engaged by critical and competent actors. We can really only speak of successful democratic transition to the degree such authenticity is achieved, for if we stay with the minimalists and address popular conceptions of democracy only in terms of degree of acceptance of the new order, it is in the end impossible to distinguish between normative commitment and simple acceptance of a status quo, between reflective approval and mere socialization. The latter in turn reveals some disconcerting continuity between old and new systems, at least in terms of the normalization that both can seek. Such normalization assumes different forms under state socialism and nascent liberal democracy, but in both cases it is the silencing of critical voices that is sought. Under state socialism, criticism is equated with subversion; potential opponents of the regime must be convinced that there is ultimately no alternative to it. Under the new democratic order, criticism of the institutional status quo can be interpreted by minimalists only as anti-democratic feeling, rather than possibly representing desires for a different, perhaps more authentic, democracy (Powers, 1998).

Our focus on discourses means that we believe it matters what democracy and democratization mean to people. Certainly there are those who believe it does not matter much. To some, democracy is, in Przeworski's terms, "only a system of processing conflicts without killing one another" (1991, p. 95). In this light, acceptance of democratic rules is a result of strategic calculations on the part of key actors, who conclude that their expected long-term net material gain from accepting democratic rules (notably, free elections) is greater than that which would be obtained from (say) trying to seize or hold on to power through coercive means. If, as rational choice theorists tell us, the political world is made up only of rational egoists (*homo economicus*), then it matters not at all what key political actors think democracy is or should be, let alone what nonelites think. Such "elite pact" accounts of transition take nonelites into account only in terms of their potential for upsetting the pact: for example, by engaging in protests that induce an authoritarian reaction on the part of the old regime signatories.

From a very different direction, neoinstitutional macro-sociologists such as Skocpol (1979) and Rueschemeyer, Stephens, and Stephens (1992), who consider that political development is the remorseless working out of structural forces, would see discourses of democracy as being as irrelevant as all other human ideas in explaining the course of history. Different again, development (or what Fish, 1998, pp. 233–4, calls "strong modernization") theorists who believe that successful liberal democracy is positively associated with prosperity, mainly because economic growth produces a middle class that possesses the necessary democratic virtues, would direct our attention away from discourses (except as intervening variables, determined by economic development) and toward the influence and interaction of economics and social structures (i.e., classes – see, e.g., Lipset, 1959; Pye, 1966; Moore, 1967; Rostow, 1971). Those more skeptical about the impact of the transnational capitalist political economy on democracy – believing that there is no scope for popular control of collective decisions, that all governments must in the end please financial and capital markets (see, for example, Block, 1977) – might also think that popular discourses about democracy cannot make much difference. Relatedly, world systems theorists such as Wallerstein (1974) would see a country's location in a particular zone of the world economic system as the key determinant of its public policies.

Another kind of determinism that figures large in analyses of the post-communist world emphasizes culture rather than structure. For example, Hellén, Berglund, and Aarebrot (1998, esp. pp. 365–6) distinguish between the Baltic states and the Central and East European states on the one hand,

and Romania and Bulgaria on the other. Like many analysts (for example, Vachudová and Snyder, 1997), they identify a "North–South divide" in CEE, and argue that "There is, in fact, a good case to be made for the notion that the resilience of authoritarian features in the Balkans has much to do with the clientelistic heritage in that particular region."[11]

We agree that deep history can influence current politics and, as mentioned above, deploy it ourselves in order to understand differences in discourse configurations from country to country. However, we have three criticisms of cultural determinism. First, cultural determinists too often treat a complex society in overly monolithic terms. As we will demonstrate, different groups can in fact recall very different periods and events in their society's history. Thus we address histories in the plural when considering the influence of the past (though we do occasionally speak of "deep history" in a generic and aggregated sense). Second, cultural determinism is too reductionist and monocausal. Not only deep histories but also contemporary experiences influence attitudes, discourses, and developments. The relative importance of these factors can vary from one individual or group to another. Third, and most important, cultural determinism can condemn a society to nondemocracy because that society has allegedly had the "wrong" experiences. We reject this sort of stereotyping, arrogance, and lack of political imagination when it comes from observers from comfortable Western democracies. Some of the worst culprits here do however hail from the countries we are considering – especially those seeking to establish their own country's Western credentials. Our findings ought to lead to the reconsideration of such positions. Empirically, our study will demonstrate the point we have just made about diversity; there are one or two surprises in store (as there were for us when the results began to arrive). Also, it is a truism that none of the existing established democracies would exist if a prerequisite for democracy is prior democratic experience.[12]

A further kind of determinism that we reject is advanced by some of those who share our emphasis on discourses and their causal force. Most notable among discourse analysts, Michel Foucault has demonstrated that discourses surrounding sexuality, mental health, criminality, and the like exercise an essentially normalizing function: they construct human subjects in particular ways. Thus the idea of an autonomous human subject begins to

---

[11] Hellén, Berglund, and Aarebrot (1998, p. 366) do go on to argue that this does not condemn Bulgaria and Romania; both may be able to consolidate democracy because of weak cleavage crystallization. Allowing for contemporary social structures and alignments supports our point that culture(s) can play a role, but should never be seen as decisive.

[12] For further empirical evidence that the concept of national culture can be misleading when used to assess the likelihood of successful democratization in post-communist societies, see Fish, 1998, esp. pp. 230 and 232–3.

look suspect, though not wholly inconceivable. Foucault himself deployed a notion of "governmentality" to argue that political discourses in modern societies have constructed individuals in particular ways that make them amenable and easy to govern. Foucauldians such as Barry Hindess (2000) extend this idea to democracy: discourses of democracy are just another means of disciplining individuals, making them compliant subjects of the liberal democratic state. Liberal constitutionalists would of course applaud such discourses, and not recognize the kind of coercive potential emphasized by Foucault. Along these lines, Francis Fukuyama (1989, 1992) argues that the "end of history" represents the global triumph of a particular discourse – liberal democracy plus capitalism – over all others. Fukuyama is hardly a Foucauldian; he believes that there is an essential human nature consisting of the desire for recognition (*thymos*) plus material self-interest which capitalist democracy is uniquely able to satisfy. But if one sees the desire for recognition plus rational egoism as historically contingent rather than human essences, or at least as aspects of humanity that are invoked much more by liberal society than by its predecessors, it is easy to reconcile Fukuyama's argument with a notion that discourses are mainly sources of constraint. The end of history is in this light simply a discursive closure. Indeed, Fukuyama recognizes as much at the end of the book, where he bemoans the "men without chests" who populate the end of history, where there is nothing noble left for people to fight for.

While our conception of discourses owes something to Foucault, our treatment is actually closer to Bourdieu's notion of a discursive field. As we pointed out earlier, our results for each country model such a field. Political actors are constrained (and in part constituted) by the structure of this field. But these actors in turn, via their own interventions, contests, and interactions, can affect the boundaries and structure of the field, as well as the particular positions (discourses) that exist within it. We believe, then, that discourses offer resources as well as constraints: that intelligent individuals can, if only sometimes, reflect upon the content of the discourses in which they move, and make good choices within and across discourses. (Arguably, Foucault himself moved closer to this position late in his life.) We do not maintain that this happens all the time: if it did, the whole concept of discourses would lose its force, as individuals would not be subject to them in the slightest. But such reflection and choice can happen some of the time, and especially at important times. It is especially likely in societies with unsettled political and economic orders – and all post-communist societies still fall into this category (even allowing for the substantial differences between a Hungary or Slovenia at one end of the spectrum and an Albania or Serbia at the other). Moreover, it can be argued that one characteristic of today's world is that traditions, established authority, and discourses are questioned

as they never have been before. Social theorists such as Ulrich Beck and
Anthony Giddens (Beck, 1992; Beck, Giddens, and Lash, 1994) describe such
developments under the headings of "detraditionalization" and "reflexive
modernization." Reflexive modernization is development become conscious
of itself. Modernization was once thought of in terms of a path on which
all societies were embarked; choice came only in whether to move or stand
still, to walk faster or slower, and to go via the route marked democracy
or via the one labeled dictatorship. Reflexive modernization questions the
destination of the path, and is ready to question and even reject aspects of
its content – for example, risks associated with biotechnology or chemical
pollution.

While our intent here is not to demonstrate that these concepts work
as empirical accounts of contemporary post-communist societies in particular, notions of reflexive modernization and detraditionalization help
provide a context for our inquiry, because we believe that democratic development *should* proceed in reflexive fashion; indeed, that this is a large
part of what makes it democratic. To the extent this can happen, the rational choice theorists, neoinstitutional macro-sociologists, development
theorists, and economic determinists we mentioned earlier provide partial
and so ultimately unsatisfactory accounts of democratization and its possibilities. This is not the same as saying that they are devoid of insight or
completely wrong, but merely that they highlight the influence of necessity
and so miss the influence of freedom in democratic innovation (for a critique of development theorists who imply that there are no choices to be
made, see Di Palma, 1990). Here we seek to redress the balance in favor of
freedom. (For an attempt to work out the balance of freedom and necessity in democratic innovation in developed liberal democracies, see Dryzek,
1996a.)

Like all political theories, theories of democracy necessarily rest on assumptions about the dispositions and capabilities of the persons who will
make up any political order. Many democratic theorists have sought universal applicability, and so have made assumptions about the essence of what it
means to be a human being: be it the liberal's model of an individual capable of exercising choice, the republican's model of individuals who can find
fulfillment only in public life, the public choice theorist's *homo economicus*,
the conservative's model of ordinary people driven mostly by passion and
prejudice rather than by reason, the feminist's model of a nurturing and
connected (female) person, or the Marxist's model of new socialist person.
We prefer to treat such matters of disposition and capability as contingent
on particular times and places – hence as questions to be studied empirically,
rather than stipulated theoretically. Thus our inquiries are grounded in the
way people in post-communist societies think about themselves, about

politics and democracy, and about how they and others can (or cannot) engage in political action.

We have argued in this chapter against several existing determinisms. We are happy to report that a number of analysts had by the late 1990s begun to reassess their earlier positions (compare for example the tone of Jones, 1993, 1997, and 2000, as changes in Georgia led him to more optimistic prognoses). But we are not only concerned about arguments in the scholarly literature. Precisely because, as democrats ourselves, we are interested in what ordinary citizens believe and do, we are concerned about images created in the mass media, which often have far more influence on public attitudes than do scholarly analyses. Unfortunately, while stereotyping (particularly cultural determinism) appears to be on the wane among scholars, this cannot be said so readily of the mass media. It would take at least another full-scale project systematically to analyze the presentation of our thirteen countries in the Western mass media. We believe that many readers will recognize the stereotyping to which we refer (and we do cite various examples throughout the book). Still, our primary objective is not to discredit the analyses of others, but rather the constructive one of presenting an alternative way of looking at democracy and democratization.

Before turning to our country studies, we need to say a little about methodology: specifically, how we have utilized Q methodology and political discourse analysis in producing the map of discourses of democracy for each country. This methodological discussion constitutes chapter 2; readers more interested in the substance of what we have found and what we have to say about discourses of democracy and democratization in post-communist societies may be forgiven for passing lightly over chapter 2.

2

Methodology

As should be clear from chapter 1, we seek to model the capabilities and dispositions toward democracy of individuals, and map the discursive field of democracy and democratization which these individuals constitute (and are in part constituted by) for each society. Thus we are interested in how democracy looks *subjectively* to people. Accordingly, we deploy the best-developed paradigm for the investigation of human subjectivity, Q methodology (Q was invented by the psychologist William Stephenson; see especially Stephenson, 1953).[1] Q will be joined with political discourse analysis with the intention of uncovering particular kinds of structures embedded in political language. Our approach is interpretive in that it seeks to come to grips with the way the world looks to the people we study. But unlike interpretive methods such as depth interviewing and ethnography, the interpretations are constrained by statistical results. It should be remembered throughout that statistical tests should inform, but not substitute for, interpretive judgment.

Q methodology

Q methodology is used to model patterns of subjectivity within and across individuals. By way of contrast, familiar R methodology techniques, such as survey research, model patterns within and across variables.[2] In Q methodology, the whole subject's orientation to a particular domain is modeled at

---

[1] For the best textbook exposition, see S. Brown, 1980. For current developments, subscribe to the list Q-METHOD@LISTSERV.KENT.EDU.

[2] The origins of the terms Q and R date to the early days of factor analysis in psychology, when Q designated any method based on correlations across persons, while R designated methods

once as the basis for the analysis of patterns across individuals. This modeling is done through reference to the subject's reactions to a set of statements drawn from the domain in question – in our case, the domain of democracy and democratization. This set of statements is called the Q set or Q sample. An individual's reaction to any one of these statements is not treated in isolation, on a par with a question in survey research; rather, it only takes on meaning in the context of the individual's reactions to all the other statements in the set.

Normally a Q sample contains forty to seventy statements; much more than seventy and the burden on the individual asked to sort the statements becomes too great. For each country in our study we obtained sixty-four statements pertaining to democracy for our Q sample; the relatively large number of statements facilitates the making of fine distinctions. The Q sample was different for each country. Obviously it would have been much easier to apply a common set of statements to all the countries studied. Such is the way of survey researchers, but this would have involved gross violation of some important epistemological and methodological principles (which we will discuss shortly). Using a different Q sample for each country does nothing to preclude systematic comparison across countries of a kind essential to our inquiry; but the comparisons across countries will have to use words rather than statistics. Nor does this use of national Q samples preclude finding discourses that transcend national boundaries, and in the concluding chapter we will examine such possibilities. (On the other hand, a measurement strategy that *began* with transnational discourses could not easily pick up national peculiarities, which is why we prefer a bottom-up approach.) We are certainly not committed to any Herder-like *Volksgeist* notion that each national society must have a unique outlook. The question of whether there is more similarity within countries than across countries is an empirical one, which we can investigate.

Each subject was asked to order the sixty-four statements into thirteen piles in a quasi-normal distribution. The extremes of the distribution were coded +6 for "most agree," and −6 for the "most disagree" category. A coding of zero indicates indifference. This quasi-normal distribution is reproduced in figure 2.1. The ordering produced by each subject is called a Q sort; the Q sort represents a model of the individual's orientation to the domain of democracy and democratization.

The source of the sixty-four statements is a crucial matter. In investigating what democracy and democratization actually mean to our subjects, it is

based on correlations across tests (that is, variables). However, though Q methodology as it is now understood deploys Q factor analysis, it is much more than simply a method of factor analysis, as will become clear in the following discussion.

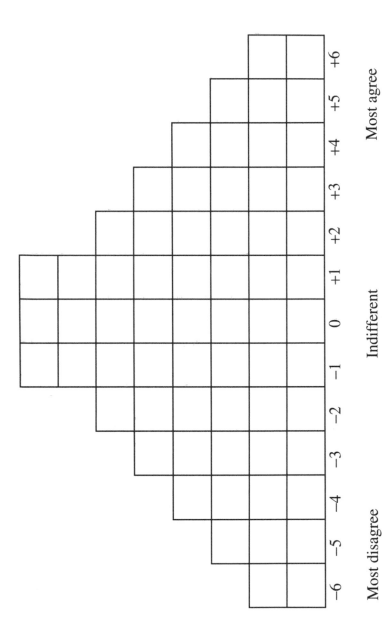

Most disagree   Indifferent   Most agree

Figure 2.1 Q sort template, sixty-four statements

Note: The template contains sixty-four cells, corresponding to the sixty-four statements in the Q sort.

vital that the statements are in language the subject is likely to use and understand. We concur with Kitzinger (1986, p. 153) that "the theoretical basis on which Q methodology is founded relies on the axiom that researchers should acknowledge and present the reality constructions of different women and men without prejudging or discrediting them, and without insisting on the superior (more 'objective') status of the researcher's own construction of reality." To do this, we need to present these "reality constructions" in terms of everyday language – another reason to use statement sets drawn from the country in question.

Our epistemological commitment here is a *reconstructive* one (Dryzek and Berejikian, 1993, pp. 49–50). We aim to reconstruct the social competences of the individuals engaged in processes of political change, and their associated languages of human interaction. The development of such accounts is sometimes referred to as "reconstructive science" (Habermas, 1979; Johnson, 1991). "Reconstructive" here does not refer to the reconstruction of society and its institutions, but rather the social scientist's reconstruction of the capabilities and dispositions of the individuals being investigated.

Our own reconstructive approach is designed to let the individuals we study speak for themselves about their own capacities as they engage other people, social practices, and institutions – the practices and institutions of politics. (Here we depart from Habermas and Johnson, who are interested mainly in reconstructing the competences of ideal individuals, not real ones.) These individual capacities and dispositions help construct (even as they are in turn constructed by) those social entities which we call discourses of democracy. We seek to uncover the self-described capacities of individuals as constituents of actual or potential political orders, and their dispositions or opinions about matters of fact and value that concern democracy. Each individual's capabilities and dispositions are interrelated in all kinds of ways. The capabilities at issue are interactive ones, so they exist only in relation to the individual's dispositions toward his or her social context.

We measure these capabilities and dispositions for each individual using the Q sort. The Q sorts for different subjects can then be compared using statistical techniques – most usefully and most commonly, factor analysis (which we will describe in more detail later). Factor analysis can reveal the structure of agreement and dispute across the individuals from whom we obtain Q sorts. Again, unlike R factor analysis, Q factor analysis seeks patterns across individuals, not variables. The individuals who load highly on a given factor demonstrate a high degree of commonality with each other, and dissimilarity with individuals who load highly on different factors, or negatively on the same factor. (A loading here is just the correlation coefficient between an individual and the "ideal type" of the factor in question.)

Combining Q methodology and political discourse analysis

In modeling an individual's orientation to the domain of democracy and democratization, we need first of all to define that domain. Q methodologists
use the term "concourse" rather than "domain." A concourse is "the volume
of discussion on any topic," containing the interplay of opinions, ideas, evaluations, and attitudes (S. Brown, 1986, p. 58). The concept is operationalized
as the population of statements about some topic in a particular society –
in our case, the topic of democracy. We define the democratic concourse
as composed of statements concerned with the collective construction, application, distribution, and limitation of political authority. (Astute readers
will note that the fact that the concourse is defined by the analysts rather
than the subjects is a minor, but unavoidable, violation of the reconstructive
principle.)

Obviously the analyst cannot work with all the statements that could be
made within the concourse, and so needs to design a representative sample of
the statements to use in the Q sorts. The reconstructive principle we have just
elaborated means that the statements selected should be drawn from those
actually made by individuals involved with the concourse of democracy in
the society in question. We used two kinds of sources for statements: discussion groups and publications such as newspapers and magazines. By far the
largest proportion of statements came from our discussion groups, which
have proven the most effective and efficient means to generate statements.

For each country we organized four discussion groups of around ten participants each. Each group lasted around one hour. The groups were held
in at least two different locations in the country. Participants were recruited
by newspaper advertisements and networks of personal connections (when
advertising was difficult or inappropriate). In one case (Czechia) participants were located through the services of an opinion polling organization.
In another (China), conversations with individuals were substituted for discussion groups because of the political danger involved in organizing groups
to discuss democracy. We tried to secure variety in terms of the social and
political characteristics of the individuals participating (though such variety
is less crucial at this discussion-group stage of the research than in the later
individual Q sort interviews). The individuals involved in the discussion
groups were not the same people as the subjects for whom we subsequently
obtained Q sorts in individual interviews.

The discussion groups all worked, in the sense that people did talk, and
sometimes argued. In a few cases it took some effort to begin the conversation: for example, in Armenia the participants began by asking what
they were required to say. Even after being convinced that it was their own
opinions that were being sought, they still wanted to talk in Russian rather

than Armenian, as Russian was the language appropriate to "official" political occasions – into which category the discussion group appeared to fall. Eventually they were happy to speak Armenian.

The group discussions were tape-recorded and then transcribed, so that particular statements about democracy and democratization could be isolated. The list of statements produced by the discussion groups was supplemented by statements from published sources, until we had around 300 statements for the country. Our reconstructive commitment meant that we did not edit statements, except to correct grammar or substitute a noun for "it." Some of the statements were ambiguous or contained more than one opinion, but that is the nature of political language. Ambiguities are generally resolved in the act of sorting the statements – that is, the meaning an individual ascribes to a statement is illuminated by how he or she reacts to related statements. We sought and obtained statements referring both to the individual making them and to the character of the political world in general – in the society in question, or in some ideal polity, or in some actual or imagined past or future. An example of the former kind of statement is "We should not be allowed to decide on everything because we are not specialists on everything" (Poland); of the latter, "Since Europe is moving forward, it cannot and will not tolerate an undemocratic Bulgaria" (Bulgaria).

We reduced the 300 statements for each country to 64 using a sampling procedure based on some principles of political discourse analysis (Seidel, 1985; Alker and Sylvan, 1986). Q methodologists frequently use a cell structure to inform statement selection as a heuristic device for ensuring that a reasonably broad spread of different kinds of statements is identified and used. When it comes to mapping political discourses, we need to make sure that the key elements defining and separating these discourses are identified. The key elements of a political discourse are:

1. An ontology – that is, a set of entities whose existence is recognized (for example, nations, the international system, individuals, politicians, the mafia, social classes, states, civil society).
2. Agency ascribed to these entities. Agency is the capacity to act. Some entities will be ascribed agency – for example, citizens in models of participatory democracy. Some entities will be denied agency – for example, a cynical discourse might see the state as fully controlled by the rich, thus possessing no agency of its own.
3. Motives of agents. Some motives will be highlighted, others ignored or denied. Motives might relate to survival, personal advancement, the public wellbeing, securing the confidence of investors, self-interest, and so forth.

4. Natural and unnatural political relationships. Such relationships might refer to conflict between nations or social classes, political equality, harmony, competition, or hierarchies based on wealth, ability, degree of political interest, age, gender, or experience.

Statements should be sought from each of these four categories, which together constitute one dimension of a cell structure for sampling statements from a concourse. A second dimension for this cell structure emphasizes that all statements embody claims about the world. Toulmin (1958) classifies the claims that can be made in arguments into four types:

1. Definitive – concerned with the meaning of terms.
2. Designative – concerned with matters of fact.
3. Evaluative – concerning the worth of something that exists, or might exist.
4. Advocative – concerning something that should or should not exist.

We can combine these two dimensions to construct a four-by-four cell structure or matrix for categorizing statements, as shown in table 2.1. The (approximately) 300 statements for each society were each coded according to the cell they fell into. As far as possible, statements with no clear cell location were eliminated, and four statements were chosen at random from those coded in each cell. (Occasionally there were fewer than four statements in a cell, in which case a search was made for an additional statement or statements.) This procedure yielded the sixty-four statements for our Q sample.

An example of a "definitive, ontology" statement from cell 1 in table 2.1 is "Democracy is discipline, social order, and consciousness" (Russia). An

Table 2.1. *Matrix applying political discourse analysis to sampling statements from a concourse*

	Discourse element			
Type of claim	Ontology	Agency	Motives	Natural and unnatural relationships
Definitive	1	2	3	4
Designative	5	6	7	8
Evaluative	9	10	11	12
Advocative	13	14	15	16

Note: The numbers identify the cells from 1 to 16.

example of a "designative, agency" statement from cell 6 is "Continuing to reorient and adjust itself, the former *nomenklatura* preserves in its hands control over the state apparatus in the majority of the republics of the former Soviet Union" (Ukraine). An example of an "evaluative, motives" statement from cell 11 is "People are ignorant about politics, and yet they vote. They do not know what they do, but they do it" (Poland). An example of an "advocative, natural relationship" statement from cell 16 is "We are not equally capable, neither equally clever, we do not have the same contacts, nor equal money, but, with respect to the state, the society, the system of government, it should be possible for me to realize my rights under conditions of equality of rights" (Yugoslavia).

Selecting subjects

Around forty individuals in each country were selected for individual in-terviews, the essence of which was completion of the 64-statement Q sort. Q is an intensive methodology, and always works with a relatively small number of subjects; adding more subjects beyond forty would yield little additional information, unless the additional individuals were of a kind not already represented or intimated at all in the original forty. Given the rel-atively small numbers of persons, population sampling techniques of the kind used by survey researchers, such as quotas or random samples, are in-appropriate. We selected our subjects carefully to maximize their *variety* in terms of social characteristics and political partisanship. The relevant social characteristics included age, income, education, occupation, rural/urban residence, ethnicity (in ethnically diverse societies), gender, and religion (where appropriate). Concerning political partisanship, we looked for sup-porters of particular parties, and of none; for individuals actively involved in politics, and for those indifferent to politics. Interviews were conducted in more than one location in each country, in some cases in as many as five sites. Of course, this still means that in a large country like Russia or China many regions of the country are not represented.

Given the small number of subjects, we cannot argue that they are statisti-cally representative of the population of the country. Yet generalization from our subjects to the society as a whole is still something we can claim, though in a way that is quite different from the way most (R methodological) so-cial scientists conceptualize it, for the patterns – specifically, discourses of democracy – that we identify in our group of subjects represent the patterns existing in the larger society (S. Brown, 1980, pp. 66–7). That is, each dis-course that we find among our subjects represents a discourse that exists in the larger society, and the relationships we find between discourses among our subjects represent the relationships that exist in society at large. This is why we stress variety in subject selection: we can be confident in the comprehensiveness of our coverage of discourses to the extent of the variety we have secured in the social and political characteristics of our subjects. In other words, if a discourse exists in society, we are likely to find it among our subjects, given the degree to which we are careful to include very different kinds of people in our analysis.

Given their small number of subjects, Q methodologists must have confidence in their individual observations. This is very different from large-n statistical procedures, which utilize large numbers of subjects precisely because they lack confidence in individual observations. We can, as we have noted, generalize from the content of the discourses we find among our small number of subjects to the content of the discourses that exist in the larger society. What we cannot say is just what proportion of the society in question subscribes to each discourse (though occasionally we speculate, utilizing knowledge of the society from beyond our Q study). Such questions could be answered easily, though expensively, by administering a sample survey based on our Q results to a random sample from the population (and if we can find suitable surveys on which to piggyback some questions, we may do so in the future). But though survey researchers typically regard such questions as crucial, we do not. When it comes to any given discourse, it perhaps matters less how many people subscribe to it than who these people are, the likelihood of them acting on the discourse in question, and the political significance of that action. Simply counting heads is not decisive in establishing importance. (For example, in retrospect we would say that any discourse subscribed to by the few hundred people who constituted the pre-1989 Czechoslovakia opposition mattered hugely, even if it were not shared at all by the more compliant millions.)

Factor analysis and narrative interpretations

The patterns we find across individuals in each society are elucidated using Q factor analysis, that is, a factor analysis of all forty individual Q sorts for each country.[3] Each factor represents a discourse of democracy for the society in question. The number of factors we report for each society normally varies between two and four. The greater the number of factors we could identify, the more nuanced the pattern of democratic discourses within the society therefore appeared. We used no mechanical formula to determine

---

[3] We used centroid factor analysis followed by varimax rotation. As its name implies, varimax is intended to capture variation or variety in the results – that is, to draw sharp distinctions between factors, as opposed to (say) blending them into a consensus point of view.

the number of factors to report. More conventional R factor analysts often use a "scree test" that decides on the number of factors to report based on the cumulative percentage of variance that the factors explain (if an additional factor explains little compared to its predecessors, it is not reported). Given our interpretive commitments as Q methodologists, we take a different approach. So while statistics *inform* and *constrain* our interpretations (and so are included in the presentation of results), they do not *determine* these interpretations. If statistical tests (such as the scree test) point in different directions than interpretive plausibility, we are guided by the latter. So if a factor proved little different once interpreted to a factor already reported in the analysis, we would not report it, because it adds little or no additional information about the country. Always we report the factors explaining the greatest amount of variation across the subjects (that is, we would not skip a factor accounting for a substantial amount of variation in favor of one that accounted for less). Our judgments were also informed by the number of people loading on a factor; if there were only one or two people loading on it at the .01 level of significance, we would not report the factor.

To interpret each factor, an idealized Q sort can be computed which represents how a hypothetical individual loading 100 percent on that factor and zero on any other factor would order the sixty-four statements. We report the idealized Q sort for each factor in a table for the country in question. In a second table for each country we report the loadings (correlations) of each of our forty-odd subjects on each factor. These loadings can in principle vary from −1 to +1 (reported in the tables for ease of presentation as −100 to +100). A loading of +1 indicates perfect agreement between individual and factor, while −1 would indicate perfect disagreement. While we report statistical significance for the loadings, noteworthy substantive loadings as a rough guide are those that are greater than .4 (and less than −.4).[4] To give a sense of the kind of individuals loading on each factor (which in turn can inform our interpretation of the factor), we also report in the table of loadings the gender, occupation, and political self-description of each person.

In keeping with our focus on language and discourse, we present our factor interpretations in the form of narratives, which we have found makes for parsimonious, vivid, and effective presentation. (However, readers unhappy with the substance of these accounts are welcome to construct their own alternative narratives from the tables we present.) We do not give an example of such a narrative here, for narratives can be found in each substantive

---

[4] Statistical significance is computed based on the standard error, which is $1/\sqrt{n}$, where n is the number of statements. We work at the .01 level of significance, which designates loadings greater than 2.58 times the standard error (S. Brown, 1980, p. 283).

chapter – indeed, they form the core of the results and analysis for each country.

The narratives are not constructed by simply cutting and pasting statements with extreme scores (-6, -5, $+5$, $+6$) on the factor in question. Although statements with these extreme scores always merit special attention, we do not simply run them together and call that a narrative. Each narrative also reflects how the statements appear in relation to one another on the factor – seeming ambiguities and paradoxes may require resolution. For example, our Bulgaria factor B, which we call "Democratic Nationalism," appears to support tolerance and respect for others while denying equal rights to all ethnic groups. Interpretation of this factor requires addressing questions about who seems to qualify for liberal citizenship in its supporters' eyes. The comparative ranking of statements in different discourses is also important; so if a statement is ranked zero (indifferent) in factor A, that may be very significant for the interpretation of factor A if the statement is given extreme scores (of either agreement or disagreement) on factors B and C for the same country. Our interpretations assume that each discourse or factor represents a coherent point of view. In this light, if there are internal inconsistencies within a discourse, they need to be explained, not just criticized or dismissed. We should also add that the interpretations that appear in our narratives are informed by our knowledge of the society in question. The nature of any social scientific interpretation is such that no apologies are necessary here.

The narratives we present together constitute our representation of the discourses of democracy for the society in question. We will do our best to explain the patterns we find within each country through reference to the experience of that society, and the crossnational currents in which it is enmeshed, in terms of both recent and deeper history. We will also draw connections and contrasts between the discourses we find and particular theories and models of democracy and democratization. We shall point to instructive contrasts in the results we generate from different countries, as well as locating discursive currents that transcend national boundaries. Throughout, the intent is to use these findings to develop a deeper understanding of post-communist political transformations.

While we have elucidated and justified our methodology in this chapter, in the end the proof of its utility lies in the power and leverage it can give us in each of the country studies, and in discerning patterns across countries. It is to these studies we now turn.

PART II

Pre-transition countries

We begin our comparative scrutiny of discourses of democracy in the post-communist world with two countries that are not exactly "post," but not really "communist" either. (As we write, Yugoslavia is moving toward the "post" category.) China and the Federal Republic of Yugoslavia (Serbia and Montenegro),[1] despite their geographical distance, both retained in the late 1990s an effective monopoly of state power on the part of the communist party, or at least its direct successor(s). Alone among the countries we survey, they had not yet undergone any post-communist political transition, in the sense that there is no clear break with the totalitarian legacy. China has undertaken substantial changes in the economy that look a lot like capitalism. Economic change in Serbia and Montenegro has featured more in the way of collapse of the economy than of capitalist and market-oriented developments, though its baseline involved less in the way of state central planning compared to other communist countries.[2]

When it comes to their politics, both China and Yugoslavia experienced unsuccessful democratic protests against the regime – China in 1989, Yugoslavia in the winter of 1996–7. These protests initially looked much like those of the 1989 "Autumn of the People" in Central and Eastern Europe; but they ended in failure. Yugoslavia's "autumn" came with greater effect in late

---

[1] At the time of our study, the Federal Republic of Yugoslavia (Serbia and Montenegro) had not been recognized internationally as the sole successor to what is commonly referred to as "the former Yugoslavia"; hence Yugoslavia's seat at the United Nations remained empty.

[2] The general economic collapse in Serbia and Montenegro was accompanied by state-sponsored pyramid schemes. Hyperinflation impoverished much of the population, while making it easier for the state to finance war. On the chronology of the Yugoslav inflation, see Dinkic, 1995, pp. 26–44.

2000. This suggests that the regimes the protestors confronted were a lot more resilient than those that collapsed so easily once their Soviet sponsorship was withdrawn. In the Chinese case, failure came through military suppression of the movement; in Yugoslavia, through a mixture of factors: suppression, concession, a crude appeal to nationalism, and weak and divided leadership of the opposition forces. This mix was consistent with the means used by the old regime, which did not involve the kind of heavy-handed repression common in other communist countries. Both regimes have had to cope with Western opprobrium, though for Yugoslavia this resulted from sponsorship of war in Croatia, Bosnia, and Kosovo, rather than repression of the democracy movement. The political and economic consequences of this opprobrium have been much more severe in Yugoslavia than in China, whose development along the capitalist road was barely affected by the fallout of the Tiananmen Square massacre in June 1989.

Yugoslavia and China offer us an opportunity to make the kind of empirical observation that is unavailable in our other cases. It would have been highly instructive to map the discourses of democracy prevailing under Soviet-era regimes in these countries, then compare them to the discourses we found in the late 1990s. This would have enabled us to test propositions concerning the degree to which discursive legacies affect post-communist political development. Unfortunately, empirical research on popular conceptions of democracy was not possible prior to the revolutions of 1989. It did prove possible – if occasionally a little tricky for us to execute – in China and Yugoslavia in the 1990s. We cannot yet make a before/after comparison in each case, because as yet there is no "after" (though as we write there may soon be in Yugoslavia). However, it is possible to make comparisons between the kinds of discourses that we find in these two pre-transition societies and those found in the post-transition countries, with a view to determining the kinds of discursive shifts that can occur with political transition.

3

China

WITH YALI PENG

China began the twentieth century as a monarchy and an empire, and ended it as a communist state. Communist control over the whole of mainland China was secured in 1949 with the defeat of the Nationalists and their retreat to Taiwan. This was the culmination of several decades of revolution, war, and unstable political arrangements from 1911 on. Though China became a republic, and formally committed to democracy under the nationalists by the 1920s, this commitment remained largely an abstraction. With the Japanese invasion in 1937, the communists and nationalists joined forces. But the relationship was under constant strain and, following the end of the Second World War, they resumed open fighting with each other.

The communist struggle had begun in the early 1920s; after failed attempts to base a revolution in the cities, the Chinese Communist Party (CCP) guided by Mao Zedong developed a strategy of revolution rooted in organization of the peasantry, applied from 1927 on. This kind of protracted struggle based in the countryside was very different from the Leninist model of a seizure of power in the main cities. Not only did the Chinese communists come to power based almost entirely on their own efforts, with very limited outside support, but they also developed their own model of revolution. This lends the CCP regime a degree of legitimacy shared only by Yugoslavia and Russia in this study.

The decades after 1949 were also tumultuous. Until the death of Mao in 1976, the country was subject to a series of bewildering shifts in political direction, often inspired by Mao himself. The most cataclysmic of these was the Great Proletarian Cultural Revolution unleashed in 1966, in which young Red Guards set upon supposedly conservative and reactionary elements, including even party leaders.

At the time of Mao's death, China remained a largely agrarian society at a
level of economic development not radically different from 1949 (though the
country could at least feed itself). The years since then have been dominated
by a pragmatic party leadership (notably Deng Xiaoping, who died in 1997)
much more interested in political stability and rapid economic development
than in Maoist political radicalism (though lip service is still paid to Mao
himself). Economic development has taken the form of the introduction of
market capitalism, though styled "socialism with Chinese characteristics" by
the party leadership. With occasional individual exceptions, that leadership
shows little interest in political reform, and the CCP retains a monopoly on
political power and the definition of state ideology. That monopoly faced
its most serious challenge from a student-led "democracy movement" in
1989. But this was short-lived: the movement was soon crushed by force,
and China has still had almost no experience of democracy of any sort.

The general pattern in the East European countries covered in this study
is that economic reform and marketization in particular follow in the wake
of a political transition in which the communist regime collapses or is overthrown. In China, however, market reform has proceeded now for more
than two decades in the absence of any significant moves toward political transition. The Communist Party has a *de facto* monopoly on political
power, and there are hardly any nongovernmental organizations, let alone
any *competing* political parties. Pluralism only really goes as far as factions
within the Communist Party leadership. Thus it is a straightforward matter
to classify China as one of our two pre-transition cases. Describing China
as "pre-transitional" implies that one day there will be a transition to some
other type of system. We cannot predict that any such move will be toward
a more liberal democratic system. But we should note that China has liberalized its politics to a degree, as indicated by the fact that we brought
this research to a successful conclusion – hardly imaginable two decades
ago. However, the research had to involve "Q methodology with Chinese
characteristics," as we departed somewhat from the discussion group and
individual interview procedures we used in other countries; we believe that
this departure has little bearing on the results.

The results bear upon political possibilities for China's future. But they
should also provide insight into the discursive software that helps constitute
current Chinese political reality. After all, China can style itself a "people's
democracy" in the Marxist-Leninist tradition. But the question of how the
symbols of democracy play into the Chinese context is complicated by the
events of 1989, where the "democracy movement" positioned itself against
the regime. Lei Guang (1996) argues that the Chinese word *minzhu* conveys
a distinctly different concept from the Western word *democracy*. As a result,
it is now clear that the 1989 "democracy movement" cannot be understood

Table 3.1. *Statement scores on four factors for China*

Factor A is Radical Liberal Democracy.
Factor B is Established Conservatism.
Factor C is Concerned Traditionalism.
Factor D is Alienated Egalitarianism.

Statement	Factor			
	A	B	C	D
1 Confucianism does not think of individual needs as conflicting with collective interests. Rather, it encourages a moral constraint based on compromise. Every individual should exercise self-restraint, for it will lead to cooperation and social harmony.	0	+2	+3	+1
2 The people are the most important, the state is second, and the ruler is the least important.	+3	+2	+1	+5
3 If more people are better educated, China will turn to political democracy.	0	+1	+1	+3
4 The present electoral system has set up a framework for democracy. Although it does not have much impact now, it may become more significant in the future with further political and economic development.	−1	+1	0	−2
5 The most serious social problem today is corruption of government employees.	+1	0	+6	+2
6 The current electoral system is a mere formality.	+5	−2	+2	+6
7 The Chinese almost fail to understand the spirit of freedom of speech. When perceiving "threat," they would rather give up freedom for the sake of "order."	0	0	+1	−2
8 The "Oceanic Civilization" is full of vitality and has led the West into a modern society, because it values science, democracy, commercialism, and competition – things the "Yellow-River Civilization" has been unable to nurture.	+1	−3	−3	0
9 Diverse opinions, views, schools, and even political thinking are normal phenomena of a healthy society. They cannot be regarded as factors of instability and be repressed.	+5	+1	+1	+1
10 With their own unique current situations, historical traditions, and cultural backgrounds, countries can exchange ideas, but they cannot copy each other's models.	+1	+5	+3	+1
11 Elections may not select the best qualified individuals, but they can eliminate corrupt and bad individuals.	+4	0	+1	−4

Table 3.1. (*cont.*)

Statement	Factor			
	A	B	C	D
12 To guarantee democracy for the people, we need to enforce the rule of law, and make the democratic process part of our institutions and laws, which will not be subject to changes in the leadership.	+4	+3	+4	+6
13 The practice of "the rule of law" is to protect citizens' rights and freedom by limiting the power of the state and guarding against the abuse of power.	+5	0	+5	+3
14 Nobody wants to see chaos in China, which would only impede economic development. The delay of economic development would in turn slow down the progress of democracy and civilization.	+2	+6	+5	+4
15 There is no such thing as proletarian or socialist liberalization. Liberalization is bourgeois by nature. It is in opposition to our current system and policy.	−5	−1	−3	−2
16 Implementing direct elections in a country when one-quarter of its population is illiterate is like popularizing light music in the countryside when people have difficulty feeding themselves. It is far removed from reality.	−2	+2	0	0
17 There would be no national unity or prosperity without the leadership of the Communist Party or the socialist system.	−6	+6	+4	−4
18 I cannot describe what democracy is and I have never thought about it seriously. But I feel that democracy is a good thing and I can benefit from it.	−1	−1	+2	0
19 Democracy is based primarily on reason and moral standards. The restraint of law and rules is only secondary.	−1	−1	0	+5
20 No political force is strong enough to replace the Communist Party yet. In this situation, free competition of a multiparty system is not only unrealistic, but also would cause chaos.	−3	+4	+1	−2
21 Comprehensive representation means that the People's Congresses must have representatives from different nationalities, regions, and social groups. This formal inequality guarantees a substantive equality.	−2	+1	−1	0
22 The kind of democracy the Chinese people need is socialist or a people's democracy, not individualistic bourgeois democracy.	−4	+4	+2	−1

Table 3.1. (*cont.*)

Statement	Factor			
	A	B	C	D
23 To build a healthy society, it is imperative to carry out privatization on a large scale; this is also the necessary means to fight corruption and increase efficiency.	+3	−4	0	−2
24 The root of many social abuses is that the state controls too many things. We should follow the philosophy of "small government, large society" and greatly reduce the role of the government.	+3	0	−4	+1
25 Those who oppose democracy on the grounds of poor quality of the people are using an unfounded excuse. No matter how ignorant an individual is, he can always tell good people from bad ones.	+1	−2	+3	0
26 Political reform must advance democracy as economic reform deepens. Economic reform would encounter difficulties without political reform.	+2	+4	+3	+2
27 I have no influence on government policy-making and the appointment of officials.	+2	−2	−4	+3
28 "Socialism with Chinese characteristics" is actually capitalism. Our country now in fact has capitalism under the leadership of the Communist Party.	0	−6	−1	+4
29 During the Cultural Revolution, "fighting against liberalization" was a popular slogan, and it has a feudal-autocratic nature. Therefore, it should be abandoned.	+2	−3	−3	−3
30 My concern is to make money and live a good life. I am not interested in politics. I do not care whether we have democracy or not, or who is in charge of the government.	−3	−3	−5	−3
31 To love the motherland does not just mean to love its natural beauty and long history, but also to love the socialist state under the leadership of the CCP.	−4	+5	+1	−3
32 Some people advocate absolute freedom and unlimited democracy. This will only lead the country in the wrong direction. Democracy with Chinese characteristics should have the party as a mainstay and source of unity to ensure stability.	−1	+3	+3	−1
33 The Americans say that our policies are very changeable. Actually, ours are more stable than theirs.	−4	+2	−2	−5

Table 3.1. (*cont.*)

Statement	Factor			
	A	B	C	D
34 People in the coastal areas are different from people in the interior areas. The differences reflect an increasing gap between the two regions in political, economic, and attitudinal aspects.	0	−2	−2	+3
35 Democracy means that what the leaders say should represent the masses' voice, and leaders should work for the people and represent people's interests.	+3	+3	+2	+2
36 Democracy can be developed only gradually. There would be chaos if we blindly copied the Western model.	−2	+4	+4	0
37 Democracy is inseparable from freedom. It means that I can say whatever I want to say and do whatever I want to do.	−5	−5	−6	−1
38 The People's Congresses are institutions to elect and supervise government officials. But the irony is that many members are government officials themselves.	+1	−2	−2	+2
39 If we give complete democracy to the people in elections now, either no representatives would be elected or there would be factious fighting.	−2	−1	−1	−1
40 In a country as large as China with a big population, regional diversities, and so many minorities, direct election at higher levels is not viable. The primary reason is that the people are poorly educated.	−2	+2	+2	−1
41 The 1989 democracy movement was inspired by fervor rather than reason. The participants did not understand how to govern the country.	−2	+1	−1	−1
42 The People's Congresses generally are still rubber stamps, but they have a bit more power than before.	+1	−3	−3	−1
43 The priority for China is to concentrate on economic development instead of Western-style democracy. Economic development will eventually lead to democracy.	−1	+1	0	+1
44 Today's China is a society without ideas. People think only about money. This is a good thing.	−3	−5	−6	−5
45 With Marxism-Leninism being discredited and Confucianism knocked down, Buddhism should be restored to unite the Chinese people's thought.	−3	−6	−5	−6
46 People rebel only when they are starving. Very few peasants are starving nowadays, so there is no crisis in Chinese society.	−3	−1	−4	−5

Table 3.1. (*cont.*)

	Factor			
Statement	A	B	C	D
47 The country is facing a serious potential crisis because of deteriorating public safety, corruption, moral degradation, stratification, economic difficulties, and widespread discontent.	+1	−4	+4	+4
48 In politically developed countries, policies are debated by scholars before they are implemented by politicians. In China politicians implement policies before they assign scholars to verify their feasibility.	+3	−1	−2	+1
49 At the county level, a rural deputy to the People's Congress represents four times as many people as an urban deputy does. At the provincial level, the ratio is 5:1; at the national level, 8:1.	−1	0	−2	−4
50 The direct elections at the county level and below are fully fair and competitive.	−4	+1	−3	−6
51 The cities are political and economic centers where the working class lives. Having more urban than rural deputies in the People's Congresses embodies the leadership of the working class.	−1	−1	+1	−3
52 Democratization does not mean we should copy the Western model. Democracy as an abstract idea can have different expressions when applied to societies with different historical and cultural traditions.	+1	+3	0	−1
53 The essence of democracy is judging individuals by their ability. Those having high moral standards and competence should be given the responsibility to rule the country.	+4	+1	+6	+5
54 Human rights in China constitute primarily the right to life. To be protected from starvation and secured a better life is the 1.2 billion Chinese people's number one human right.	−1	+3	−1	+4
55 A modern society should protect its citizens' freedom from the repression of the state. Democracy is a necessary means to guarantee that protection.	+4	0	0	+3
56 The Chinese military should no longer be controlled by the party.	+6	−5	−5	+2
57 If China turns to capitalism, there will be stratification with wealth for a few millionaires and poverty for the majority of the population.	−5	+5	+2	+2
58 The development of socialist democracy is important in the establishment of a market economy.	+2	+2	0	+1

Table 3.1. (*cont.*)

Statement	Factor			
	A	B	C	D
59 It is national defeatism to blame a geographic disadvantage and a "Continental Civilization" for China's historical failure and contemporary backwardness.	0	0	−1	−4
60 The failure of public ownership lies in the fact that distribution of benefits is not determined by production but by power. Those having power can gain control of social products for nothing.	+6	−3	−1	+1
61 In an abstract sense, freedom and democracy are not absolutely good. For today's China, they are relatively "evil," because freedom would make China lax, and democracy would cause it to collapse.	−6	−1	−4	−3
62 An urgent task of reform is for the political system to regain authority it has lost. However, a new power structure is needed to achieve this goal.	0	−4	−2	−2
63 A middle class is gradually forming in China. It will have political demands. Once economic power is combined with political power, it cannot be overlooked.	+2	−2	−1	0
64 In today's society power brings money.	0	−4	+5	0

simply as a struggle for democracy in any standard Western sense,[1] nor can the activists in the 1978–9 "Democracy Wall" movement be understood as speaking the same language as the students in 1989. Thus, in China perhaps even more than elsewhere, we need to pay close attention to the variety of meanings that can be embedded in the language of democracy and associated concepts.

Before we proceed to analysis of our Chinese results, a few words about methodology are appropriate. In our Central and East European cases, the main sources of statements for the Q study were the discussion groups we conducted in each country, though these groups were normally supplemented by statements taken from written sources, especially newspapers and magazines. Discussion groups proved unfeasible in China, and, as a substitute, conversations conducted in private with individuals were used as a source of statements. Of the sixty-four statements used, thirty-one were from

[1] Our wording here allows that there are different models of Western democracy, while suggesting that there are certain agreed fundamentals that cut across country-specific details.

these conversations. The remainder of the statements were from published sources, mainly newspapers, books, and magazines. Some of the statements were made by political figures holding widely different views (within the establishment), such as Deng Xiaoping, Jiang Zemin, He Xin, and Yan Jiaqi.

Sixty subjects were interviewed in late 1994; they included government officials, private business owners, scientists, white-collar employees, teachers, students, workers, peasants, and soldiers, among others. The subjects were drawn from three geographical locations: Beijing (the nation's political and cultural center), Hainan (an economically more developed offshore coastal province), and Guizhou (an interior province with much less economic development).

The researcher normally spent one to two hours talking with each subject about political issues, the economy, social problems, their welfare, their concerns, and so forth before letting them order the statements. It took most subjects two to three hours to produce a Q sort – a longer average time than for any of our other countries. On a few occasions, several subjects together discussed the statements among themselves and did a Q sort collectively, which seems rather different from what one might expect in an individualistic Western society, where we expect people to respond to social scientists individually. However, in China the culture encourages an articulation of "collective" opinions on issues of political and social significance. These collective Q sorts were perfectly consistent with our goal of modeling the way people approach and communicate about democracy. (In table 3.2 the individual listed for a collective Q sort is the one the researcher initially intended to interview.)

Chinese political discourses

Factor analysis of the sixty subjects produced four discourses, which we label Radical Liberal Democracy, Established Conservatism, Concerned Traditionalism, and Alienated Egalitarianism. (In the narratives, numbers in parentheses refer to the statements from the first table.)

China factor A: Radical Liberal Democracy

Democracy and freedom are absolutely desirable. They won't make China lax or cause the country to collapse as some people allege (61). Therefore, it is improper to claim that absolute freedom and unlimited democracy will lead the country in the wrong direction, and that democracy can be developed only gradually. It is also unfounded to claim that there would be a chaos if we "blindly copy" the Western model (32, 36). On the contrary, democracy is a necessary means to protect citizens' freedom from state repression. Diverse political views are a normal phenomenon of a healthy society, and they cannot be treated as

Table 3.2. *Subject loadings on factors for China*

Subject and political self-description	Factor			
	A	B	C	D
1 F, retired English translator, our hope is in the twenty-first century	50*	28	7	23
2 M, retired bank employee, I know nothing about politics	−33	67*	6	−6
3 M, state employee-turned-business owner, I'm optimistic	71*	11	−19	11
4 F, secretary, democracy is more than votes	4	53*	−1	5
5 F, manager, democracy can't be too loose or too tight	61*	36	24	−5
6 M, state official, education and economy are the keys	53*	73*	24	17
7 F, teacher, I see conflict between the ruled and ruler	71*	−14	−1	21
8 M, county court judge, I favor "checks and balances"	66*	14	21	24
9 M, office worker, politics should be active and relaxed	62*	−16	20	13
10 M, teacher, parliamentary democracy is the only option	78*	−27	4	1
11 M, private business employee, democracy is the trend	74*	−19	8	15
12 F, linguist, I hope the party regains prestige among the people	16	−27	−31	28
13 M, army officer, stability is the priority	−31	80*	22	12
14 F, doctor, democratic policy-making is the core of reform	76*	−1	−7	−9
15 F, army movie technician, some people have turned to Buddhism	61*	23	−1	−15
16 M, librarian, I am optimistic about China's future	51*	6	3	7
17 M, party school teacher, I am confused	36	−4	−9	0
18 F, researcher in journalism, democracy is unrealistic	58*	15	15	28
19 M, social scientist, stability is the means, not the goal	73*	−12	−2	0
20 M, writer, democratization will be long and painful	35	−12	−30	9
21 F, high school student, we must punish corrupt officials	50*	−20	27	40
22 M, retired factory cadre, the future is bright	4	55*	37	−3

Table 3.2. (*cont.*)

	Factor			
Subject and political self-description	A	B	C	D
23 M, high school student, I don't know much about politics	−22	72*	29	11
24 M, soldier, we must stop corruption	−21	35	52*	23
25 F, bank employee, I hate corrupt officials	46*	13	51*	14
26 F, worker, we should reduce number of cars for officials	1	37	62*	13
27 F, cashier, there will be no corrupt officials if we have democracy	20	−15	38	53*
28 M, tobacco company employee, we must strengthen the rule of law	62*	−26	1	6
29 M, employee of defunct state business, prices are too high	35	2	15	37
30 M, deputy county head, we should stick to CCP leadership	−10	77*	15	6
31 M, high school teacher, I favor capitalism and democracy	73*	−22	19	24
32 F, retired bank employee, no public funds for banqueting	5	32	54*	28
33 F, trade school teacher, we must reform political system	44	8	−14	66*
34 F, kindergarten director, there is mass discontentment	30	1	63*	15
35 M, peasant, freedom cannot be limitless	−22	26	41	11
36 F, retired worker, only revolution can change politics	37	−43	30	20
37 M, peasant, the government has no correct positions	25	14	29	50*
38 M, peasant, we need political stability and public safety	−3	23	48*	47*
39 M, village party head, the peasants bear a heavy burden	−19	22	61*	24
40 M, peasant, now money can buy everything, even life	31	3	64*	21
41 M, government official, reform is the only way out	12	60*	25	9
42 M, businessperson, China should have an Eastern democracy	53*	7	9	32
43 M, shoe repairer, I don't know what democracy is	32	43	21	16
44 F, worker, I used to be a political activist	33	−15	14	40

Table 3.2. (*cont.*)

Subject and political self-description	Factor			
	A	B	C	D
45 F, shop owner, I have no views about political things	38	35	61*	1
46 M, government employee, democracy is based on education	6	74*	8	26
47 M, peasant, we should have a clean government	35	25	15	63*
48 M, unemployed worker, society today is rotten	−5	−1	33	42
49 M, migrant peasant laborer, I am not interested in politics	0	18	48*	16
50 M, migrant peasant laborer, democracy is peace	7	35	33	11
51 F, computer operator, democracy is worth trying	−15	50*	26	18
52 F, company stock portfolio clerk, China has its own problems	62*	18	6	40
53 F, office worker, the most serious problem is corruption	0	−1	58*	−26
54 F, office clerk, I'm not knowledgeable about politics	8	38	18	−8
55 F, maid, I don't know what I should do for democracy	22	31	45*	−2
56 M, driver, we cannot do without the party leadership	−9	68*	34	−11
57 F, secretary, democracy is important for the market economy	2	46*	−6	−2
58 M, worker, I am scared by the present society	12	17	47*	12
59 F, college student, only the socialist road is correct	−6	73*	19	−16
60 F, state employee, ownership reform is the priority	45*	10	43	12

Subjects 1–20 were interviewed in Beijing; 21–40 in Guizhou; 41–60 in Hainan.
* Denotes a loading significant at the .01 level.

factors of instability or be repressed (9, 55). To practice "the rule of law" is to protect citizens' rights and guard against the abuse of power by the state. Human rights are more than the right to live (13, 54). The policy of "fighting against liberalization" is feudal-autocratic in nature, and should be abandoned (15, 29). Unlike Western culture, Chinese culture is lacking in the spirit of science, democracy, commercialism, and competition. We must change the culture (8). It is not valid to believe that there would be no national unity or prosperity without the leadership of the Chinese Communist Party and the socialist system. Neither is it valid to say that a multiparty democracy is not viable because no other political force is strong enough to replace the CCP (17, 20). To love China does not necessarily mean to love the socialist system under the leadership of the CCP (31). It is also wrong to assert that what the Chinese people need is a "socialist," rather than a "bourgeois," democracy (22). The current electoral system is not fair or competitive. Rather, it is a mere formality, and the People's Congresses are just rubber stamps (6, 42, 50). It is unjustifiable to use a poorly educated population as an excuse for not holding direct elections above the county level (16, 40). Public ownership favors distribution of benefits to those with power and fosters corruption and inefficiency. Therefore, large-scale privatization and reduction of the government's control of society are imperative to build a healthy society. Capitalism does not necessarily bring stratification (23, 24, 57, 60). A new power structure is needed for the Chinese political system to regain the authority that it has lost since the reform. In the process of political development, a middle class combining economic power with political power may play a role in future politics (62, 63). Finally, the Chinese military should not be controlled by the party (56).

The discourse represented by factor A, as its label suggests, is radical in its views about democracy. It advocates individual freedom, private property rights, free elections, dissident opinions, and a military under state, rather than party, control. Moreover, Radical Liberal Democracy rejects the ideas that national unity and prosperity depend on the leadership of the Chinese Communist Party (CCP) and the socialist system (a direct challenge to Deng Xiaoping's Four Cardinal Principles); that to love China means to love the current political system; that capitalism would mean stratification and that the Chinese people need a "socialist," rather than a "bourgeois," democracy. Radical Liberal Democracy is the most liberal of the four discourses. However, we should also note that it is not completely consistent with liberal democracy in the Western sense, for Radical Liberal Democracy cares about national unity and social stability (14), and supports a meritocracy in which the best and most moral rule, suggesting acceptance of some degree of benevolent rule without popular consent (53).

China factor B: Established Conservatism

A free, competitive multiparty system is unrealistic since no other political force in China is strong enough to replace the CCP. There would be no national unity or prosperity without the leadership of the party or the socialist system (17, 20). Therefore, to love the motherland means to love the socialist state under the leadership of the CCP (31). Democracy with Chinese characteristics should have the party as a mainstay and source of unity. Abstract freedom and unlimited democracy will only lead China in a wrong direction (32). A return to capitalism would produce a few millionaires and a large number of poor people, rather than creating a middle class. Hence, advocacy of privatization is wrong. Public owner- ship has not proven merely to conceal benefits gained by the few with power (23, 57, 60, 63). The kind of democracy the Chinese people need is socialist democ- racy, rather than bourgeois democracy (22). It is totally incorrect to believe that the situation in China now is capitalism under the leadership of the Communist Party (28). It is true that economic reform would encounter difficulties without political reform to advance democracy, but democracy can be developed only gradually. There would be chaos if we blindly copy the Western model. Nobody wants to see chaos in China because it would impede economic growth and slow down political reform (14, 26, 36). The 1989 democracy movement was inspired by fervor rather than reason. The participants had no understanding of how to run the country (41). Democracy as an abstract idea can have different forms contingent on distinct culture and history. With their unique current situations, historical backgrounds, and cultural traditions, countries can exchange ideas, but they cannot imitate each other (10, 52). Probably, democracy is relatively "bad" for China here and now (61). It is invalid to argue that the "Yellow-River Civilization" is inferior to the "Oceanic Civilization" of the West because it has been unable to nurture the spirit of science, democracy, commercialism, and competition (8). The direct elections at the county level and below are fair and competitive. That more urban than rural representatives are elected assures the leadership of the working class (6, 21, 49, 50). People's Congresses are not rubber stamps (42). The current electoral system has set up a framework for democracy. Direct elections above the county level are premature because a large portion of the population is still poorly educated (4, 16, 40). There is no urgent need to have a new power structure (62). There is no crisis in Chinese society, and corruption is not as serious as people believe. Power does not bring money (5, 47, 64). Finally, it is dangerous to think that the Chinese military should be removed from the control of the party (56).

In sharp contrast to Radical Liberal Democracy, factor B's Established Conservatism rejects liberal democratic beliefs. Established Conservatism values political stability, CCP leadership and socialism, the gradual devel- opment of democracy, and reform measures based on China's own peculiar national characteristics (*Guo qing*). This conservatism also results in a de- fense of the status quo, evidenced in opposition to the need for a new power structure in the political arena and privatization in the economic structure, the denial that the country is in any kind of crisis, and refutation of the asser- tion that so-called socialism with Chinese characteristics is in fact capitalism under CCP leadership.

China factor C: Concerned Traditionalism

Our country is facing a deep crisis because of official corruption, deteriorating public safety, moral degradation, polarization, broken state enterprises, and mass discontent (46, 47). I am very worried that power brings money in our society, and that corruption of government employees has become the most serious problem (5, 64). Yet I do not agree that today's China is a society without ideas, and that people are concerned only with making money. It is also incorrect to say that people are not interested in politics any more, and that they don't care whether we have democracy or not (30, 44). As an individual, I do have some influence on government policy-making and the appointment of officials (27). I do not like the idea that we should follow the philosophy of "small government, big society" and reduce the role of government (24). Too much individual freedom and democracy will probably lead us in the wrong direction. We should follow the Confucian idea of viewing individual needs as not conflicting with collective interests, and encouraging a moral constraint based on compromise. Self-restraint will lead to cooperation and social harmony (1, 32). There is no reason to believe that the Chinese civilization is inferior to the Western civilization when it comes to science and democracy (8). Even if I cannot tell what democracy is, and I have never thought about it seriously, I know it is something good and beneficial. I don't agree that democracy is a relatively "bad" thing for China here and now (18, 61). To guarantee democracy for the people, we need to enforce the rule of law, which is to protect citizens' rights and freedom by guarding against the abuse of power (12, 13). But democracy can be developed only gradually. Implementation of the Western model too quickly would cause chaos, which would impede economic development and slow down the process of democratization (14, 36). Sometimes I feel that it is unjustifiable to oppose democracy on the ground of a poorly educated population. An ignorant individual can still tell good people from bad ones (25). But sometimes, when I view the matter from a different angle, I tend to agree that it is not viable to hold direct elections at higher levels because many people are not politically competent (40). The Communist Party still holds an important position in Chinese political life that is more or less difficult to replace. Therefore, to some extent patriotism requires commitment to the socialist state under the CCP leadership (17, 20, 31). It is not a good idea to end the party's control of the military (56).

Though sharing some views with both of the first two discourses, the Concerned Traditionalism of factor C seems to care more about clean government and social morality than about democracy. Based on its belief in Confucian social harmony and compromise between individual and collective interests, C's traditionalism is concerned about corruption and the potential crises it sees facing society. Though in some aspects discontented, C generally still has a favorable feeling toward the current regime.

China factor D: Alienated Egalitarianism

I don't think we have democracy. As an individual, I have no influence on policy-making or appointment of officials. The current elections are far from being fair and competitive. They are just meaningless political ceremonies. They do not have much impact now and won't have much impact in the future (4, 6, 27, 50). I am very doubtful when somebody says that, even if elections may not select the best qualified candidates, they can eliminate corrupt and bad individuals (11). I disagree with the arrangement in the current electoral system that allows greater urban representation than rural representation in the People's Congresses on the assumption that this arrangement guarantees the leadership of the working class (49, 51). It is an irony that many government officials are themselves deputies of People's Congresses. This is tantamount to letting officials elect themselves and supervise their own work. The People's Congresses do not mean much anyway (38, 42). China is now facing a deep potential crisis resulting from corruption, moral degradation, crime, and mass dissatisfaction. It is naive to believe that there is no crisis in Chinese society because peasants are not starving and hence will not rebel (46, 47). If you ask me, "socialism with Chinese characteristics" is just a euphemism for capitalism. China is now nothing but capitalism under the leadership of the Communist Party (28). Economic reform has created an increasing gap between the coastal and interior areas in political, economic, and attitudinal aspects (34). Although the implementation of democracy presupposes the rule of law, democracy is primarily based on reason and morality. Its essence is to judge individuals by their competence and virtue, rather than by connections. People are the most important, and the ruler is the least important (2, 12, 19, 53). Democracy is democracy; it does not change regardless of where and when it is practiced. It probably does not make much sense to say that the Chinese people need a "socialist," rather than a "bourgeois," democracy. And it is groundless to claim that there would be no national unity or prosperity without the leadership of the CCP or socialism (17, 22, 52). Sure, chaos is bad for the country and democracy may not mean an individual can do whatever he or she wants, but it is also unjustified to claim that absolute freedom and unlimited democracy will lead the country in the wrong direction (14, 32, 37). There may be something in the Chinese culture and China's geographic position that is responsible for the country's lagging behind in the world community (59). How can democracy be achieved? Perhaps if more people get better educated, China may finally turn to democracy (3).

The Alienated Egalitarianism of factor D does not support the regime. It has little faith in the current electoral system and is even suspicious that any election would work. Alienated Egalitarianism believes that democracy can be achieved primarily through reason and moral standards, such that laws and rules are only secondary. This emphasis on public morality is similar to that associated with European republicanism (as well as with factor C, Concerned Traditionalism), though there is no plausible means through which such ideas could have affected the content of this discourse. Alienated Egalitarianism believes that the people should be more important than the state's hierarchy, but that now they do not play any role in policy-making. Its populist conviction even leads D to have a more positive attitude than the other factors toward the statement that democracy means individuals can do whatever they want. Like Concerned Traditionalism, Alienated Egalitarianism sees imminent crises in society. If C's traditionalism is discontented and concerned, then D's populism is discontented and cynical. Discontent and cynicism may have been noted before by observers of the Chinese populace, but they have not been empirically corroborated in the literature.

Absent from our discourses is any clear advocacy of Neo-Confucianism (though certain Confucian ideas may find some approval in C's Concerned Traditionalism and D's Alienated Egalitarianism), Buddhism, and Taoism. In fact, all the factors reject the argument for reviving Buddhism as an ideology to unite the Chinese people, given that other belief-systems, notably Marxism and traditional Confucianism, have been in large measure discredited (45). Any prescriptions resorting to religious or traditional sentiment are unlikely to be very successful in China.[2] Nationalism is also not explicitly present in any of the discourses. This, however, does not suggest that nationalism can be completely dismissed, especially as a force that might be used by a post-communist leadership in a bid to hold the country together in the face of potential breakup, as indicated by analysts such as Jenner (1992).

Issues in Chinese political culture

Chinese political culture is often regarded as anti-democratic because of its authoritarian tendencies, belief in hierarchy, intolerance, political apathy and ignorance, and unstable participatory mentality marked by periodic shifts from indifference to fanaticism (e.g., Zhu, Zhao, and Li, 1990, p. 992; Nathan and Shi, 1993, p. 95; Zhang, 1994, pp. 142–3). Scholars also remark that the Chinese are particularly concerned about unity, harmony, and conformity; that private interests are repressed for the sake of public interests; that individualism is constrained by collectivism; and that the people are dependent on the state for benevolent rule. If so, the path to democracy (or any desirable form of polity) in China must then be different from that in the West (Nathan, 1985, pp. ix, 49, 104–5, 132; Pye, 1985, pp. 329, 339, 341, 343; Dittmer, 1987).

Our results challenge some aspects of this conventional wisdom. First, our subjects really did care about political issues and were anxious to talk about politics throughout the whole course of this study. Some of them may be poorly educated, but they are not uninformed. The statement that it is

---

[2] Recent conflict between the Chinese authorities and the (quasi-religious) Falun Gong movement suggests only that the movement could under certain circumstances serve as a focal point for political dissent, much as the evangelical church did in the German Democratic Republic during the 1980s.

a good thing that today's China is a society without ideas and that people care about only money (44) is rejected by all four discourses. The assertion that Chinese are apolitical is not borne out in any of the four discourses.[3]

Second, this study identifies a different aspect of Chinese political culture: feelings of alienation and cynicism. These feelings are evident in Alienated Egalitarianism's suspicion of elections, rules, and laws; its dissatisfaction with urban dominance; its belief that individuals play no role in politics, and its disbelief that China's policies are stable. This discourse also has a somewhat pessimistic view of China's traditional culture and geographic location, and it strongly disagrees with the statement that peasants will not rebel because people rebel only when they have nothing to eat.

Some aspects of the conventional wisdom on Chinese political culture fare better in light of our results. While on "real-world" political issues the discourses tend to have conflicting views (especially A and B), when it comes to some "culturally related" statements they are more likely to present consensus. In terms of unity and stability, with factor A's Radical Liberal Democracy showing some reluctance, none of the discourses wants to see chaos in China (14) and all definitely agree (though Alienated Egalitarianism is hesitant) that democracy does not mean one can do or say whatever one wants (37). These concerns reflect the chronic Chinese fear of chaos (*luan*).

Also, all four discourses think that democracy means that leaders should represent the masses' voice and serve the people's interests (35). Except for B's relatively unenthusiastic agreement, the discourses strongly believe that the essence of democracy involves judging individuals by their abilities and morality, such that capable people with high morality should be chosen as leaders (53). These attitudes seem to suggest that the discourses are all to some degree related to the traditional Chinese idea of *min ben* – to rule benevolently without necessarily asking for consent from the ruled (Hua, 1992, p. 50). Thus the Chinese still place a high value on meritocracy in thinking about democracy.

Finally, what of the Chinese peasantry? Hua (ibid., p. 55) argues that theorists usually forget that "in China nothing can be done without the workers and peasants." But Chinese peasants have long been held to be a liability

[3] It might be objected that Chinese respondents are being "political" because they are being asked to. We accept that there is a difference between self-initiated and externally prompted political activity. Nevertheless, we believe that the sheer level of interest shown in participating in our research project itself suggests that many Chinese would be just as "political" as their Western counterparts if their leaders would give them the opportunity. Moreover, the onus is on those who claim the Chinese are inherently apolitical to provide empirical evidence; basing arguments on the very low levels of self-motivated political activism is hardly persuasive when, as the repression experienced by dissidents such as Wei Jingsheng, Wang Xizhe, and others testifies, the cost of engaging in such activism is extraordinarily high.

for political development. On this point, both Maoist revolutionary zealots, who regard the peasantry as petty bourgeois, and some liberal democrats, who doubt that the peasants really understand democracy, agree. Whenever there is a debate about something that can or cannot be done in the country, a poorly educated, impassive, backward, and narrow-minded peasant population is always cited as a factor in the debate. The Radical Liberal Democracy of factor A generally does not agree with the idea that democracy is unrealistic because China has a large poorly educated rural population, while the Established Conservatism of factor B tends to be in favor of gradualism in democratization because of the poor preparation of the rural population. The interesting case is the Alienated Egalitarianism of factor D, which is the most outspoken when it comes to defending the rural sector against urban dominance and expressing dissatisfaction on behalf of the peasants (46, 49, 51). This should come as no surprise because, of the five individuals who have a significant loading on D, three are peasants themselves (see table 3.2). This probably helps explain why Alienated Egalitarianism gives strong agreement to statement 54 (see table 3.1), which is included primarily to test the debate in the international community about China's official human rights policy. Judging from this discourse's responses to other statements, it might be expected that this item would meet with disagreement. This apparent inconsistency can be resolved once we see that D's Alienated Egalitarianism relates this item not to the context of the debate on human rights, but to the issue of practical livelihood which is important to the peasantry.

Eight of our sixty subjects are peasants (including two migrant workers), to which we can add one street shoe repairer and one house maid who are of peasant origin. Three turn out not to load significantly on any of the four factors; one loads significantly on both C (Concerned Traditionalism) and D (Alienated Populism); four subscribe to factor C and two belong to factor D (see table 3.2). None of the peasants identifies with either Radical Liberal Democracy or Established Conservatism, but this does not suggest to us that they are indifferent to democracy, rather that they use a distinct language when talking about democracy. For example, they are concerned about a corruption-free and clean government and officials' morality; they do not believe that it is fair for urban areas to have more representatives in the People's Congresses; and they question whether elections can have any beneficial results.

These results can help us to make sense of the 1989 "June 4th" incident in Tiananmen. It may not be so much that the peasants in the People's Liberation Army (PLA) believed the government's propaganda about the protestors. Rather, they were operating within a different discourse. They were probably not convinced that the pro-democracy demonstrators had

property rights, a free market, and a withdrawal of the state from economic management. They argue that today the Russian people are suffering because Russia has attempted to follow this path. The social democratic model does not favor an East Asian model either, for, while part of China has developed along the East Asian line quite successfully, the strategy cannot easily penetrate the rest of the country due to historical and cultural factors, as well as the sheer size of the country. As Bowles and Dong (1994, p. 75) point out, not all China is Guangdong. The path proposed for China would retain social ownership while democratizing the economy and politics, giving the market economy and political democracy a stronger form than in the leading Western powers. This democratic socialism, built on China's own characteristics and innovations, should be one of "national emancipation and popular empowerment" (Unger and Cui, 1994, p. 87).

All four of these models claim justification based on some degree of democracy, and three at least find resonance in the discourses we have identified. "Socialism with Chinese characteristics" fits the Established Conservatism of factor B. Liberal democracy finds some reflection in A's Radical Liberal Democracy and, to a lesser extent, D's Alienated Egalitarianism. East Asian developmental corporatism is consistent with C's Concerned Traditionalism. The social democratic model finds no support in our discourses.

The four discourses we have identified are truly Chinese discourses of democracy in the sense that they cannot be equated with either liberal democracy in the Western tradition, or an orthodox Marxist ideology and its CCP version of socialism with Chinese characteristics. For example, the Radical Liberal Democracy of factor A is the most liberal of our four discourses. Yet its concern for national unity and social stability, its identification of meritocracy with democracy, and its acceptance of some degree of benevolent rule without popular consent conflict with liberal democratic ideas. Similarly, the willingness of B's Established Conservatism to accept democracy as a legitimate political concept creates some distance from the official Four Cardinal Principles.

Any move to democracy in China would almost certainly have a much better chance of success were it to involve more than one of the four discourses. Though they use different languages in talking about democracy, there is some common ground among the four discourses with respect to the desirability of democracy (12, 26, 39). All four agree with Deng Xiaoping's statement that, to guarantee democracy, the democratic process should be made part of the institutions and laws of the country (12); they all favor increasing democracy as economic reform deepens because they think that economic reform would encounter difficulties without political reform (26); none believes that freedom and democracy are relatively "evil" in an abstract sense for today's China (61), though B's Established Conservatism predictably retains some reservation on this score; and they all reject the idea, though not strongly, that the masses cannot be given complete democracy now through elections for fear of stalemate and faction fighting (39). The idea of democracy has become a universal concept in the Chinese political context.

This shared commitment might form a general base for political alliances. Also, A's Radical Liberal Democracy and D's Alienated Egalitarianism reluctantly accept the belief of B's Established Conservatism and C's Concerned Traditionalism that any model of democracy must be uniquely Chinese (10). In addition, though not as strongly as B and C, both A and D also agree that chaos is a bad thing, and that stability is necessary for economic development, which in turn will lead to democracy (14). These compatibilities could produce a "developmental coalition," which would agree upon the priority of economic development and the need for stability, with an understanding by each party that political reform will emerge in the long run. Given their shared approval of meritocracy and their acceptance, to some degree, of benevolent rule without popular consent (35, 53), a "political coalition" is also possible. For this to happen, factor B would have to drop its insistence on the Communist Party's monopoly of power, factor A would have to modify its demand for a full-fledged Western-style liberal democracy and total privatization, the excessive corruption that factors C and D are most concerned about would have to be checked, and, finally, the interests of the peasantry would have to be incorporated into the process.

These requirements for compromise are substantial. It is quite likely that the current CCP leadership, as represented by B's Established Conservatism, will not be willing to retreat from its hold on power, even if it does give way on more extensive privatization of the state sector. At the same time, A's Radical Liberal Democracy may not accept anything less than a multiparty democracy and free market based on private property rights. The most high-profile conflict when it comes to the prospect of democratization in China pits advocates of liberal democracy against the "socialism with Chinese characteristics" of the CCP regime. This conflict is reflected in these differences between the discourses of Radical Liberal Democracy and Established Conservatism.

We have also uncovered two more subordinate discourses that seem to be especially energized by their discontent with rampant pursuit of self-interest under the present regime, which is coupled with their strong senses of crisis and cynicism. Because of strong vested interests and lack of political checks, the regime may not be able to reduce corruption or bring about a clean government as desired by C's Concerned Traditionalism and D's Alienated Egalitarianism. And due to the financial needs of many local governments, the peasantry may continue to be oppressed and exploited (see Peng, 1996).

These problems notwithstanding, we have shown that there exist substantial discursive resources for those interested in democratic reform in China. It is important to stress that the relevant discourses have many distinctively Chinese features which would have to be borne in mind in any transition. Just as in our other pre-transition case, Yugoslavia, there prove to be indigenous discourses relevant to democratization which do not simply involve importation of a Western model of liberal democracy. Here we can see just how dangerous are those liberal triumphalists such as Fukuyama (1989, 1992) and Sartori (1991), and all those transitologists for whom a one-size-fits-all liberal constitutionalist version of electoral democracy is a universal model. If such a model is inserted into contexts where it is does not mesh with any indigenous discourses, then the supporting software necessary to make it work is simply not there. As the case of Russia shows, the consequence can be widespread alienation, not just from the state, but also from the very language of democracy. We argue here not as apologists for a regime and system that claims that China's distinctiveness means that it can have no substantial democracy of any sort, but as democrats who believe that democratization must attend to particular real-world configurations of discourses and material circumstances, in China no less than elsewhere.

4

Yugoslavia

WITH SINIŠA NIKOLIN

Contemporary Yugoslavia dates only from the 1990s. It is all that remains of a much larger Yugoslavia created after the First World War as the Kingdom of Serbs, Croats, and Slovenes (under Serbian King Peter), although it also included Bosnia, Hercegovina, Montenegro, and parts of Macedonia. The new country was renamed Yugoslavia (Land of the Southern Slavs) in 1929. There was a limited form of parliamentary democracy during the 1920s. But this was short-lived, and the country became a virtual dictatorship under King Alexander in 1929. (For a claim that democracy in Serbia was well developed prior to the First World War, but usually overlooked in histories of the period, see Suster, 1998.)

There had been ethnic tensions within Yugoslavia from its earliest days, particularly between the two largest groups, Croats and Serbs. These reached a peak during the Second World War, when the fascist Ustaše declared a separate Croatia (which included parts of Bosnia and Hercegovina). The Serbian position was more complex. The new anti-fascist Yugoslav government fled into exile in London in 1941, while Serbia itself was controlled partly by the Serbian nationalist Chetniks. In 1943, the Western allies discovered that many (though not all) Chetniks were collaborating with the Nazis. Given the existence of a fascist state in Croatia, and the fact that the London government-in-exile had little real power within Yugoslavia, the West increased support for Josip Broz Tito's communists. Tito's partisans were also very committed to the pan-Yugoslav cause, which suited the West's desire to see Yugoslavia hold together. Under Western pressure, the communists and the government-in-exile formed a short-lived coalition in 1945. By the end of the year, the communists were in power and the monarchy had been abolished.

A few points about the communist era relevant to our study need to be highlighted. First, the communists came to power largely through their own efforts; to the extent that external forces assisted them, these were from the West rather than the Soviet Union. This distinguishes Yugoslavia from all the other states considered in this volume except Russia and China. A serious rift between Tito and Stalin resulted in Yugoslavia leaving the Soviet camp in 1948.

Second, partly in order to distinguish their brand of communism clearly from the Soviet bloc's, Yugoslav leaders such as Tito and Kardelj soon developed their own version of "socialist" or people's "democracy." In addition to symbolic gestures, such as renaming the party a "league" (a term considered more in line with the Marxist tradition than the Leninist), the Yugoslav communists developed the concept of self-management. They contrasted this with the more centralized and bureaucratic state socialism of the Soviet bloc. They also developed a system of delegative democracy, which they maintained was superior to representative forms. Although both concepts proved highly problematic in practice, the Yugoslav model of socialism and "democracy" was indeed very different from that practiced in other Central and East European states and the Soviet Union. Hungary, perhaps the most liberal of the Soviet bloc states, was in many ways more repressive than Yugoslavia. For instance, it was much easier for Yugoslavs to travel in the West or read Western magazines than it was for other Central and East Europeans.[1]

The most popular explanation of Yugoslavia's breakup in the 1990s attributes it to long-standing nationalist tensions that bubbled to the surface. But there is an important "chicken and egg" question here. Inasmuch as there were always *some* ethnic tensions within Yugoslavia, we need to ask why the situation changed so dramatically at the beginning of the 1990s, and – most importantly from the point of view of our study – address the implications for democratization and attitudes toward democracy.

The simple and most common answer is that disintegrative nationalism was suppressed by the regime. Yet though repression was sometimes severe – in the 1930s and under the communists until 1966 and from 1974 to 1980 (Tito's death) – it was much less severe during the 1980s. Another suggested explanation is that the various ethnic groups in former Yugoslavia were inspired by what they saw happening elsewhere in CEE. But the Soviet Union did not break up until 1991 (nor Czechoslovakia until the end of 1992). By the time of the August coup in Moscow that triggered the disintegration of

---

[1] Though the Yugoslav authorities could be quite intolerant of dissidents and some nationalists, for instance: see Sher, 1977 on the Praxis group and Bertsch, 1973 on disintegrative nationalism. We are talking only in relative terms.

the Soviet Union, Slovenia and Croatia had already declared independence (in June 1991, following declarations of sovereignty in July and December 1990 respectively). The Slovenian parliament had proclaimed Slovenia's right to secede as early as September 1989, *before* the 1989 "Autumn of the People."

Genuinely contested elections were held in all six of the component republics of Yugoslavia in 1990. While four of the six voted to replace their communist systems with more democratic ones that were also more oriented to the particular republic than to Yugoslavia as a whole, Serbia and Montenegro voted to retain leaders who were only marginally reformed communists. The republics were opting for quite different types of system. Obviously it is important here that the republics could opt for different systems, and indeed eventually opt for secession. Yugoslavia's federalism gave enormous power to the republics, with a notionally weak center that held only so long as Tito, his successors, and the League of Communists could exercise power throughout Yugoslavia. As Bunce (1999b, p. 111) points out, this situation was really confederalism rather than federalism, doubly flawed because it defined republics on the basis of nationality. The 1974 constitution legalized self-determination and secession, and left it unclear whether these rights were awarded to ethnic groups or people who live in a particular territory (the word *narod* in Slavic languages has both meanings; Dimitrijevic, 1996, p. 454). Once the power of the center declined, this arrangement enabled unscrupulous politicians to play ethnic nationalist cards. Since the late 1980s, ruling elites had adopted nationalist ideology to secure popular legitimacy, and could use the institutional setup of six republics and two autonomous provinces that had been formalized under the 1974 constitution to claim state-like prerogatives (see Dimitrijevic, 1994, p. 7). At one extreme, nationalism in Slovenia was reformist and pro-European; at the other, in Serbia, the elites' nationalism was unionist and dominating from the outset, seeking in the late 1980s the preservation of Yugoslavia under Serb control.

The person the Serbs elected as their president in 1989 – Slobodan Milošević – was committed to holding Yugoslavia together under a centralized system at almost any cost, and, when that failed to work, to extending political control over Serb-populated areas outside Serbia. To non-Serbs, Yugoslavia now looked to be governed by a prime minister dominated by a Serb president committed to Serb domination of a barely reformed system. Milošević cultivated a Serbian perception of underrepresentation in Yugoslav institutions, which worked on a one-vote-per-republic basis. This configuration of circumstances exacerbated ethnic differences that in and of themselves were insufficient to cause the breakup of Yugoslavia. In all events, Yugoslavia began formally to disintegrate from 1991 amid warfare, first in Slovenia, then in Croatia and Bosnia, and later in Kosovo (for more details, see Glenny, 1993; Cohen, 1995).[2]

By the time of our study, then, the Federal Republic of Yugoslavia consisted solely of Serbia and Montenegro. Serbia in the 1990s turned into the fiefdom of Slobodan Milošević, president of Serbia and then (from 1997) of Yugoslavia. Under Milošević, whose hold on power began in May 1986 (when he became head of the Serbian Communist Party and chair of the Serbian presidency), the Serbian (and to no small extent the Montenegrin) political system was transformed into a husband-and-wife team: Milošević led the Socialist Party of Serbia, while his wife controlled the Yugoslav United Left (other associated parties were New Democracy, and, in Montenegro at that time, the Democratic Party of Socialists).

The idea of a Greater Serbia was eventually frustrated by military defeat and external pressure. The economic consequences were quite disastrous, exacerbated by sanctions imposed by the United Nations. By the end of 1995, the wars in both Croatia and Bosnia were over (the latter through the Dayton Agreement), and sanctions were partially lifted. But aggressive ethnic nationalism lingered among all parties to that conflict, and in Serbia no less than in the other states, the same elites remained firmly in control. The 1999 Kosovo conflict exacerbated Serbia's economic problems and deepened its political isolation (some distant moral, but not material, support for the regime came from China and Russia). At the same time, Milošević's control did slip a little vis-à-vis Montenegro. In the late 1990s, the previously compliant Montenegrin government, under a new prime minister, began to pursue more reformist policies and greater cooperation with the international community. This resulted in a split of the ruling party in Montenegro (Democratic Party of Socialists), with Milošević's supporters forming the Socialist Popular Party.[3] The Milošević regime was not merely nationalistic and xenophobic; its rhetoric also featured socialism and intrusive state centralization, which is but the flip side of the nationalist coin in a country in which almost 40 percent of the population (including Kosovo) is ethnically non-Serb.

Yugoslavia looked at one stage as though it might have a belated "Autumn of the People" in 1996–7. Although the Milošević bloc had an effective monopoly on state power in Serbia and Montenegro, other parties were allowed to contest elections. The problem was that they were not allowed to win, or at least to assume office (unless they were Milošević fronts). Local elections on November 17, 1996, were won in seventeen towns, including

[2] Dissolution did not have to lead to war, as a glance at the dissolution of the Soviet Union and of Czechoslovakia suggests (see Pesic, 1996, p. 3).
[3] To reward these loyalists, their leader was installed as the president of the Yugoslav federal government, and newly elected deputies to the federal parliament from Montenegro were not permitted to take their seats, which were retained by members loyal to Milošević.

Belgrade, by the civic opposition, in many cases organized into the Zajedno (Together) coalition. The result was surprising, in that the Milošević regime had retained monopoly control over the media, and in the past had used the police, the army, gerrymandering, and falsification of votes in order to prevent such an occurrence. The regime responded by canceling the local election results, which in turn provoked two months of street demonstrations on the part of many citizens, students, and Zajedno supporters; these spread to almost every town in Serbia. The Zajedno leadership was itself taken by surprise by such an outcome.[4]

These nonviolent demonstrations were aimed not just at having the local election results confirmed, but also at removing the regime. Success at the former was achieved, under pressure from the demonstrations and a commission sent by the Organization for Security and Cooperation in Europe to investigate the election results, though arguably at the expense of the latter. Thus members of opposition parties were installed in local government, but the civic opposition immediately left the streets, and the leaders of opposition parties soon began squabbling with each other. Political parties in Serbia did not generally reflect social cleavages, or any tradition of pluralism. Most of the former (until 2000) opposition parties were themselves quite nationalistic. Zajedno itself was gone by the spring of 1997, having lasted less than a year. The regime remained intact if weakened, leaving Milošević with only minor constraints on his ability to retain and consolidate power, by effectively marginalizing opposition parties and their local governments. At the same time Milošević entered into an alliance with the ultranationalist Serbian Radical Party. Yugoslavia remained a pariah in the international community, still more so in the wake of the 1999 Kosovo conflict with NATO, and its economic situation throughout the 1990s remained catastrophic. At the time of writing, however, the situation looked to be changing markedly after the results of the September 2000 presidential election in which Milošević was defeated by Vojislav Koštunica, the candidate of the democratic opposition. At first Milošević refused to accept the verdict, but massive street demonstrations and the unwillingness of police and army to repress them forced his hand. Yugoslavia's reintegration into the international community began almost immediately, and it was allowed to resume its seat at the United Nations. However, the new regime retained many nationalistic aspects.

Our discussion groups were conducted in the winter of 1996–7, during the period of mass anti-regime demonstrations. Given the context, there was no difficulty in inducing people to talk with great energy about democracy and what it could mean for Serbia and Montenegro. By the time we

---

[4] Interviews with Vesna Pesić (Civic Alliance) and Zoran Djindjić (Democratic Party), leaders of the Zajedno coalition in November/December 1996.

conducted the forty individual Q sort interviews in late 1997 and early 1998, matters were quite different: protest had disappeared, and effective opposition was nowhere to be seen – not in the streets, not in party politics, not in local government. (The exception was armed resistance by members of the Albanian majority in Kosovo.) As we present and interpret these results, we should bear in mind the capacity of censorship, prohibition on foreign news sources, state control of most of the media, and the marginalization of independent media to constrain the terms of political discourse. However, as the experience of protest makes clear, there are spaces for alternative voices to be heard, and we did find them in our results. Thus we are confident that our results represent relatively enduring political traditions, not passing reactions to events. We conducted interviews in Serbia, including Kosovo, and in Montenegro, including ethnic Albanians/Muslims (subjects 9–13 in table 3.2) and other ethnic minorities, as well as majority Serbs. Interviews took place in villages as well as towns and cities. Let us now turn to the presentation of the results.

Discourses of democracy and authoritarianism in Yugoslavia

We interviewed forty subjects in Serbia and Montenegro, selected in the usual way to maximize variety in social characteristics and political ideology. Factor analysis produced three discourses of democracy, which we label, respectively, Democratic Future, Participatory Self-Management, and Electoral Authoritarianism. We present each discourse in the form of a narrative, the raw material for which can be found in table 4.1. (In the narratives, numbers in parentheses refer to the statements from the first table.)

Yugoslavia factor A: Democratic Future

Democracy is something that has to be lived and fought for, not just learned from looking at other countries (20, 61). It extends rule beyond the select few (16, 37, 40). Ordinary people should not be apathetic and ignorant of politics (25). In a democratic state there is political equality (5), majority rule (43), elected and replaceable government (44), parliamentary sovereignty (6), separation of powers (29), a constitutional and orderly state in which there is respect for human rights and dignity (2, 47), freedom of the media, freedom of association, and critical thinking (8, 57). None of these currently exists in Yugoslavia, where there is a rule of fear, which the judiciary reinforces (and so deserves no respect) (24, 48). Political parties are not central, and perhaps we should be suspicious of them (4, 5, 33). Governments should meet people's material needs and guarantee their standard of living; without democracy, no real quality of life is possible (10, 35). The best way to secure this is to guarantee equality of opportunity, and how well people then do depends on their capabilities (45). Clever

Table 4.1. *Statement scores on three factors for Yugoslavia*

Factor A is Democratic Future.
Factor B is Participatory Self-Management.
Factor C is Electoral Authoritarianism.

| | Factor | | |
Statement	A	B	C
1 Democracy is the rule of the majority, the rule of the people.	+1	+6	+4
2 A democratic society is a society in which the government is elected and replaceable, in which the normal needs of man, human dignity, and civil rights are the basis of policy.	+6	+5	+3
3 An important element of democracy is elections in which the outcome is uncertain.	0	+4	−3
4 There is no democracy without the existence of political parties.	−1	+3	−5
5 Democracy is when I have the right to judge the policy of my party.	−3	+2	+1
6 In a democracy parliament would be the basic political and legal institution in which, through legislative activity, the basic framework would be established for individuals to live free of economic and ideological restraints.	+4	+4	−1
7 Democracy is the people as the corrector of the government, as the control over government.	−2	+3	0
8 The minimum condition for the implementation of democracy is the freedom and independence of the mass media and the free association of people into political organizations.	+2	+2	−4
9 For an individual the most important thing is the possibility to express himself and the possibility of free choice.	−1	+1	0
10 Democracy should promote the quality of my life and that of my family, that is primary for me. But, it is also some standard of living, a quality of life for society.	+5	0	+5
11 In a multiparty democracy it is a perfectly normal phenomenon that after the elections the new majority in parliament passes new laws in accordance with its political standpoints. After all, that is why parties struggle to get into power.	−5	+2	−2
12 To be free means that there are no external obstacles, except for generally valid laws, for an individual to do what he wants.	−3	−1	−2
13 Democracy means the rule of the people, the equality of each person.	0	+6	0
14 Democracy is when man's basic rights are realized on the level of local self-government, regionalization, and decentralization of the state.	+1	+1	+1

Table 4.1. (*cont.*)

		Factor	
Statement	A	B	C
15 Democracy means equality under the law; this means that both the one that has and the one that has not the right, when he goes to ask for some right, can expect equal treatment.	+1	+3	+3
16 Democracy is the rule of the people over the cattle, and not that cattle rule over people.	−5	−2	+4
17 Democracy is not the only condition for the development of people's consciousness.	−2	+4	+2
18 The process of political democratization, if started, cannot stop with the recognition of democratic procedure.	+1	−1	−2
19 The students' support for the democratic political culture of civil society, the rule of law, and democratic expression of opinion are necessary assumptions for democratic transformation of political society in Serbia.	−1	0	−6
20 Democracy is something that has to become known theoretically through books, by studying, over the radio, the television, how it is in England, in France.	−6	−6	−2
21 In a democracy, parliament is the place where political struggles are institutionalized, so social contradictions and political conflicts are not resolved on the streets with nonparliamentary methods that cannot be controlled and prevented from turning into violence.	0	+3	+6
22 There are those who are interested in being in power and those who are not.	−1	−4	0
23 In a democracy those who are shouting are not automatically right, and if several thousand students take to the streets, then these are not the demonstrations of the nation.	−4	+1	+2
24 There is not a single democratic country in the world in which it has become customary for the judicial ruling to be attacked in the press by the participants in the legal proceedings, and neither is it customary for the court to defend its decisions in the same fashion.	−3	−2	+1
25 Democracy is as in Switzerland. People don't know who their head of state is, or head of government, nor are they interested.	−4	−6	−1
26 In democratic systems, the police must not protect the government as such, but must be the guarantors and protectors of democratic principles.	+2	+5	−4
27 The government has to be willing to provide information about its work.	−3	+1	−3
28 People can, out of fear, as happened here with us, vote for an authoritarian government to stay in power, fearing a change of government.	−2	0	−3

Table 4.1. (*cont.*)

Statement	Factor		
	A	B	C
29 In a democracy we have the separation of powers, replaceability of government, the right to information, and a body of rights that is secure and undisputed.	+3	+4	−5
30 I think it is democracy when all the languages can be heard in the street, and when schooling is provided in one's own language.	0	+2	+1
31 A characteristic of modern democratic rule over a state is representative democracy, in which at all levels of government the people choose their representatives, who rule on behalf of those who elected them.	+1	+1	−1
32 The division of power works such that parts of government are autonomous in their functioning, so that when my rights are curtailed I can seek and get protection from another part of government.	0	+1	−2
33 Contemporary democracy cannot be imagined without a parliament and a multiparty system that are the alpha and omega of democracy.	+2	+1	−3
34 Extreme opinions should be respected, even those that are, by definition, against the basis of democracy, against freedom.	−5	−3	−6
35 The quality of life cannot be realized without democracy.	+3	−2	−1
36 Democracy is something that functions.	−2	−3	+2
37 Not all the people should be given the possibility to make decisions on everything, hence the principle of self-management that has proved to be a totally idiotic model.	−4	−3	+2
38 There is not a single democratic country in which elections are won or lost with the help of the court. The court should not be a means of politics but the means to safeguard democracy.	+2	+3	+4
39 Democracy would be total freedom of thought and expression, and a dialogue about even the most minuscule social changes and projects for the future.	−2	+5	−1
40 I really would not like the people to rule, because that rule, as was demonstrated in the last ten years, has been life-threatening.	−6	−5	−1
41 What could be characteristic of democracy is the respect for opinion, political pluralism, meaning from the most extreme to the most moderate, from fascism to communism.	−4	−1	0
42 For democratic transformation, besides the people's discontent, it is necessary to have freedom of expression of political will, freedom of public information, and discontinuity with the old regime.	−2	+2	−4

Table 4.1. (*cont.*)

	Factor		
Statement	A	B	C
43 Democracy is the rule of the majority, not of the minority; and the state is responsible for the protection of both the majority and the minority from aggressive groups or individuals who, by claiming needs and rights, prevent the realization of the rights of others.	+4	0	0
44 Democracy is the respect for election results and for the will of the voter.	+3	+2	+3
45 Democracy means that the state creates equal conditions for all. The order in which people finish then depends on their capabilities.	+4	−4	−5
46 The fundamental precondition for a system to be really democratic is the existence of pluralism of different political forces, which express the interest of different social groups.	+2	0	−3
47 Democracy entails an ordered state in which the rights and dignity of each citizen are respected, as are the integrity and identity of minorities, and local self-government.	+6	+1	+5
48 Rule with the aid of fear, in the long run, does not give the right results.	−3	−2	+1
49 The basic guarantor of democratic processes is a real multiparty and parliamentary system, which must be the fundamental and the most influential controller of government.	+1	−1	−4
50 All the problems should be resolved within the institutions of the system, and every other way represents nondemocracy and an attack on people who think differently.	0	−2	+3
51 Economic democracy means equal access to economic goods. The abolition of political and of economic monopolies go together.	0	−2	0
52 Freedom of public information has to be especially respected at the time of elections and during the preelection campaigns.	−1	0	0
53 People should be educated for democracy to work.	+1	−1	+1
54 People should be allowed without pressure to use their own will, their brains, to think what is suitable for them in terms of political democracy. I could freely learn about plans, programs, ideas and choose what suits me most.	+2	0	+3
55 My will should, under conditions of equality of rights, at the elections, at referenda, be respected, and the set of the free wills of all individuals be weighed.	+1	−1	−1
56 Those that want to speak their mother tongue should be given maximum rights, to avoid secession and fratricide.	−1	−1	+2

Table 4.1. (*cont.*)

Statement	Factor		
	A	B	C
57 Real democracy is impossible if in a country there do not exist reasonably high levels of education, the freedom and independence of the mass media, and developed critical public thinking.	+5	−5	+1
58 For the judiciary the real challenge of democracy is fair decisions, for everyone to have recognized what belongs to them; in equal treatment of equal cases, in unequal treatment of unequal cases.	0	0	+2
59 Democratic elections must create the possibility for citizens to give their votes also to nonprofessional, nonparty politicians, candidates from different communities, movements, and groups of citizens.	−1	−3	−1
60 For democracy, it is necessary to win over those who fear change.	+4	−5	+1
61 No nation can choose to be happy without democracy. That is why we will fight for democracy, for equality of chances, for the right to free opinion and free elections.	+3	−4	−2
62 We are not equally capable, nor equally clever; we do not have the same contacts, nor equal money; but, with respect to the state, the society, the system of government, it should be possible for me to realize my rights under conditions of equality of rights.	+5	−4	+4
63 Clever people who have a vision – who, as it has been demonstrated, were right – should not be removed, totally expelled, which was happening in the one-party system.	+3	−1	+6
64 The majority should be based on one person, one vote, so that every vote is equal in value to every other.	−1	−3	+5

people should be allowed to flourish and lead, which has not happened in the past (63). Government should also ensure that the rights of the majority as well as the minority are protected (43). A democratic system also needs stability and continuity, so after elections the new majority should not just pass any laws they like, reflecting party positions (11). Still, we should not fear change (60). Also with democracy comes responsibility, and extreme opinions that are against democracy should not be tolerated (34, 41). Democracy does not mean that anyone can do what they want (12). Otherwise, pluralism is fine (46). If students and other people take to the streets, then everyone should listen; they too are part of democracy (23).

Table 4.2. *Subject loadings on factors for Yugoslavia*

Subject and political self-description	Factor		
	A	B	C
1 M, farmer, nationalist	36*	−25	1
2 F, salesperson, democrat	−5	−77*	22
3 F, teacher, democratic left	19	−49*	−7
4 M, farmer, communist	16	−22	41*
5 F, worker, radical right	−5	−77*	6
6 M, postman, socialist	0	−60*	10
7 F, farmer, liberal	11	−80*	13
8 M, craftsman/pensioner, communist	5	−46*	19
9 F, housewife, no interest	24	−88*	−1
10 M, professor, democratic right	46*	−40*	2
11 F, student, liberal	12	−70*	32*
12 M, clerk/pensioner, neutral	26	−30	7
13 F, worker, radical nationalist	18	−41*	1
14 M, student, Serb Peasant Party	38*	−38*	0
15 F, countryman, Democratic Socialist Party	58*	−33*	39*
16 M, engineer, Liberal Party	2	−28	−1
17 M, sailor, communist	16	−48*	19
18 M, army officer, liberal left	20	−43*	−2
19 F, teacher, democrat	22	−53*	6
20 M, police officer, Democratic Center	46*	−57*	4
21 F, secretary, democrat	46*	−15	−2
22 F, economist, eternal opposition	35*	−11	−3
23 M, student, liberal democrat	36*	11	23
24 F, unemployed, anti-political	34*	−25	−4
25 F, restorer, humanist	45*	−33*	6
26 M, agricultural technician, realist	28	−18	3
27 M, student, democrat	21	−28	16
28 M, salesperson, green	62*	−14	10
29 F, bank clerk, for regional autonomy	61*	9	23
30 M, retired military, apolitical	50*	−26	3
31 M, engineer, center liberal democrat	60*	−5	14
32 M, manager/trader, democrat	71*	−1	−1
33 F, pensioner, socialist	23	−14	45*
34 M, student, democrat	36*	−26	14
35 M, businessperson, social democrat	62*	2	17
36 F, small firm employee, leftist	1	−32*	1
37 M, student, democrat	55*	−18	21
38 F, housewife, dissatisfied with the regime	59*	−1	30
39 F, typist, democrat	28	2	1
40 M, driver, democrat	45*	−22	8

* Denotes a loading significant at the .01 level.

Factor A clearly looks forward to a democratic future beyond the existing regime. We can infer condemnation of the existing regime for its sultanistic tendencies, in which both power and wealth are monopolized by the Milošević family and the rest of the ruling caste, while everyone else has to cope with unemployment, low wages, and inflation. This discourse's call for more equal opportunity can be interpreted in this light. Democracy means not just a set of institutions (some of which are already in place, at least formally), but also a change for the better in the character and composition of the political elite, and a change in political practices. What currently exists in Serbia and Montenegro is seen by the Democratic Future discourse as a travesty which features falsified election results, upheld by a corrupt judiciary, state control of the mass media, and the rule of fear. These policies reinforce the fear of change so characteristic of populist nationalism. The Milošević regime claims to rule on behalf of "the people" are therefore seen as hollow.

Democratic Future believes that this situation can be changed, that democracy is indeed worth fighting for, and one day might come to Yugoslavia. This hoped-for democracy has many familiar liberal, open society, and representative components. In light of the dominant role of Serb nationalism in politics in Serbia and (to a lesser extent) Montenegro,[5] this discourse looks at first sight quite tolerant of national minorities, and not especially nationalistic. Its tolerance does not stretch to extremists of the right and left, but on the face of it would not seem to exclude national minorities. However, when politics features sharp ethnic divisions, strong support for majority rule may cover some nationalistic leanings, because majority can mean "Serb majority," not necessarily a majority that can encompass Albanian, Hungarian, and other national minorities. Still, there is no explicit nationalism in this factor. And its intolerance for extremism is noteworthy.

Two features of the Democratic Future discourse at first sight suggest that it has some republican aspects (in the sense discussed in chapter 1). These features are, respectively, an equivocal attitude to party politics and a fairly heroic view of the demands upon citizens in a democracy, and in struggles for democratization. The lukewarm attitude to parties may be a reaction to what the existing dominant parties have actually done in Yugoslavia. While there has actually been no shortage of parties, most of them were created by Milošević in order to create confusion and discredit alternatives to the ruling bloc; thus it is no surprise

---

[5] As mentioned earlier, Montenegro's government became more reformist in the late 1990s. This government even engaged in "positive discrimination" on behalf of the Albanian minority in Montenegro, setting aside seats for Albanians in the republican parliament and government.

to find that Democratic Future sees little intrinsic value in having *many* parties.[6]

In keeping with its demanding conception of citizenship, our Democratic Future discourse stresses the need for an active civil society, if necessary in opposition to the state (though whether this would carry over into some future post-transition state is open to question). Again, though, the discourse's acceptance of extraparliamentary political action may be a reaction against a system in which parliament had long been a puppet of the ruling party. This was no less true under Tito than under Milošević.

Democratic Future represents the kind of discourse to which proponents of democratic transition might look for support. But this does not exhaust the discursive options that could support transition, as we shall now see.

Yugoslavia factor B: Participatory Self-Management

Democracy is above all the power of the people over government, and majority rule (1, 7, 13, 40). A real democracy would involve participation by everyone, and free debate on every detail of policy, as has been shown by the principle of self-management in our recent history (22, 37, 39). This is not the same as just giving everyone an equal vote – this has not prevented a bad regime remaining in power (64). Democracy can exist in any sort of society, whether or not there is a high level of education or openness to change (57, 60). People are equally capable and equally clever (62). Democracy is not just about parties and elections, but also about life more generally. A democratic state should ensure equality in the distribution of income, not just equality of opportunity (45). Constitutional government with parliament at its center and a separation of powers is needed; that is where conflicts should be resolved, not on the streets, where a lapse into violence is always possible (6, 29, 38). To achieve the rule of the people and put the old regime behind us, we need free elections in which parties compete to form the government, and then carry out their policies (2, 3, 4, 11, 44) – although there is an important role for nonparty politicians too (59). The role of the police should be to protect constitutional democratic principles, not to protect the government's policies (26). Within a constitutional system, all people have equal rights to participate, and are equal before the law (13, 15). But extreme opinions need not be tolerated (34). Freedom of the press, freedom of expression, and free association are all important (8, 42). To get to know democracy, it has to be used, not just observed in other countries (20), and people need to be interested and involved in politics (25). In the end, though I favor democracy, it is clear that people can develop and achieve a good quality of life without

[6] No less than forty-four political parties contested the first multiparty elections in Serbia in 1990 (Mihajlovic, *et al.*, 1991, p. 281). Subsequent elections at different levels saw the reappearance of many parties unheard of publicly between election campaigns, as well as the splitting up of parties that appeared too large and consolidated for the taste of the incumbent regime.

democracy (17, 35); many people are happy without democracy, and so will not fight to achieve it here (61).

Where factor A draws its inspiration from the future, factor B looks (selectively) to Yugoslavia's past. As mentioned earlier, the economy and later the polity under Tito were organized on principles of self-management, a far cry from the sort of central economic planning and centralized politics that prevailed in the Soviet bloc. Self-management attracted attention and admiration from some Western democratic theorists, especially those who favored participatory democracy – such as Carole Pateman (1970).[7] Participatory democracy did not initially extend beyond the workplace into the state. However, some of its basic principles were incorporated into the delegate system, mentioned above, which eventually became an important feature of Yugoslavia's version of "socialist democracy" (see Rusinow, 1977; Lydall, 1986). The tradition associated with self-management provides the basic resources for factor B's enthusiasm for participatory democracy, which is why we label it "Participatory Self-Management." This factor believes in many of the basic institutions of liberal democracy, constitutional government, associated liberal rights, and multiparty elections. In all these features it departs from the kind of state that prevailed under Tito. But in some respects Participatory Self-Management is more socialist than liberal, for it believes in equality of reward rather than equality of opportunity. This can be interpreted in social democratic terms or, perhaps more likely, as remembrance of a past in which the state was perceived to have done an effective job in redistributing income.[8] Participatory Self-Management believes in direct, participatory democracy in which all people should be active and involved, rather than in a limited representative democracy. This perhaps provides belated and indirect support for Pateman's contention that experience of self-management in the workplace produces more competent citizens, for this discourse clearly sees a continuity between workplace and politics.

In keeping with its orientation to Yugoslavia's past, Participatory Self-Management is not especially optimistic about the future, being resigned to the fact that many people can accept life without democracy, especially if a nondemocratic regime can deliver the goods in material terms. Still, this does not mean we should dismiss any role that Participatory Self-Management might play in political development in Yugoslavia. Pessimism is not integral to the core of this discourse, and one can imagine its supporters being drawn into more active engagement on behalf of particular kinds of democratic

---

[7] David Miller was another political theorist interested in self-management's possible contribution to theories of participatory democracy.

[8] In fact, income was ever less evenly distributed from the mid-1970s, although the wealthier groups and republics continued to complain about having to subsidize poorer groups and republics.

reform. Its existence should remind us that democratization does not have to be a unidirectional process heading toward a particular liberal model, but might also draw profitably upon other indigenous traditions. In most of the post-transition countries in this study, discourses that look to the past evidence nostalgia for the security and basic material needs provided by some authoritarian regimes. Yugoslavia differs from these other cases in having a tradition of democracy – though not liberal democracy – in its communist past. The resource that this provides has been almost universally ignored by outside observers interested in bringing democracy to Yugoslavia, most of whom are beholden to the liberal state form.

Yugoslavia factor C: Electoral Authoritarianism

Democracy means rule by and for the majority, not by the cattle (1, 16). We do not need students and troublemakers demonstrating on the streets telling us what to do and how to be democratic, and political conflicts should not take place beyond existing state institutions, especially parliament (19, 21, 23, 50). We need a firm government that promotes our standard of living, basic needs, social equality, and equal dignity as human beings (2, 10, 15, 62, 64). Separation of powers and so-called rights and freedom of expression only get in the way of effective government (29, 32, 42, 61). A government and parliament of one party is best. Elections are fine and their results need to be respected, but we do not need competing political parties and elections in which the outcome is uncertain, or too many political organizations to make trouble and destabilize the situation (3, 4, 8, 11, 33, 44, 46). Nor should the media be allowed to make trouble (8). Extreme opinions that threaten the state need to be controlled (34). Above all we need order (47). The police are there to ensure that the government's policies can be carried out, and order maintained (26). Our courts should be respected (38). There were problems with the old system when clever people were removed who should have stayed in power (63), but overall we should be happy with the democratic government we have, and the stability and continuity that have been achieved (28, 36, 42).

The discourse represented by factor C can claim to be democratic, in that it supports the authority of elected government and parliament. But its democratic aspect is more akin to the kind of one-party democracy that prevailed under Tito: elections took place, but only for the ruling party. Indeed, the discourse *could* be seen as compatible with the minimalist democratic approaches discussed in chapter 1, especially the delegative democracy variant of minimalism, which is one of the reasons we reject the claim that these conceptions are genuinely democratic. The democratic credentials evaporate quite quickly on closer examination, for it turns out that Electoral Authoritarianism is above all interested in order and stability of the sort provided by the Milošević regime. The other two factors would see such concern as a result of the fear of bloodshed of the order that has occurred in past wars induced by regime propaganda in order to perpetuate a grip on power. Electoral authoritarianism has no interest in procedural checks and balances, extraparliamentary opposition, freedom of expression in the media, or political rights more generally. Thus the discourse supports an extreme concentration of power, accepting Milošević's claim that the alternative is anarchy. Its respect for the courts has nothing to do with judicial enforcement of the rule of law and constitutional government, but rather stems from the degree to which the courts at all levels have done the regime's bidding, for example in confirming falsified election results. The discourse is nationalistic in the sense that it does not believe in looking outside Serbia for political models; its enthusiasm for majority rule can be interpreted in terms of rule by the Serb majority.

In one sense, the presence of the Electoral Authoritarianism factor shows that the Milošević regime did have a supporting discourse in society, on which it might lay some claim to institutional legitimacy, though of course a lot would turn on just how widely held this discourse is.[9] Among our subjects, Electoral Authoritarianism showed a weaker presence than the other two discourses; but nothing about their relative strength within Yugoslavia can be inferred from this relative frequency, because our sample of persons is not representative. All we can say with confidence is that these three discourses do actually exist in Yugoslavia.

The prospects for democratization

The three discourses of democracy we found in Yugoslavia represent, respectively, hope for a different future, a past, and the present. Participatory Self-Management represents the ideals of economic democracy and "the mystique of self-management" in the Tito era, while being hostile to the authoritarian state of that era. Electoral Authoritarianism represents the dictatorial and nationalistic populism of the Milošević regime. Democratic Future looks forward to the introduction of an essentially liberal democracy. This does not of course mean that any post-communist future for Yugoslavia can only draw upon the discourse of Democratic Future. Despite its adherents' pessimism, Participatory Self-Management might provide the discursive resources for a kind of democratic transition unlike those that were secured in our other countries. Rhetorically at least, it might play an important role, for in Serbia there is well-developed populist hostility to the Western liberal democracies, and hence the model of democracy associated

---

[9] The scale of support for Milošević himself declined rapidly in 1999, after Serbia was humiliated by the international community over Kosovo; but this does not mean that Electoral Authoritarianism necessarily waned in its level of support.

with them, and which they are seen as trying to impose. This kind of attitude appeared to persist into the presidency of Vojislav Koštunica. In contrast to the situation in most of the countries of the former Soviet bloc, many Serbs and Montenegrins retain a pride in the political model developed by their leaders during the communist era. As emphasized at the beginning of this chapter, the communist regime in Yugoslavia was not imposed from the outside, and maintained a distance from the Soviet model. Moreover, the country played a leading role in the nonaligned movement. Hence, many Serbs did not share the desire felt by so many other CEE citizens to reject past external domination by embracing as much as possible of the model of the former dominator's archenemy. There is a widespread perception in Yugoslavia that the old regime worked quite well in some respects, including even economic ones, until things started to go seriously wrong in the 1980s. It is possible to downplay this more recent communist past, and look back nostalgically to the 1950s and 1960s. Thus the models associated with the old system are not so easily jettisoned. Participatory Self-Management could be deployed to show those hostile to the West that there is an indigenous Yugoslav democratic tradition on which to draw. Milošević himself was aware of other aspects of the Yugoslav tradition and drew upon them, notably through a rhetoric of social welfare (guaranteed life employment, pensions, free health, and social services).

Comparing these Yugoslav results with those of our other countries, Democratic Future clearly bears a family resemblance to the various liberal democratic and republican discourses that we have found. Electoral Authoritarianism finds some resonance elsewhere, mainly in those discourses that evidence a nostalgia for the communist past. In Serbia and Montenegro there was of course no clear need for such people to feel nostalgic at the time we undertook this study, for the past was still very much present.

If we examine the kinds of people who load most strongly on our three factors, the political self-descriptions of those loading most heavily on factor A, Democratic Future, and factor C, Electoral Authoritarianism, produce few surprises (except perhaps for a nationalist with a moderately high loading on factor A). Most of those loading heavily on Democratic Future have the word "democrat" somewhere in their self-description; of those who do not, terms such as "humanist," "green," "dissatisfied with regime," and "opposition" come as no surprise. Similarly, finding descriptions such as "socialist" and "communist" for our individuals on factor C is expected. More interesting is the mix of self-descriptions among those on factor B, Participatory Self-Management. Self-descriptions here include "communist," "socialist," "radical right," "radical nationalist" (but note that this was an ethnic Albanian, not a Serb), "no interest," "liberal left," "democrat," and "liberal" – in short, factor B seems to cut across many of the traditional ideological divisions. This suggests it could act as a bridge between different factions in a deeply divided society as that troubled society undertakes its democratic transition. (A less optimistic reading here would point out that this discourse, just like Electoral Authoritarianism, has yet to make a clear break from Yugoslav-style communism and populism.)

The Participatory Self-Management discourse does, then, play a potentially pivotal role when it comes to the prospects for democratization in Yugoslavia. Its pessimism about the prospects for democratic change could be a self-fulfilling prophecy, and it might be hard to enlist the discourse in support of the development of even a minimalist liberal model of democracy, for Participatory Self-Management has both participatory and socialist welfare state leanings, the latter even revealing some commonalties with Electoral Authoritarianism. On the other hand, Participatory Self-Management does want to see the back of authoritarianism and the introduction of constitutional government. Thus it might be capable of building a bridge to those supporters of the Milošević regime who can see democratization only in terms of the imposition of a foreign model; Participatory Self-Management could show that this is not necessarily the case.

A truly successful authoritarian regime would secure its survival by producing discursive hegemony in the sense that political divisions would play into its hands; the division between the ultranationalists (represented by the Serbian Radical Party) and Milošević might fall into this category. But our results show that two out of three discourses were happy to see the back of this regime, which suggests that it was unsuccessful in securing the requisite hegemony, and to that degree had to rely on fear and manipulation to secure its rule, especially given its lack of success in achieving proclaimed nationalist goals in Croatia, Bosnia, and Kosovo. Our methodology does not, of course, enable us to ascertain the relative number of supporters of each discourse in society at large in Serbia and Montenegro. Still, these two oppositional discourses offer resources to reformers and highlight the vulnerabilities of the old regime – vulnerabilities that were starkly revealed by the September 2000 election and associated protests. At the time of writing, and even allowing for the fragilities in post-Milošević arrangements, the prospects for democracy in Serbia and Montenegro looked brighter than ever before. It remains to be seen what *kind* of democracy will emerge; our research suggests it will be somewhat different from the Western norm.

PART III

Halting transitions

The three countries examined in this section have two things in common –
they are all former Soviet states, and they have all had very troubled starts,
albeit in slightly different ways, in their transitions from communism.[1] This
trouble shows few signs of abating. Belarus and Ukraine were relatively reluctant to let go of communism; their Soviet-era leadership had resisted
glasnost and *perestroika*, and there was little in the way of popular anti-
Soviet protest either before or during the breakup of the Soviet Union. Not
surprisingly, neither embraced either liberal democracy or the market economy with much enthusiasm, and in their politics and economics both reveal
substantial continuity with the Soviet era. Belarus and Ukraine were under
communist control for much longer than were the "outer empire" states,
and were affected more directly by the collapse of the Soviet Union. While
the economies of many East European states were closely linked to the Soviet
economy, primarily through Comecon, they were not actually constituent
parts of a single economy, as were the former Soviet republics. Nor were the
political elites of Central and East European countries actually part of the
Soviet elite – unlike the elites of Belarus and Ukraine. No Pole or Hungarian
sat on the Soviet Politburo. This has meant that the elites of the former Soviet
republics have had more ground to cover in terms of creating new state identities (as well as institutions) than many of their counterparts in CEE. Of
course, the breakup of the other two federal communist states, Yugoslavia
and Czechoslovakia, means that elites in the various successor states to these
two also have problems not encountered by Poles, Hungarians, Bulgarians,

---

[1] Cultural determinists might think we have missed a third commonality: these three states
were the only former Soviet republics to be predominantly peopled by Eastern Slavs.

or Romanians, for instance. But neither were the elites in Slovakia, Slovenia, and so forth part of the "mighty bear" and they did not have as far to fall when the old system collapsed.

While Belarus is, of all the post-transition countries examined in this study (i.e., excluding China and Yugoslavia), closest to being a pure dictatorship, Russia and Ukraine could as of the end of 1999 better be described as stalemated countries, moving in no coherent direction. Since then, Russia may well have started moving again under President Putin, though it was still too early to be certain at the time of writing. Following the breakup of the Soviet Union, Russia pursued political and economic reform far more quickly than Ukraine and Belarus, even experiencing a brief burst of Poland-style economic shock therapy. But Russia soon relapsed into a situation in which political leaders were prepared to use violence against each other, and to try to manipulate the constitution for their own ends rather than behave according to constitutional rules. The Russian economy collapsed, civil society did not develop, and corruption became an enormous problem. Ukraine, for its part, escaped Russia's political strife, but featured continued domination by Soviet-era apparatchiks with little real interest in political and economic reform. But Ukraine and Russia at least continued to hold reasonably free – if not entirely fair – elections, whereas Belarus moved quickly to a situation in which all power was concentrated in the hands of an authoritarian president.

While Ukraine has only ever inched forward in terms of post-communist reform, Russia and Belarus have moved backward (though our caveat about Putin's Russia applies here too). In this they might not seem entirely unique: Bulgaria, Lithuania, Poland, and Hungary have all at some point in the 1990s elected communist successor parties and/or presidents to replace anti-communist governments. But in the latter four cases the former communists did not try to turn the clock back in either political or economic terms; and indeed themselves subsequently gave way in free elections. Thus Bulgaria, Lithuania, Poland, and Hungary are focusing on the future rather than the past (ongoing lustration issues notwithstanding).

5

Belarus

Of all the countries analyzed in this book, Belarus is arguably the one with the least developed identity; only Moldova might compete. The territory of what is now Belarus (formerly known as Belorussia, and sometimes in English as White Russia) was a part of Kievan Rus' from the tenth century, and later experienced Russian, Polish, and Lithuanian rule. By the late eighteenth century, it was part of the Russian Empire. This relationship has persisted, apart from a few brief periods during or shortly after wars. Even now, its relationship with Russia is the closest of all the Commonwealth of Independent States members.

Belarus's nationalist phases have been short-lived, and support for them limited. There was a half-hearted attempt to become independent of Russia in 1917, even a formal declaration of independence in 1918 (associated with the poet Yanka Kupala; see Holtbrügge, 1996, p. 49), after Belarus had temporarily come under German rule. Following brief Polish control, Belarus returned to Moscow's tutelage by the 1920s, expanded by the transfer of some Russian territory. The Germans occupied the country during the Second World War. Thereafter Belarus remained part of the Soviet Union until the latter's collapse in 1991. Nationalism at that point was strong enough for Belarus to declare independence, but again such sentiment was weak and short-lived.

Belarus was in many ways an economic success story in the Soviet era, in comparison both with other parts of the Soviet Union and with its own past. This experience perhaps explains why, by the 1980s, there was little support for *glasnost* and *perestroika* in the Belarusian communist elite, and little popular agitation for political change, let alone breakup of the Soviet Union (see Mihalisko, 1997, pp. 236–9).[1] This legacy *perhaps* also helps explain why Belarus was both a latecomer to post-communist democratization and soon returned to authoritarian rule, though the fact that Ukraine shares much the same legacy but has so far avoided a similar return means that we must be wary of such arguments.

Belarus played little role in the fall of the Soviet Union in 1991; its communist leadership was firmly behind the Soviet hard-liners who tried to oust Gorbachev in the failed coup of August 1991. The Belarusian party never developed a reformist faction. Although the Communist Party was formally disbanded in the wake of the breakup of the Soviet Union, it soon re-formed itself under a slightly different name (the Party of Communists of Belarus), and the Soviet-era parliament elected in 1990 stayed in office until 1995.

In 1988 a group of intellectuals formed the Belarusian Popular Front as a nationalist, reformist, and liberal democratic movement. In 1990 the Front won 26 of 360 seats in parliament, but could never make the step that, for example, Czechoslovakia's dissident intellectuals made into becoming a dominant political force in the post-communist era. In the rigged 1995 elections, it won no seats in the Supreme Council (parliament), and two of its leaders then gained political asylum in the United States.

As we have indicated, Belarus has never experienced a sustained national movement, nor a democratic one. Its identity in relation to Russia in particular was and remains unclear (Mihalisko, 1997, pp. 232–6, suggests that the Second World War crystallized an essentially Soviet patriotism in Belarus, which is not the same as the claim by many Western observers that Belarusians consider themselves to be Russian). In the March 1991 Soviet referendum on the future of the Soviet Union, Belarus had the highest support of any republic outside Central Asia (at 83 percent) for a reformed Soviet federation. On the other hand, Belarus had opted in January 1990 to replace Russian with Belarusian as its official language. As Zaprudnik (1993) observed, Belarus was at a crossroads in terms of its identity.

Even the actions and attitudes of strongman President Alyaksandr Lukashenka toward Russia need to be treated cautiously. While he is sometimes portrayed in the Western media (and, as we will see, by some of his own people) as caring more about union with Russia than about his own country, his push for integration has always recognized limits. His behavior can be interpreted in terms of wanting his country to regain former power

---

[1] We say "perhaps" because growing wealth can sometimes encourage either autonomist or separatist nationalism; Scotland and parts of Yugoslavia provide examples. But in these cases, there was a feeling that these relatively small countries would be wealthier if independent, because of the presence of valuable resources – oil in the case of Scotland, German tourists (!) in the case of Croatia and Slovenia. Belarus has few natural resources, and is highly dependent on Russia for energy; see Markus, 1995a. Nor is it a magnet for German tourists.

and status, in a most peculiar form of nationalism. Belarus was once part of a superpower, though with its own representation in the United Nations and, formally, its own nuclear arsenal; Lukashenka himself has advocated the reestablishment of something like the Soviet Union. Given that he has sought union with Russia premised on essential equality of the two (very unequal) partners, perhaps he preferred to be a big fish in a big pond rather than a big fish in a little pond. Despite these somewhat contradictory signals, Belarus has been very unnationalistic in conventional terms since the early 1990s, in the terms of Marples's (1999) book subtitle "a denationalized country."[2] The Lukashenka regime is more populist than nationalist.

The leaderships of both Russia and Belarus once again committed themselves to closer political and economic integration in late 1999 – as they had done on numerous occasions since 1992. But the government of Russia continued to prove less inclined actually to implement any such arrangements than simply to make positive noises. Russia was, however, happy to allow the capital of the CIS to be Minsk (i.e., the Belarusian capital). This was a relatively painless way to keep the Belarusians on-side while appearing not to want to dominate what could develop into a successor to the Soviet Union.[3]

Belarus has no ethnic conflicts of any note; the population is 78 percent Belarusian and 13.5 percent Russian, but given that Belarusians tend not to seek identity in opposition to Russian-ness and have a reputation for tolerance and inclusiveness (see Urban and Zaprudnik, 1993, pp. 114–15), the presence of a substantial Russian minority prompts no ethnic conflict.

An absence of ethnic conflict combined with relatively high industrialization and economic development (at least in comparison with the rest of the former Soviet Union) might lead some conventional development theorists to predict that Belarus is relatively well-placed for progress toward consolidated liberal democracy. (More sophisticated theorists would argue that economic development provides protection against democratic regimes reverting to authoritarianism, rather than a stimulus for democratic transition; see Przeworski, et al., 2000.) But that has not happened, and our analysis of discourses of democracy and authority in Belarus can help to explain why. The timing of our study in the immediate wake of Belarus's return to authoritarianism was actually a little unfortunate, because the discursive landscape seems to have been flattened by this event, or at least polarized into supporters and opponents of this dramatic move. Thus we need to dig

---

[2] In an earlier study, Marples (1993, esp. pp. 266–72) referred to "the retarded development of a Belarusian national identity," although he also argued that factors such as the Kuropaty forest revelations and Chernobyl had begun to raise national consciousness in Belarus.

[3] The CIS has so far been a great disappointment to those who harbored these aspirations, however; see Sakwa and Webber, 1999.

deeply into our results for a more nuanced picture, to find the relatively enduring patterns that we believe our methodology can reveal.

Belarus's first reasonably free and fair post-Soviet national election was held in 1994, but for the presidency, not parliament. Thus until 1994 Belarus continued to be led by communists – indeed, communists who had been anti-Gorbachev hard-liners. This election was won by Lukashenka, running on a populist, anti-corruption, pro-Russian platform (but even his main opponent, former prime minister Vyacheslau Kebich, proposed closer integration with Russia). Lukashenka's election campaign had no party backing. He was not a Soviet-era apparatchik; he had been the manager of a state farm, and a deputy in the last Soviet-era parliament, but had no formal ties to the communist power structure (for a brief but pithy biography, see Markus, 1995b, p. 52). Once elected, Lukashenka wasted little time in consolidating power and reversing Belarus's belated and tenuous democratization. The 1995 parliamentary elections were conducted under presidential manipulation that included a ban on media coverage, prohibition on private funding of candidates, minimal and delayed public funding, and nullification of results in areas where turnout fell below 50 percent. This last provision meant that the elections did not produce a parliamentary quorum. Under such conditions, only the well-organized Communist Party could flourish. Lukashenka consolidated presidential power with a successful (but manipulated) referendum in November 1996 that marginalized parliament, allowed the president to appoint a substantial bloc of members of parliament, and extended the presidential term to seven years (see Timmermann and Ott, 1997, pp. 98–102).

Our study of Belarus was conducted in the wake of this referendum, which gave virtually unlimited constitutional power to the presidency. Lukashenka had already shown a marked disposition to use the powers of his office to restrict opposition and curtail freedom of political expression, but now went even further. Thus by the end of the 1990s Belarus was easy to classify as a backslider into authoritarianism – indeed, arguably the most authoritarian of the post-communist European states, Serbia excepted.

It is against this background that we conducted first our discussion groups on democracy and then, in late 1997, our forty individual Q sort interviews, in Minsk and in the rural area of Molodechno. Let us turn now to an analysis and discussion of our results, which reveal a degree of polarization unmatched in any of the other countries we are studying.

Belarusian discourses of authority and democracy

We identified three Belarusian discourses: Liberal Democracy, Presidential Populism, and Reluctant Authoritarianism. Actually it might be more accurate to say we identified two, because the first two of these three are mirror images of one another. Technically, one of the factors was bipolar, with substantial numbers of subjects loading heavily at both positive and negative ends. Such bipolarity indicates extreme polarization. This is our factor A; the notation we will use for the Liberal Democracy end of it is A+, for the Presidential Populism end A−.[4] But it should be borne in mind that A+ and A− do not indicate variations on A, rather direct opposites. (In the narratives, numbers in parentheses refer to the statements from the first table.)

Belarus factor A+: Liberal Democracy

Democracy is the most desirable form of government, involving respect for human rights, political freedoms, a free press, public assemblies and rallies, a multiparty system, and constitutional government (2, 4, 7, 9, 10, 27, 29, 39). Democracy of this sort will provide for a smoothly functioning market economy (11, 30, 45), and openness to the world (42). Democracy is not perfect; our experience shows that democracy itself can be terminated using democratic procedures (17). This shows that the essence of democracy is not majority rule, for the majority can get it badly wrong, and repress the minority (13, 32, 40, 52, 61). In Belarus we have seen the unwarranted removal of democracy and establishment of control by a president who has no idea of what democracy is really about, who authorizes the use of force against those who dissent, who in the end serves another country (Russia) (1, 12, 19, 24, 35, 43, 58). We have an elected president, but we do not have a democracy (37).

Our Belarusian factor A+ reveals a fairly uncomplicated affinity with liberal democracy, combined with a strong negative evaluation of the status quo of presidential authoritarianism. The liberal aspects of the discourse extend not just to human rights, freedom of speech, constitutional government, openness, and a market economy, but also to the classic liberal suspicion of majority rule: the "tyranny of the majority," to use John Stuart Mill's expression. Liberals have always been suspicious of what the mediocre majority might do, and so have stressed the need for constitutional protection against majority rule no less than against tyrants. Liberalism's accommodation with democracy has always been uneasy, and arguably remains incomplete in Western political philosophy and practice.

Liberal fears of majority rule have often proved unfounded. But in Belarus the liberal nightmare has come true. A majority in a free and fair presidential election chose a populist demagogue, to whom the majority subsequently granted near-absolute power in a referendum. Not surprisingly, this Liberal Democracy factor ends up being somewhat equivocal about democracy

---

[4] The positive and negative symbols are of purely notational significance; they do not imply any judgment (positive or negative) about the content of discourses A+ and A−.

Table 5.1. *Statement scores on two factors for Belarus*

Factor A+ is Liberal Democracy.

Factor A− is Presidential Populism, such that a negative score for a statement
  indicates *agreement* with the statement.

Factor B is Reluctant Authoritarianism.

		Factor	
Statement		A	B
1	The November 1996 referendum was a step from chaos to stability and real democracy.	−4	−1
2	Independent media are part of any democratic society.	+5	+1
3	When talking about democracy, it is useful not to stick to the narrow horizons of West European political thought.	−1	+1
4	Personal rights and freedoms are the basis of democracy.	+6	+3
5	The president is the spiritual leader of a nation.	−1	+3
6	Should the executive and the legislative branches fail to reach an agreement, the president has the right to dissolve parliament.	−3	0
7	There should be many parties in Belarus, so that anyone can find something to his taste.	+4	0
8	The president is the guardian of the constitution, not the violator.	−1	+4
9	In a democratic country people don't fear that they might be punished for their thoughts.	+6	+2
10	In a democratic country people adopt a constitution to secure the rights of everyone, rather than of one single person.	+4	+2
11	In the West people can earn money without stealing or killing.	+5	+6
12	The president is willing to reflect the views of his people.	−4	+5
13	Democracy is the power of the majority.	−2	+1
14	The separation of powers in its Western meaning is nothing but anarchy.	−2	−1
15	The president and parliament look for compromise.	0	−1
16	The market and democracy are the attributes of the West.	+1	−1
17	Our experience shows that democracy can be easily terminated under democratic procedures.	+3	−2
18	Nobody needs to follow the Western pattern of development.	−1	−1
19	The use of force against those who think differently has become a norm in Belarus.	+3	−3
20	The democratization we have now involves a tremendous reconstruction of human consciousness.	+1	0
21	People who have one taste of freedom won't give it away so easily.	+1	+1
22	Centralized power is necessary to keep the country stable.	−1	+4
23	The constitution of 1996 was constructed in a way that will justify all actions by the president.	+2	−4
24	The president has the right directly to appoint a certain number of members of parliament, the Central Elections Committee, and the Constitutional Court.	−6	0

Table 5.1. (*cont.*)

Statement	Factor	
	A	B
25 The goal of the leader should coincide with the preferences of the people.	+1	+5
26 These new democrats want to get money from the West.	0	0
27 The independent journalists simply want to tell the truth but the president doesn't.	+4	−4
28 Only these new rich people need democracy.	−2	−2
29 The idea of human rights and democracy suggested by new "democrats" has nothing to do with human development and the creation of a civilized society.	−2	+1
30 Democracy should bring about the conditions for the smooth functioning of the economy.	+5	+1
31 No doubt there are rich people and poor people, since there are smart people and not very smart ones.	+3	−2
32 In Belarus the political minority is suppressed by the majority.	+4	−3
33 Who needs any democracy when there is nothing to eat?	0	+2
34 Many so-called democrats who support pro-Western ideas appeared recently.	0	0
35 Is this democracy, when the authorities throw opposition leaders into jail?	+2	−3
36 Although even the new constitution has a democratic outlook, there is no democracy in practice.	+1	−2
37 Belarus is a democratic country because we have a democratically elected president.	−5	+2
38 Parliament has always disorganized the country. They never find solutions.	0	+2
39 We don't need any public rallies; they destabilize the situation.	−3	+5
40 The president is supported by the majority, so all that he does is right.	−6	+4
41 Criticizing the president became popular in the so-called democratic circles.	−1	−1
42 The international reactionary forces want to rob the Belarusian people.	−4	−2
43 A person who publicly praises Adolf Hitler can't have even a vague idea about democracy.	+3	−3
44 The president is very ambitious. His goal is the Russian throne and he will do everything to get there.	+2	−5
45 The ideas of liberalization, privatization, and private property will lead our country to a national catastrophe.	−5	−1
46 The fact that the president is able to speak the language of the people appalls these "democrats" and their sponsors.	0	0
47 In the Soviet Union everyone was equal.	−2	−5

Table 5.1. (*cont.*)

	Factor	
Statement	A	B
48 The beginning of the reforms in Belarus was not natural; they were imported from Moscow.	+2	−3
49 We have been living without any democracy for ages, so what is the use of it?	−1	−2
50 We have two communist parties now. Isn't this a democracy?	0	−1
51 According to the opinion polls about 40 percent of the Belarusian population entirely support the policies of the president and the government.	+1	+1
52 The people expressed their will at the November 1996 referendum and gave the president carte-blanche to do as he likes.	−3	+3
53 Those who disagree with our policies will have to leave the country.	−5	−5
54 Parliament, which was dismissed in November 1996, used to be the attribute of a really democratic society.	+1	−6
55 The president is the only person who is able to oppose the old bureaucratic apparatus.	−3	+3
56 The destiny of our motherland is to be decided by our spiritual leader.	−3	+4
57 Whatever ambitions our president might have, they shouldn't threaten the people.	+2	+2
58 The president wants to serve another country, but we don't.	+3	−6
59 The president should stand for social equality among the people.	+1	+6
60 All the opposition parties, including communists and nationalists, have united against the president in order to support our freedom.	0	−4
61 The majority is always right.	−4	0
62 The new parliament represents the opinion of the public better than the old one.	−2	+1
63 It is more efficient when every local boss is directly responsible to the president.	−1	+3
64 There is no opportunity for the opposition to get into power in a peaceful way.	+2	−4

itself. Democracy is endorsed as a symbol, and an umbrella under which the standard range of liberal principles can shelter; but it is condemned for providing no protection against resurgent authoritarianism. By the lights of our factor A+, the people in Belarus have got it badly wrong. But it is not clear who then might get it right. The Liberal Democracy discourse contains more lamentation than hope, and it is unclear about how liberal democracy in Belarus might be redeemed. There is certainly no intimation of an alternative or unconventional route to democracy of the sort we can find even in Yugoslavia. Democracy is, reflexively, a system that has to be designed for people as they are; but people in Belarus have apparently not measured up. Thus democracy might be possible, but not with people as they are. Unfortunately democracy does not allow for the election of a new people. On the other hand, it does allow for a developmental process in which people gradually learn citizenship, a process that should not be ruled out.

Our Liberal Democracy discourse is consistent with the platform of the democratic reform-oriented parties in Belarus, most notably the Belarusian Popular Front. But these parties have never mounted a serious electoral challenge; in the only free and fair national election to date in 1994, their candidate finished a distant third to Lukashenka and the Communist Party candidate. (The October 2000 parliamentary elections were neither free nor fair, and were boycotted by the opposition parties.) If the discourse of Liberal Democracy in Belarus represents a commitment to liberalism in fairly un-compromising and unsullied form, that may be because those sympathetic to such a discourse have yet to get anywhere near the levers of power – and so, for example, are not chastened after the fashion of the corresponding discourse in Russia. In the long run, this lack of association with post-communist failure may not be altogether a bad thing for, perhaps unlike the situation in Russia, liberal democracy might therefore get one more chance. On the other hand, it is not hard for impotence and purity to coexist.

Let us now turn to Liberal Democracy's mirror image, or absolute negation.

Belarus factor A−: Presidential Populism

With the establishment of presidential authority approved by the people, we have moved from chaos to stability and real democracy, in which the president carries out the views of the people – this is true majority rule, where everything the president does is right (1, 12, 17, 24, 32, 37, 40, 52, 61). The president is our spiritual leader, the only person who can oppose the old bureaucracy (55, 56). In this real democracy, we do not need multiple parties, an autonomous parliament, freedom of speech, so-called rights secured by a constitution, or journalists and protestors to make trouble (4, 7, 10, 27, 29, 39). We need a firm hand that can defend us against both international reactionary forces who want to rob us (42) and troublemakers at home. Anyone who does not like this should leave the country (53). We have no need of a Western-style market economy, which would lead us into catastrophe (11, 30, 45). Economic development does not need this so-called democracy (30).

It is easy to discern in factor A−, Presidential Populism, enthusiastic approval for the kind of politics embodied by the Lukashenka regime. It would be equally easy to dismiss this support as mere authoritarianism, but Presidential Populism's self-image is democratic and, as table 5.2 shows, several of those who load highly on this factor describe themselves as democrats. This discourse in fact constitutes an extreme form of what O'Donnell (1994) calls "delegative democracy" (see chapter 1). The president is seen as embodying the will of the people, and with some justification can be regarded as the people's choice. This factor is anti-pluralistic, illiberal, and intolerant, suggesting that those dissatisfied should leave the country. But on a populist interpretation, it is democratic, and proclaims itself to be so. Presidential Populism believes in an easily defined and unitary public interest, though unlike the republican model it would see little point in wasting time in debating competing views of what is in that public interest. A unitary and uncomplicated notion of the public interest here means unitary and uncomplicated political authority.

When it comes to economics, Presidential Populism rejects a Western-style market economy, just as it rejects Western-style liberalism. On the other hand, this discourse evidences little nostalgia for the communist past, nor is it at all nationalistic. Just what economic model it favors is less clear. Economic development is seen as stemming from the exercise of a firm and uncorrupt hand at the top, but just how this can deliver the economic goods without resort to Soviet-era central economic planning is not specified.

Presidential Populism is enthusiastic about strong centralized authority. Our third discourse, to which we now turn, is less enthusiastic, but concedes the necessity thereof.

Belarus factor B: Reluctant Authoritarianism

Democracy means constitutional government and personal rights and freedoms (4, 9, 10). But in Belarus today we need strong presidential power to keep the country stable and ensure economic development (22, 33). Luckily the president guards the constitution and does not violate it, and is willing to reflect the views of the people (8, 12, 23, 25). So Belarus is a democratic country, because the president is elected and supported by the majority; so what he does is always right (32, 37, 40, 44, 52, 58) . The president is our spiritual leader, the only person who can oppose the old bureaucracy (55, 56, 63). Irresponsible journalists, opposition parties, troublemakers in parliament, and public rallies upset the situation, and so needed to be controlled (27, 38, 39, 54, 60). But opposition should still be allowed within reasonable boundaries, and opposition parties are still allowed to seek power in a peaceful way; those who disagree with current policies should not have to leave the country (35, 53, 64). Our society does not have to be divided into rich and poor (31); it is most important that the president stand for social equality (59). Such equality did not exist in the Soviet Union (47).

Table 5.2. *Subject loadings on factors for Belarus*

	Factor	
Subject and political self-description	A	B
1 F, pensioner, neutral	28	63*
2 M, pensioner, neutral	17	41*
3 M, unemployed, liberal	84*	−15
4 M, economist, liberal	81*	−6
5 M, manager, anarchist	67*	15
6 M, translator, nonpartisan	72*	−8
7 M, pensioner, democrat	19	61*
8 F, salesperson, democrat	−25	50*
9 F, salesperson, neutral	60*	7
10 F, teacher, neutral	69*	30
11 F, accountant, socialist	−16	72*
12 M, ex-military, democrat	−56*	49*
13 F, self-employed, anti-socialist	84*	−7
14 F, housewife, nonpartisan	−3	80*
15 M, executive, patriot	−31	52*
16 M, military, democrat	82*	0
17 F, medical, democrat	78*	25
18 F, physician, centrist	84*	6
19 F, teacher, nonpartisan	12	68*
20 M, journalist, leftist	−50*	60*
21 M, truck driver, anti-nationalist	25	60*
22 M, plant worker, democrat	80*	−8
23 M, computers, nonpartisan	81*	12
24 M, unemployed, democrat	−72*	33*
25 F, economist, nonpartisan	76*	−13
26 M, manager, conservative	53*	28
27 M, sales agent, nationalist	79*	1
28 M, railway worker, democrat	−81*	25
29 M, unemployed, liberal	81*	−8
30 M, driver, neutral	66*	9
31 M, clerk, communist	−85*	21
32 F, salesperson, liberal	53*	17
33 M, self-employed, anti-communist	72*	−4
34 M, farmer, nonpartisan	−20	75*
35 F, farmer, neutral	58*	31
36 M, manager, reformist	87*	4
37 M, self-employed, democrat	86*	−2
38 M, factory worker, socialist	−67*	31
39 M, musician, liberal	81*	3
40 M, student, nationalist	88*	−10

*Denotes a loading significant at the .01 level.

The Reluctant Authoritarianism of factor B concedes the necessity of strong presidential authority as necessary to ensure stability and promote economic development, even treating it as democratic, for roughly the same reasons as does Presidential Populism. Thus can this discourse too regard Belarus as a democracy, on the grounds that centralized authority is exercised by a democratically elected president whose powers have been confirmed by a majority of the people. However, Reluctant Authoritarianism is far from enthusiastic about this state of affairs – for this discourse also has liberal commitments to constitutional government and a range of individual liberties. Its democratic commitments are also more pluralistic than Presidential Populism, and it recognizes the legitimacy of opposition, provided it takes place within reasonable bounds. That opposition need not be banned from seeking office itself. Also unlike Presidential Populism, Reluctant Authoritarianism is not hostile to a multiparty system. And it does not believe that those unhappy with the status quo should leave the country.

Reluctant Authoritarianism is socialist in its advocacy of state-promoted material equality, but it does not regard the communist past as a model for equality, or for much else. Its economic model is even less clear than that of Presidential Populism, which at least knows that it does not like the market economy. Reluctant Authoritarianism allows that the market works well for the West, but shows little sign of wanting to develop this kind of market system in Belarus (see table 5.1, statement 11). Its liberal aspect is, then, political rather than economic.

The prospects for democracy in Belarus

At first sight it might appear that the prospects for democratic development in Belarus are weak, for the only discourse that champions democratic values is reconciled to the fact that the majority in Belarus voted to do away with democracy. Thus this discourse of Liberal Democracy sees little hope for the realization of its own ideals in the future. Moreover, Belarus's authoritarian presidency does not rule simply by fear and coercion; instead, it has the more secure basis of the active backing of two of our three discourses.

Still, a more positive reading of these results is possible. All three of the Belarusian discourses are committed to democracy of a sort, however limited that notion may be in two of them. This situation compares well with that of Russia, where two out of three of the discourses we found are hostile to the very idea of democracy. None of the three Belarusian discourses has any enthusiasm for a return to the Soviet past, nor is there any trace of nationalism, let alone aggressive ethnic nationalism. If nationalism is anywhere in the three Belarusian discourses, it is associated with Liberal Democracy's hostility to rapprochement with Russia. This link echoes the nineteenth-century association of liberalism with nationalism in Western and Central Europe.

A further factor working in favor of democratization in Belarus is that the post-communist economic trauma occurred under a nondemocratic regime, such that the idea of democracy was not discredited by association with economic collapse and increasing criminality and corruption. Bearing in mind the fact that the level of GNP per capita is about the same in Belarus and Russia (at US$2,200 and $2,300 respectively, according to the World Bank's *World Development Report 1999/2000*), such that they are equal in terms of the material preconditions for liberal democratic persistence, we therefore stick our necks out and predict that as of 2000 the prospects for democratization are better in Belarus than in Russia.

At the time of writing Lukashenka has not managed to impose totalitarian control – despite his efforts in this direction. Mass protests against him have taken place, notably in September 1999 (see Anonymous, 1999). Some of these involved trade unionists who strongly disapproved of the move to universal contract labor and criticized his mismanagement of the economy (many unions also supported a boycott of the 2000 elections). Well under half the electorate bothered to vote in the October 2000 parliamentary elections (turnout was nearly total in the communist era). Lukashenka revealed his willingness to compromise under pressure (including international pressure), in changing the parliamentary electoral laws in a manner that could marginally undermine his own position – though the fact that he then managed to circumvent some of his own rules is hardly encouraging. As was the case with Slovakia under Mečiar and Yugoslavia under Milošević, where observers' views had to be revised quickly in 1998 and 2000 respectively, the simple presence of an authoritarian leadership does not mean that a country is condemned to an authoritarian future.

6

Russia

WITH TATIANA ROGOVSKAIA

Russia has very little in its deep history to recall in support of any post-communist democratization process. For centuries, the country was part of the large Russian Empire under a tsarist autocracy. The final years of this autocracy, especially after October 1905, saw some modest reforms such as an elected Duma (parliament). But these were limited in both the nature and extent of the suffrage and the actual powers of the Duma. The tsarist system was overthrown in February 1917,[1] replaced by a weak provisional government that lasted only eight months. In October 1917 Lenin and the Bolsheviks took power in a coup. The Bolsheviks did permit elections to a constituent assembly in January 1918, but disregarded the results, which were not to their liking. Following a civil war (1918–20) and a revolt by many of their own supporters (the Kronstadt revolt, 1921), the Bolsheviks decided not to tolerate the other political parties they had permitted since 1917; by mid-1921, the country was a one-party dictatorship. In the following year, the Soviet Union (Union of Soviet Socialist Republics) officially came into existence. Political power then became ever more centralized.

However, we do *not* maintain that the absence of a democratic tradition precludes a country's democratic development. While evidence suggests that some experience of democracy and constitutionalism facilitates any particular democratization project, if such experience were a *sine qua non*, existing Western states could never have established themselves as democracies. Russia's troubled start with democracy, as elaborated below, has more to do with acute identity problems not shared by any other country we analyze. These problems help explain the profound disagreements of the past decade

[1] In line with standard practice, we use the Julian calendar for describing events in 1917.

or so within Russia concerning political and economic institutions. These differences in turn help to explain why the capable and effective state that such a large country may well require at this stage of its democratization process, and that the March 2000 presidential election suggested many Russians want, has been difficult to establish.

The Soviet Union came to an abrupt end in December 1991 in the wake of a failed coup by hard-liners against Mikhail Gorbachev. Russia, as one of the constituent republics of the Soviet Union, was by far its largest successor state. Power was transferred to the Russian government as elected under the Soviet system, and in particular to the administration of President Boris Yeltsin, who had played a major role in resisting the hard-liners in the August coup attempt. Thus Russia's political transition to post-communism began in earnest in 1991. Although the process had started under Gorbachev with economic and then political reforms (*perestroika*, *demokratizatsiya*, and *glasnost*), these were in the end tinkering with the Soviet system. Moreover, the August 1991 coup confirmed the continuing presence of hard-line communists wanting to reverse the Gorbachev reforms. Progressive as these reforms were, they were still introduced in a system with few safeguards to prevent a reversion to a more Stalinist, or merely Brezhnevian, political economy.

Since 1991, Russia has experienced anything but smooth sailing in democratization and marketization. Indeed, progress on both fronts soon came to a halt, in what at times became such a mix of force and farce that it might with some justification be called the *Rossky Horror Picture Show*.[2] Democratization suffered a setback in September–October 1993 with a confrontation between the president and parliament that was resolved only through violence, with the president sending in the tanks. In the wake of this confrontation, the powers of parliament were curtailed under a new constitution (December 1993), and authority was concentrated in the executive branch. Still, this new arrangement did not amount to elected presidential dictatorship, and Russia retained a substantial dispersal of power. Parliament retained a legislative role, and through an elaborate no-confidence procedure could force the president to call new parliamentary elections (which could conceivably produce a composition more hostile to the president than even the relationship between Yeltsin and the Duma sometimes was). Parliament itself featured multiple parties with no dominant coalition, and regional (we include here republican) governments have played a prominent role, often challenging or

---

[2] Rossky (or Rosskii) is a word we have made up; it is midway between the two actual Russian words for Russian (see n. 7 below and the accompanying text). Readers with Russian will appreciate that the pathetic pun we have introduced here could be made even more convincing by mixing Cyrillic and Latin scripts, since the Latin "s" equates to the Cyrillic "c." The word symbolizes nicely the confusion in Russian identity that we explore later in the chapter.

even ignoring the central government (see, e.g., Tolz and Busygina, 1997). President Yeltsin secured reelection in June 1996, but throughout the 1990s his opponents constituted a majority in the Duma.

We classify Russia as a stalled or halting transition because, at the time of our empirical study in 1997–8, its major political players were only weakly committed to pursuing their ends through constitutional means, as distinct from trying to manipulate constitutional structures to their own advantage. Corruption had emerged as a major problem. The authority of the state was only as strong – or more often weak – as President Yeltsin.[3] There was little in the way of a supportive civil society (though see Marsh, 2000 for evidence of some encouraging recent developments on this front), nor was any democratic leadership from within the state filling the gap. Successful politicians were – and still are as of mid-2000 – often demagogues seeking to play a strongman role, if they are not recycled communists. There was still no real party *system* as such, in the sense of a small number of parties with relatively clear identities. Admittedly, the Communists, the ironically named Liberal Democrats, and Yabloko *had* become constants by the end of the 1990s. But the fact remains that none of the parties that came second, third, and fourth in the December 1999 parliamentary elections, and which then collectively came to dominate the new parliament, was more than six months old. (These parties were, respectively, Unity, formed September 1999; Fatherland–All Russia, August 1999; Union of Rightist Forces, August 1999.) On the other hand, elections for parliament and president have been held that were reasonably free and fair; though as an adequate indicator of democratic transition, this criterion would satisfy only the adherents of a minimalist or electoralist definition of democracy, which we dismissed in chapter 1.

Russia has however enjoyed a measure of stability, as indicated for example by the relative ease with which the country "recovered" from the August–September 1998 ruble crisis (though see Breslauer, *et al.*, 2000 for a problematization of this recovery) and the (often uneasy) *modus vivendi* that existed most of the time between Yeltsin and the Duma. However, the Chechen war and (possibly related) terrorist attacks in Moscow and other Russian cities connote instability, as does the rapid and frequent turnover of prime ministers in the late 1990s (there were at least five between March 1998 and July 1999).[4] Any apparent stability was perhaps largely a matter of actors waiting to see what would happen after Yeltsin's departure, as well

---

[3] There were signs at the time of writing that the newly elected president, Vladimir Putin, was intent on changing this situation, with some success (see our concluding section).

[4] Six if one includes the few hours in March 1998 that Yeltsin was prime minister – or seven if one counts Chernomyrdin twice for his two separate terms in this period.

as a "discourse stalemate" that we will describe later, not mass or even elite acceptance and internalization of a new order.

Economic transition, too, was soon arrested following an attempt in 1991–2 under Deputy then Acting Prime Minister Yegor Gaidar to introduce the market via "shock therapy," along lines pioneered in Poland, but which in Russia achieved little before being abandoned (see Murrell, 1993). Russia's economic performance in the 1990s was catastrophic – albeit no worse than in many other states of the former Soviet Union – with national income in free fall, ever-increasing inequality in wealth and income, minimal foreign investment, and the oligarchs and so-called mafia coming to play dominant economic roles. Perhaps surprisingly, economic decline produced little or nothing in the way of mass protest – unlike, for example, the situation in Bulgaria in 1996–7. (Theorists of revolution would not be surprised; empirically, one constant across time and space is that misery alone never causes revolution.)

Russian discourses of democracy and reaction

The discussion groups we held in the winter of 1996–7 in Rostov and Moscow were conducted in order to generate statements for the subsequent Q sort interviews (see chapter 2), but they proved revealing in their own right. First, to many of the participants, "democracy" was something about which they could talk, but which seemingly had nothing to do with them. It was not a concept they could "own." Perhaps there was some legacy here of the tradition of "speaking without meaning" when it came to politics, of the sort that prevailed in the Soviet Union before *glasnost*.[5] Thus for some people the transition from the discourse of communism to the discourse of democracy is merely the replacement of one empty concept by another equally empty. The project assistants conducting the discussion groups were treated by some participants as ideological commissars, by others as being the unwitting tools of some mysterious controlling power, by others as spies. Some wondered if we were recruiting for Jehovah's Witnesses or some other religious sect. Such attitudes are perhaps indicative of a wholesale lack of trust in post-communist Russia: lack of trust in institutions, and in other people if they might be working for "the authorities." One assistant described the discussion group atmosphere as "angry active ignorance."

---

[5] This tradition is also perhaps reflected in the fact that the main extreme nationalist grouping in the 1990s styled itself the Liberal Democratic Party, while Our Home Is Russia sounded nationalistic but was in fact a party of centrists tied very closely to the state, concerned mainly with maintaining its members' proximity to the levers of power. Both parties declined in the late 1990s. But in the December 1999 parliamentary elections, Fatherland–All Russia did well – it is a far more centrist grouping than its nationalistic title would suggest.

For a number of participants in these discussions, democracy was a negative symbol. It is often maintained in contemporary Western textbooks on democracy and politics that in today's world everyone is a democrat, or at least claims to be, but in Russia that is clearly not the case. From the point of view of any conception of democracy, the focus groups were not encouraging, especially bearing in mind the "reflexive" stance we took in the first chapter, where we argued that democratic development has to occur in conjunction with popular discourses. These discussions suggested that, when it comes to democracy, Russia's weak institutional hardware is compounded by unhelpful, though not necessarily irredeemable, institutional software. In this sense the group discussions compared poorly with those we undertook in (for example) Yugoslavia, where there was at least a sense that democracy was something that could be talked about, that collective projects could be organized around the idea of democracy, and that these projects could engage people like the participants.

However, such impressionistic accounts of group discussions are less reliable indicators of the capabilities and dispositions of Russians when it comes to democracy than our more systematic individual Q sort interviews; so let us turn now to an analysis of these. Russia is a vast country, difficult to cover comprehensively, but we secured individual interviews in some widely different parts of the country: Moscow, Rostov, Arkhangelsk, Vladivostok, Novosibirsk, and Slavyanka. These took place in late 1997. Factor analysis enabled us to identify three discourses, which we label Chastened Democracy, Reactionary Anti-Liberalism, and Authoritarian Development. Again, we summarize each of them in the form of a narrative, constructed from the statement scores reported in table 6.1. (In the narratives, numbers in parentheses refer to the statements from the first table.)

Russia factor A: Chastened Democracy

Democracy means openness toward other societies and communication with them (12); it means freedom, private property, a code of effective laws, and social order (3, 4, 16, 52). Democracy is not just the transfer of power to new elites and self-interested conspirators or the freedom to rob (8, 27, 41). Thus democracy is desirable – if you have the means to make use of it (11, 25, 48). Certainly there are problems with the way democracy has developed in Russia, and the current political situation in general. It is terrible for democracy when people do not receive their wages and pensions (19), and when the mafia can defend people working in a business better than the state (22). It is bad that democracy's promise of openness to the world cannot be realized because people cannot afford to travel, and because of the way the government has mishandled foreign investment (30, 36). Privatization and market reform could and should have been handled more effectively and flexibly (36, 50). The state is not serving the people

Table 6.1. *Statement scores on three factors for Russia*

Factor A is Chastened Democracy.
Factor B is Reactionary Anti-Liberalism.
Factor C is Authoritarian Development.

Statement	Factor		
	A	B	C
1 Modern democracy is when the length of your chains increases.	−2	−3	−3
2 Democracy is a pure abstraction. The richer an actual society is, the more easily it can solve problems for all members of society.	0	−2	+4
3 Democracy is discipline, social order, and consciousness.	+2	−5	+2
4 Democracy without private property is impossible.	+5	0	−1
5 Before, the country was like a concentration camp, and everything was produced whether it was required or not.	+2	−6	−6
6 Nowadays, the state has created structures to support itself: more officials, more KGB, more police.	−1	0	−3
7 Russian democracy is when there is no control over the police or those running the regime.	−3	−1	+1
8 Democracy is the redistribution of power in the upper echelons of society.	−3	−2	0
9 Peoples' Deputies do not represent the interests of ordinary people, but rather those of commercial structures.	+1	+3	0
10 Democracy and patriotism are inseparable.	−1	−5	−1
11 Democracy is good when you have the means to use it.	+4	+1	+3
12 Democracy means openness toward foreign societies and the possibility of international communication.	+6	+2	+1
13 Now we do not have a democracy, but rather bureaucratic management.	0	0	−3
14 People cannot improve the economy because of the unstable political and financial situation.	+1	−3	−1
15 Bourgeois commodifying democracy treats a voter's choice as the subject of trade.	+2	+4	+1
16 Democracy means too much freedom, which ordinary people do not need.	−5	−1	0

Table 6.1. (*cont.*)

Statement	Factor		
	A	B	C
17 I do not know how democracy looks in America.	−2	−2	−1
18 Democracy will never be established in Russia as they have it in the West.	+1	+1	+6
19 The most terrible thing now is when people do not receive their salaries and pensions. Our present situation is not a democracy.	+3	+6	+4
20 Our problem is in criminality.	+2	+5	+5
21 In Russia people are fired if they are not pleasing to top officials.	−1	0	+3
22 In the present stage of Russia's development, the mafia can better defend a person working in a business than can the state.	+4	+2	+2
23 Russia is a theater of nominal democracy. The people in this theater are just spectators.	0	+1	+2
24 People voting all over Russia have two choices: people already in power and communists.	0	−3	−2
25 We need Russia, and the democrats want experiments.	−4	−1	−2
26 The state tries to figure out what is better for us.	−2	−4	−5
27 Democracy gave the freedom to rob.	−5	+2	−2
28 To create a democracy, we have to improve the material situation first.	+1	−3	+4
29 The legal mess in Russia now is a direct consequence of the absence of effective democratic institutions.	+4	+2	−2
30 Now we have a right to travel to see the world, but most people cannot afford it.	+5	+3	−2
31 Now is the period of redistribution of property.	+3	−2	+3
32 There is not any sense in the present situation with the market. No one invests money in the market, which does not have any relation to the population.	−1	+1	0
33 The word "democrat" has for many become a swear-word.	+5	+1	+1
34 Democracy in Russia is a mess.	−2	+2	+5
35 Democracy is good but there is no democracy in Russia. There is no public opinion.	+1	0	+2
36 Democracy opened the way to foreign investments, which were distributed improperly by the government, which made mistakes in privatization.	+3	+4	0

Table 6.1. (*cont.*)

	Factor		
Statement	A	B	C
37 It is more important for me how the government acts than whether we have a democratic society or not.	0	+5	+6
38 The state now pushes people with university degrees out from their chosen fields.	0	+4	−1
39 Before, people could not steal much, because they thought that someone might confront them.	−3	−4	−2
40 The state does not make money and is not able to collect taxes.	+2	0	+4
41 Democracy means the right of the next bunch of intriguers to sit in the next parliament and solve their personal problems.	−4	−3	0
42 Democrats have proved that they can destroy any political unification with their ambitions.	+1	−2	−3
43 Journalists have the opportunity now to insult people.	0	+5	+2
44 I hate those who called the country we lived in the "Evil Empire."	−3	−1	−5
45 All spheres of influence – that is, money and power – have already been divided among the various political groups.	−1	+1	+1
46 Russia is normally not lucky with its leaders.	+3	−1	+1
47 Now children are raised to believe in forgery and speculation, when before people were taught to respect their work and family.	−4	+3	−5
48 Democracy made our people passive and took away their trust in the future.	−6	−1	−4
49 Real democratic politics can and must be moral, as immoral politics brings totalitarianism.	+1	0	−4
50 The policy of market reform should have been more flexible.	+4	+1	+3
51 For the basis of democracy there should be a centuries-old culture, but this was destroyed in 1917.	−1	−4	−3
52 Democracy should be a code of effective laws.	+6	−2	+5
53 Real democracy must not only have a long tongue but also strong teeth.	0	−1	0
54 There should not be legalization of property created by stealing, because this spoils public morality.	−1	+3	0

Table 6.1. (*cont.*)

Statement	Factor		
	A	B	C
55 Russia needs a power like that of Pinochet or Stalin.	−6	−5	−1
56 The state does not do what it should do. It does not defend the interests of its populations either inside or outside the country.	+3	+4	−1
57 The real democrats today need real courage to recognize and admit their own errors.	+2	+1	+1
58 It is not particularly important whether a person is of democratic or communist viewpoint. You need to vote for a person who relies upon moral principles.	−2	+3	+2
59 If we had not taken the path to the present situation, we would have ended up in a primitive society.	−1	−6	−4
60 When Russians become proud of their country, only then will democracy appear.	+1	0	−4
61 It is better for some people to be beaten with a stick once a day, and then they will live in a more highly developed society.	−5	−4	+3
62 Before, if you had a problem, in a local party committee you could solve it.	−3	−1	−6
63 There was a working country before; everything should have been modernized, and not made to fall apart.	−2	+6	−1
64 All ordinary people from the so-called CIS countries want them to reunite.	−4	+2	+1

well; now as before, Russia is not lucky with its leaders (46, 56). For many people the word "democrat" has become a swear-word (33). But the mess in Russia is due to the absence of effective democratic institutions – not the presence of democracy (29). Russia may be a mess, but it is not democracy that is a mess, and the last thing we need is an authoritarian leader like Stalin or authoritarian repression (55, 61). We must look forward rather than back. The Soviet Union was more like a concentration camp than a moral system or an effective system that could solve one's problems (5, 39, 47, 62, 63); so no reestablishment of the Soviet Union should be sought (64).

The discourse represented by factor A is home to liberal, constitutional, and civic commitments, unlike the other two discourses. It is extremely cosmopolitan, seeing openness to and communication with other societies as among the most important aspects of democracy, and very frustrated that Russia's economic situation obstructs communication and travel. But Chastened Democracy is also beleaguered and defensive: effective democracy is seen as something that is intrinsically desirable, but not in prospect. This discourse recognizes that for many people democracy has become a negative concept, and understands the reasons for this. Chastened Democracy bemoans the condition of post-communist Russia as quite disastrous in both economic and political terms, with little genuine democracy. Like the other two Russian discourses, it sees little worth defending in the status quo; unlike them it is adamant that there must be no return to the Soviet system, or any kind of authoritarianism. Thus it is not democracy *per se* which is seen as having failed, but rather Russian political leadership, among other matters by proving incapable of introducing effective democratic institutions, and by making a mess of economic reform. Shock therapy is regarded as a mistake.

Any defense of existing democratic accomplishments in Russia would seem to fall to the Chastened Democracy discourse; the other two discourses have on the face of it little interest in such defense (though at the end of this chapter we will attempt a more positive reading of them). But Chastened Democracy too has little interest in defending the existing political system, except on the weak grounds that it believes the old Soviet system to be much worse.[6] Moreover, its adherents evidence little sign of expecting any better democracy in Russia in the foreseeable future. Still, democracy is not seen as a totally impossible dream.

In terms of the configuration of Russian party politics, at least until 1998–9, Chastened Democracy resonates with the platform of the Yabloko party, whose 6.9 percent of the vote in 1995 secured fifty-one seats in the Duma, making it the largest of the reform-oriented parties, indeed the only one of these to pass the 5 percent threshold necessary for candidates on the party list to enter parliament. The party did not perform quite as well in the December 1999 elections, scoring only 5.9 percent of the party list vote and securing just 21 of the 450 seats. Yabloko styles itself a liberal democratic, pro-market movement, oriented to Europe, and appeals to those who supported the liberalizing and democratic reforms of 1991–2, but who opposed shock therapy and subsequently felt deceived and let down. Reflecting Chastened Democracy's negative evaluation of the status quo, Yabloko's

---

[6] This does not mean the discourse subscribes to the "Churchill hypothesis" that Rose, *et al.* test in the East European context: "democracy is the worst form of government, except all those other forms that have been tried from time to time" (cited in Rose, Mishler, and Haerpfer, 1998, p. 11). Chastened Democracy does have a principled commitment to democracy as such.

leader, the economist Grigorii Yavlinskii, in 1998 described Russia as having "a corporate oligarchic semi-criminal system still based on former Soviet monopolies" in whose favor the government operated (*OMRI Daily Digest*, March 17, 1998). Ironically, the most consistent principled opposition to the Yeltsin government came not from nationalists or communists, but from Yabloko. Alone among the Duma factions and parties, Yabloko was not interested in deal-making. This moralistic attitude to politics echoes a republican commitment to the politics of public virtue, as opposed to the politics of interest and compromise, but we can find little direct reflection of this sort of republicanism in our Chastened Democracy factor.

A number of survey studies of Russian opinion conducted in the early and mid-1990s generally concluded that the Russian public featured a relatively high level of support for liberal democratic principles such as free speech, freedom of the press, and competitive elections, combined with low support for, and extreme alienation from, the post-communist Russian state (for a summary of such studies, see Remington, 1997, pp. 114–15). This summary judgment is broadly consistent with our Chastened Democracy discourse. Survey evidence suggests, however, that support for liberal democratic principles declined in 1998 (unpublished research by Stephen Whitefield and Geoffrey Evans cited in A. Brown, 1999, p. 9), reflecting perhaps increasing instability and political cynicism in the last three or four years of Yeltsin's presidency. Still, the discourse represents an enduring point of view, regardless of fluctuations in the proportion of the electorate willing to act upon it.

Let us now turn to a very different discourse, one that is more alienated from the status quo than the first, but less democratic.

Russia factor B: Reactionary Anti-Liberalism

This so-called democracy is a mess (34). There is no discipline, social order, or patriotism, only criminality and the freedom to rob (3, 10, 20, 27). Ordinary people do not receive their salaries and pensions, and that is terrible (19). Educated people are pushed out of their chosen field by the state (38). Journalists have the opportunity to insult people (43). People's deputies do not serve the people, but rather serve commercial interests (9). Property acquired by stealing is legalized, and this destroys public morality (54). The mafia protects people working in a business better than the state does (22). The state does not try to figure out how to do better for us, or defend the interests of people (26, 56). Votes can be bought (15). I do not care whether we have a democracy or not: more important is what the government does in response to these problems (37). It does not matter whether someone is a democrat or a communist; you need to vote for a person who relies on moral principles (58). But we do not need a dictator like Stalin, or to beat people with a stick (55, 61). Before, the country was not a concentration camp; it was a working political and economic system that should have been retained and modernized; we did not have to go down the path of privatization we have taken (5, 36, 59, 63). Ordinary people of the CIS countries want them to reunite (64). Now children are raised to believe in forgery and speculation; before, people were taught to respect work and family (47).

The Reactionary Anti-Liberalism of factor B clearly regrets the passing of the Soviet Union. Of the four statements that energize this discourse most strongly, three (statements 5, 59, and 63 – see table 6.1) refer directly to the Soviet past. That past is not regarded as perfect, but it is compared favorably to the post-communist situation, which meets with round condemnation. This does not mean that Reactionary Anti-Liberalism is an enthusiastically authoritarian discourse, and it explicitly rejects dictatorship. It is actually less authoritarian than our third Russian discourse which, as we shall see, does not regret the demise of the Soviet Union. But Reactionary Anti-Liberalism ascribes no intrinsic value to democratic procedures or liberal freedoms. It sees a need for firm action to get things done and solve problems effectively; and the Soviet regime is looked upon with favor, because in this respect it is seen as delivering the goods much better than its successor. This attitude looks to be at root a very instrumental one, not representing any idealistic commitment to communism or "socialist democracy" – it accepts that democracy is something that arrived only in the post-communist era. Indeed, this discourse is quite indifferent when it comes to democracy versus communism, and does not care whether politicians describe themselves as democratic or communist. Thus it is not anti-democratic, but it is anti-liberal in its hostility to privatization, market reforms, and excessive freedom of the press on the one hand, and its stress on the need for state-controlled social discipline on the other.

While the discourse of Reactionary Anti-Liberalism is in many ways instrumental, it does not deal only in cold calculation, and there may be an occasional lapse in logic. For example, statement 19 on the scandalous nature of nonpayment of salaries and pensions receives a strong positive response; but the incapacity of the state to collect the taxes necessary to pay state employees meets with indifference (statement 40).

In terms of the relationship between Reactionary Anti-Liberalism and the major currents in Russian party politics, one might expect to find here those communists and nationalists who opposed the Yeltsin administration's reforms most vociferously. If we look at the political self-description of individuals who load most highly on this discourse (see table 6.2), we find that they include three self-described communists, one person who liked the Soviet Union, one conservative (which in the Russian context can mean anti-reform), one patriot, and one Russian nationalist. Certainly, we would

Table 6.2. *Subject loadings on factors for Russia*

		Factor		
Subject and political self-description		A	B	C
1	M, television director, no preference	31	5	48*
2	M, teaching assistant, no preference	52*	4	16
3	M, teacher, Russian nationalist	10	59*	12
4	F, pensioner, communist	−10	41*	4
5	F, student, democrat	38*	39*	3
6	F, student, nonpartisan atheist	1	21	60*
7	M, student, democratic anti-communist	54*	19	2
8	M, unemployed, liberal left	−10	42*	13
9	M, unemployed, new communist	−25	40*	2
10	M, lawyer, interested in politics, no preference	46*	15	23
11	M, tattooist, apolitical	49*	29	2
12	F, housewife, left democrat	29	17	12
13	F, social worker, radical	−3	20	49*
14	M, translator, liberal	63*	−16	14
15	F, student, apolitical pacifist	65*	2	27
16	F, public relations manager, liberal	70*	4	31
17	M, business owner, liberal democrat	59*	8	5
18	F, journalist, social democrat	58*	13	11
19	M, student, right-centrist	−51*	19	−8
20	M, travel agent, liked Soviet Union	30	56*	21
21	M, driver, nonpolitical	26	6	28
22	F, secretary, reform democrat	55*	6	27
23	M, unemployed engineer, no preference	7	7	30
24	M, physicist, anti-political	39*	49*	4
25	M, military officer, patriot	24	42*	25
26	M, single mother, pro-reform	30	37*	18
27	F, student, liberal democrat/reform	32*	11	18
28	F, pensioner, pro-government	7	32*	5
29	M, teacher, liberal/pro-government	28	21	−17
30	M, farmer, communist	24	48*	26
31	F, accountant, democrat	30	19	52*
32	F, housewife, moderate liberal	50*	10	−9
33	M, construction worker, don't care	33*	20	60*
34	? (gender not known), engineer, monarchist	44*	21	−40*
35	F, student, conservative	6	41*	9
36	M, salesperson, democrat	31	21	6

*Denotes a loading significant at the .01 level.

expect CPRF (Communist Party of the Russian Federation) supporters to subscribe to this discourse; the CPRF has rejected aspects of the Soviet past while highlighting others for which it believes there remains nostalgia within the electorate. The Communists pay lip service to democracy, and in many ways are an instrumental party with principled edges. But of particular interest is that we also find one liberal leftist, one pro-reform, and one pro-government individual loading highly on this discourse. What this suggests is that this discourse, and especially its instrumental aspects, may extend to some of those supporting the centrist parties which have no strong ideological commitments beyond sharing as much as possible in state power. Among these, Our Home Is Russia, the party of former prime minister Chernomyrdin, which secured 10.1 percent of the party list vote and fifty-five seats in the 1995 election (only 1.2 percent of the party list vote, and a total of seven seats in the 1999 election), has followed an especially managerial approach to politics.

Reactionary Anti-Liberalism might at first sight seem to offer only bad news for those interested in Russia's democratic development. But though it has no interest in defending democracy, it has no ideologically charged hostility to democracy either, let alone a coherent outlook on the need for authoritarian political change. Demagogues might find this very frustrating. We turn now to a discourse that is more explicitly authoritarian but, perhaps paradoxically, much less reactionary.

Russia factor C: Authoritarian Development

Democracy will never be established in Russia as it is in the West (18). But that doesn't matter; democracy may be fine if you have the means to use it (11, 12, 35), but more important is that as a society we become rich, for only then can we begin to solve all our problems (2, 28). What the government does is more important than whether we have a democracy or not (37). We need stronger, more effective laws and social discipline (3, 52). It does not matter whether our leaders call themselves communists or democrats; more important is that they rely upon moral principles, and such morality does not go along with democracy (49, 58). Some people have to be beaten with a stick to make them live in a more highly developed society (61). Democracy and the situation in Russia in general are a mess (19, 34). People do not receive their salaries and pensions, criminality is everywhere, journalists insult people, people are fired if they are not pleasing to top officials, the state cannot collect taxes or manage effectively, and it does not try to figure out what would be better for us (13, 19, 20, 21, 26, 40). But that mess is not because of the absence of democracy (29). Things today may be a mess, but the old system was not so great either (44, 47, 63). It was not a concentration camp, and the economy worked in its fashion, but party committees could not solve one's problems (5, 62).

While our factor B is a reactionary discourse, looking back to the old regime, factor C, Authoritarian Development, would be classified as a skeptical discourse because it disapproves of both the Soviet Union and the post-communist regime (to use the taxonomy of Rose and Mishler, 1993). Skepticism here does not mean the discourse has no program, because indeed it does. Like Reactionary Anti-Liberalism, the Authoritarian Development of factor C cares little about ideological differences between communism and democracy, and has a very instrumental view of government. But the goals of instrumental action are much clearer: the first priority is to make Russia rich. And the means are more explicitly authoritarian: a strong state, public morality, social discipline, coercive laws, if necessary "beating people with a stick" to force them to live in a more developed modern society.

None of this is seen as compatible with democracy, which is considered synonymous with immorality and corruption. Thus economic development in Russia is going to have to be authoritarian and statist, with the constitutional democracies of the West providing no relevant model. Authoritarian Development therefore involves a perception that Russia is unique, that it must find its own path to riches (and perhaps capitalism), but not via this phenomenon called democracy.

There is little sense that authoritarianism is necessary only for some transition period, after which a more liberal and democratic politics might be sought. Authoritarian Development looks like a program for the long haul. Thus this discourse should not be equated with the position of observers of post-communist transition such as Przeworski (1991) and Brucan (1992) who have argued that the introduction of a market economy can only be effected by an authoritarian government, on the grounds that democracies are less able to cope with the transitional pain. (These sorts of arguments failed to maintain credibility among transitologists by the late 1990s.) Such observers readily concede that democracy was the political goal in the medium to long term. Another key feature of the discourse is highlighted through contrast with the position of such observers: for a discourse which puts making society rich above all else, Authoritarian Development has little to say on what kind of economic system would achieve this. The discourse appears to be quite agnostic on, for example, the appropriate mix of markets and planning, of private and public property. Perhaps this discourse represents a continuation of a persistent theme in Russian history: that if the right leadership is found everything will fall into place.

If it is not easy to map Authoritarian Development on the extant range of models for post-communist transformation, it is even less easy to associate it with any political party that existed in Russia prior to 1999. If we examine the self-descriptions of those who load heavily on this factor (see table 6.2), they appear to be a mixed bag: one "no preference," one "nonpartisan atheist," one "radical," one "don't care," one "monarchist," and (perhaps most surprising) one "democrat."

The emergence of Unity (also known as Medved in Russian – the word for bear, the Russian symbol) meant that this discourse had at last found its party home. Although it was not very clear even at the time of the 1999 parliamentary elections what Unity stood for, it *was* the party associated with Prime Minister Putin, whom Yeltsin had chosen as his preferred successor – and on whom many Russians were pinning their hopes for a strong new leader who could stand up to the Chechen rebels and terrorists. The party's – and at that time, the prime minister's – vagueness about how to improve the economy, the lack of sentimentality about the communist past, the notion that Russia is different from the West, the absence of any clear ideological orientation, the determination to deal with corruption and bring the oligarchs to heel, and the commitment to the notion that what is needed above all is strong leadership and a less fragmented, more powerful Russia (hence "Unity" and Medved) – all resonate with Authoritarian Development.

The clarification of what Putin stood for by the middle of 2000 would mostly be music to factor C's ears. His liberal economic policy – guided by the "St. Petersburg" economists, favoring marketization and privatization, as well as greater transparency – should not upset factor C, which has no strong preference in economics. If the Putin approach delivers the goods it will be happy. It would approve of his criticism of irresponsible and politically loaded media; his moves to bring the oligarchs under control and make them pay taxes; and the steps to bring the more autonomist regional governors in check as part of his institutional recentralization (on this last point, see Tompson, 2000). It would also support Putin's emphasis on the need for a "dictatorship of law," even if it would not necessarily endorse the new president's argument that the dictatorship of law is a key component of *democracy*.

The prospects for Russian democracy

Russian politics by the end of the 1990s featured a state that seemingly lacked legitimacy in the eyes of any significant sector of the population, and a government that presided over an economy that lurched ever deeper into crisis (its survival of the August–September 1998 ruble crisis only giving analysts more reason to despair of making sense of this vast country!), pursuing policies that nobody seemed to support. This might seem a recipe for social instability and unrest, but contemplation of our three Russian discourses gives some insight into the sources of staying power of state and government. None defends the status quo, but each wants to move it in a different direction: Chastened Democracy wants to move it to the West, Reactionary Anti-Liberalism to the past, and Authoritarian Development to some brighter (because richer) future. None of these projects looks especially plausible, particularly given the resistance each is likely to meet from the other two discourses. Combining this discourse stalemate with the apparent "wait and see" attitude of many Russians in Yeltsin's last years makes the lack of political unrest understandable.

At first sight, the apparent stalemate might seem to offer about as much comfort as can be drawn from our results for those interested in Russia's democratic future. But before trying to squeeze a more positive prognosis from these results, there is one more negative to be noted. Though our results do not speak directly to the issue, some significant questions are raised when we contemplate these findings in the context of Russia's acute identity problems. These can be explained in terms of five aspects, four of which relate directly to losses over the past ten to twelve years (for an analysis of Russia's identity problems that considers instead five major discourses of national identity, see Tolz, 1998).

First, Russians have for centuries been unsure in their own minds whether their country and culture are European, Asian, or *sui generis*. This confusion has led Huntington (1996) to identify Russia, like Turkey and Australia, as a deeply "torn" country. Geographically, Russia is primarily Asian – indeed the largest Asian country. In the late 1980s, however, Mikhail Gorbachev talked publicly of Russia's return to "our common European home." In clearly implying that Russia was European, he followed a line of leaders that can be traced back at least to Peter the Great in the early eighteenth century. Our discourse A, Chastened Democracy, continues this Western orientation. Yet ever since the debate between the "Slavophiles" and "Westernizers" that began in the 1830s and continued throughout the nineteenth century (see Utechin, 1964, esp. pp. 78–127), some Russians have seen their country as simultaneously the center of Slavic civilization and unique, hence *sui generis*. Discourse C's Authoritarian Development appears to share this viewpoint, rejecting Western models of democracy. This nineteenth-century debate finds many resonances in contemporary Russian politics, and hinders attempts to agree on a common Russian identity.

Second, and arguably more significant, is the fact that Russia is the heart of what was, until 1991, perhaps the world's last great empire. This empire extended into four continents – from Vietnam and Mongolia in Asia to the GDR and Bulgaria in Europe, and from Angola and Mozambique in Africa to Cuba in the Americas. Many Russians lamented the loss of this "outer" empire, symbolized in the collapse of both the Warsaw Pact and Comecon. Yet of even greater concern was the loss of the so-called inner empire – the countries that had once been component republics of the

Soviet Union itself. As first the Baltic states and Georgia, subsequently even the fellow Slavic states of Ukraine and Belarus, declared their independence, so Russians started to blame each other for the fact that their centuries-old empire had just collapsed. This empire crumbled much more quickly and decisively than had most of the European empires. Surveys revealed that many Russians had not hitherto even thought of themselves primarily as Russians, but rather as Soviets – members of a vast, multiethnic state. Thus Russians had to rethink who they were; in a sense, they had to engage in "identity downsizing." Their confusion was reflected in the language; there are few other languages in which there are similar but separate words for the ethnic (*russkii* or *russkaya*) and the civic (*rossiskii* or *rossiskaya*) identities.[7]

Third, the Russians lost not only an empire, but also, and very suddenly, their role as a universally recognized superpower. This was the country that had beaten the USA into space, so that the word *sputnik* was by 1960 almost as familiar to English speakers as to Russians. At the end of the 1960s, German chancellor Willi Brandt had urged détente, which connoted Western recognition of the Soviet Union's ability to destroy the West many times over. Come the 1990s, Russia appeared to be a country on its knees. There was now only one superpower. The criticism President Putin faced for his handling of the *Kursk* submarine disaster of August 2000 was barbed because many Russians were aware that their leader should have called in Western assistance earlier, yet frustrated that their own once-mighty navy could not achieve what a tiny group of Norwegians managed to do quite quickly once they were called upon.

Fourth, and closely related to the last point, the Soviets lost the Cold War. As the *de facto* core of the Soviet Union, many Russians felt humiliated that they had lost so unambiguously that many of their new leaders were advocating adoption of the former archenemy's political and economic system.

Finally, Russians lost their privileged position as citizens of the home of socialism – of a model that was supposed to eventually take over the world and demonstrate that Russian civilization was superior to all others. Whereas

---

[7] Various other languages distinguish the citizenship from the ethnic majority group. Hungarian, for example, draws a distinction between Hungarian and Magyar. In the Hungarian case, however, the two words are quite different, whereas even readers with no Russian will be able to see the similarity of the terms in Russian (the two versions of each Russian word are the masculine and feminine versions respectively). Sakwa (1999, p. 61) makes a reasonable (if brief) case in favor of "nationism" (different ethnic groups identifying with the nation) over nationalism; the notion of *rossiskii/-aya* might appear to represent this. Unfortunately, and as Tolz (1998) demonstrates, Russians seem at present to be unable to agree on one form of identity over the other, or indeed any at all, so that the dominant impression is of confused and contested identity.

East Europeans could blame their underdevelopment on an imposed system, the Russians had invented that system.

This identity issue places Russia in a unique position in the post-communist world. Whereas Poles, Slovaks, or even Georgians may have disagreed on the optimal transition path, they at least had a reasonably coherent identity, and little reason for any profound sense of loss.[8] They were neither fundamentally confused about who they were, nor seeking scapegoats for loss. This sense of loss, and search for scapegoats, clearly pervades our second Russian discourse, Reactionary Anti-Liberalism.

In an earlier comparative study, one of us (L. Holmes, 1993, esp. pp. xi and 21–2) referred to the "double rejective" revolutions of 1989–91, by which he meant rejection of both the communist power system and external domination. At the time, he made the point that the notion of the "double rejection" had to be modified to suit Russian conditions. The "double rejective" revolution experienced by most Central and Eastern Europeans was in some ways a "quadruple loss" revolution for the Russians. With possible, but less vivid, exceptions in Moldova and Ukraine, we have found nothing like the sense of loss that the Russian discourse of Reactionary Anti-Liberalism represents.

Further, Russia, like other former Soviet republics (except for the three Baltic states and Moldova), had experienced some seventy years of communist indoctrination, considerably longer than the other CEE communist states. The communists had also taken power under their own steam in the Russian Empire. (Yugoslav and Albanian communists were the only other European communists who managed this.)

Given all these problems, it is easy to be pessimistic about Russia's democratic future. Yet beyond pinning hopes on stalemate across the three discourses we have identified – and so stalemate in Russian politics, which would at least prevent a return to full authoritarianism – there do remain other more positive possibilities, though it may take some effort to unearth them.

Starting in the early 1990s, the Russian communists publicly blamed President Yeltsin for the breakup of the Soviet Union. Whether or not this is justifiable – and in many ways it is not[9] – it has been repeated so often that many Russians now more or less accept it (for the communists' criticism

---

[8] In the case of Georgia, note that the Soviet Union was the successor to the *Russian* Empire, which is why non-Russian members of the former Soviet Union would not be expected to have suffered the same sense of loss of status and power as the Russians. However, many Georgians are still proud of the fact that the longest-serving Soviet leader was one of them!

[9] The final trigger for the breakup was the near-farcical attempted coup of August 1991; this was led by conservative communists. At a more general level, if the communists had made a better job of running the Soviet Union, it would not have been in the dire straits Gorbachev and others identified by the mid-1980s.

of Yeltsin's role, see Dunlop, 1993). Ironically, this might serve to facilitate democratization in the future. Yeltsin's departure signaled a symbolic break with the past. Given that Putin is not too obviously tainted with the collapse of the former empire, the fact that even our two anti-democratic discourses yearn for a strong (in the sense of capable and effective but uncorrupted) state – a yearning corroborated in Russian survey evidence (see *Vremya MN*, December 6, 1999, translated in *Current Digest of the Post-Soviet Press*, 51:49 [2000], p. 19)[10] – means that one can at least envisage a future more democratic than the present that would be tolerated by all three discourses, and perhaps even supported by one or more of them. Such a future, and its presidency, would combine the aspects of a strong state that refer to capacity and effectiveness favored by Reactionary Anti-Liberalism and Authoritarian Development (without the state size favored by the former and the intrusiveness favored by the latter) with the democratic commitments of Chastened Democracy. Of course, any such presidency would fall far short of Western liberal democratic ideals (but then so did Richard Nixon), and hence of the ideals represented in the Chastened Democracy discourse. But these ideals are a remote prospect in Russia under any scenario, especially given the current weakness of Russian civil society as a political force.

As mentioned in chapter 1, one of us has argued elsewhere (L. Holmes, 1998) that, perhaps counterintuitively, the state sometimes has to play a leading role in the democratization project. For instance, it has to establish the legal and institutional bases of the rule of law. Moreover, in many post-authoritarian and post-totalitarian systems, the economic situation of many citizens is so parlous that they do not have the time or the inclination to engage in civic activism. A strong state with strong leadership can under these circumstances play a positive role in establishing the basic rules and tools of democracy, as well as putting the economy onto a stronger footing.

It might be objected that this kind of "facilitating" role smacks of both paternalism and authoritarianism, and indeed there is a danger of either or both of these. But while the current Russian constitution could allow a democratically elected president to become a virtual dictator, there is no *necessity* for this to occur. There have been many cases of strong leadership in consolidated democracies – think, for example, of Margaret Thatcher, Helmut Kohl, Franklin Roosevelt – without its presence endangering the basic democratic credentials of the systems in question. Where the democratic commitment of such leaders has been questioned, they have often been removed through constitutional electoral processes.

[10] Unfortunately, more than three-quarters of those surveyed shortly after Putin became acting president believed that even he could not bring corruption under control – see *Vremya MN*, February 23, 2000, translated in *Current Digest of the Post-Soviet Press*, 52: 9 (2000), p. 14.

These examples show that strong leadership does not have to equate with dictatorship. As long as such leaders are prepared to stand in regular and genuinely contested elections (i.e., are ultimately answerable to the electorate), are not above the legal system, do not muzzle the media, and work with, rather than over, elected representative assemblies (parliaments), then they have not become dictators. Now, the requirements for such leaders are more demanding in transitional societies, in which from the point of view of democracy there is a need to put the economy on track, reduce tensions between groups or factions with sharply different views on political fundamentals, and eventually facilitate constitutional change that would reduce the power of the executive in favor of parliament. Yet at least one good example can be found in a transitional society, in the role played by King Juan Carlos in Spain after 1975. Of course, post-Franco Spain did not have quite such profound identity problems as Russia now does – though Basque and Catalan issues did present serious boundary and identity questions.

All three of the Russian discourses we have identified recognize and lament alienation, a breakdown in trust, and the absence of civic engagement.[11] Hence, there *is* some common ground between the adherents of each discourse, and we would argue that this provides *some* reasons for, at the very least, not hastening to write off Russian democracy too soon. Putin can appeal in some senses to all three discourses. To those who maintain that there is no way Russia could be heading toward the consolidation of democracy under a former KGB officer and head of its Russian successor organization, we would point out that Khrushchev was once a leading member of Stalin's Politburo, yet condemned the former leader's "errors," then "crimes." This reveals that, in Russia at least, leopard leaders may indeed change their spots. Putin was also a deputy to the very liberal former mayor of St. Petersburg, Anatolii Sobchak.

Acknowledging that the situation in Russia has been chaotic and depressing is quite different from arguing that this means the future of democracy in that country is doomed. A dynamic, strong new presidency might just make a significant difference in a relatively short time, especially if Putin's commitment to "the dictatorship of law" really translates into the rule of law rather than rule by the coercive agencies of the state. Putin has stated that he believes political dictatorships are invariably fragile and temporary,

---

[11] Richard Rose (2000b) has argued that there remains a great deal of "social capital" in Russia in terms of being prepared to help one's neighbors, for instance. Unfortunately, not only is this kind of social capital clearly not of great significance in terms of the development of a politicized civil society, it can also reinforce the level of alienation between the state and society. The other side of the coin is that social capital helps to reduce social unrest, and – at the most basic and perhaps most important level – to ensure people do not actually starve.

and that democracy is the only truly robust and enduring political system (see Remington, 2000).[12] Our discourse analysis suggests, at least, that there are no *inherent* reasons for Russia not to become more democratic, especially if strong leadership and democracy (especially democratization) can be compatible.[13] Also, at the risk of sounding platitudinous, time heals; many of the reasons for the Russians' identity crisis might fade if the new president and parliament, between them, can put the economy back on track.[14] At the time of writing, we wonder if our classification of Russia as a stalled or halting transition will soon need updating.

[12] By late 2000 the Western media were raising doubts about Putin's commitment to democracy. Two of the pieces of evidence cited were the recentralization of power from the regions and the clampdown on the Russian media. Closer analysis shows that the situation is more complex. In the case of the former, it needs to be borne in mind that many regional governors have been far *less* democratic and accountable than the politicians in Moscow. Equally, some of Putin's actions vis-à-vis the mass media appear to have been designed to make the media more independent of often quite undemocratic owners.

[13] Our own findings suggest that many Russians want a decisive and effective leader with the capacity to impose his (or her?) political will. While part of the explanation might well be Russian political tradition, and while it might prevent Russia moving much beyond delegative democracy in the short term, we would suggest that citizens in many countries, whatever their "political culture," would seek such leadership when the state has been as weak and impoverished, and criminals as wealthy and powerful, as has been the case in Russia in recent years.

[14] In terms of creating a better relationship between the president and parliament, the "presidential party" that Eugene Huskey (1999) has argued is a prerequisite for the consolidation of a functional political system in Russia, absent in the Yeltsin era, *may* now have arrived in the shape of Unity. But prediction in politics, especially Russian politics, is a risky business!

7

Ukraine

WITH VICTOR HOHOTS AND KYRYLO LOUKERENKO

Ukraine is a large and diverse country, with a population not much smaller than that of France, Italy, or the UK. By 1991, it was one of the more industrialized and urbanized republics of the Soviet Union, and as such might look well-placed to be able to negotiate political and economic transition (though, as we pointed out in our discussion of Belarus, economic development provides a defense against reversion of democracy to authoritarianism, as opposed to being a cause of democracy; see Przeworski, *et al.*, 2000). But in addition to the weak commitments to political and economic reform of its post-communist political leaders, several aspects of Ukraine's situation in terms of religious, linguistic, and cultural divisions might seem less auspicious.[1]

The much smaller (population-wise) West of Ukraine is mainly Catholic, the East Orthodox. The East is largely Russophone. Traditionally, the West is more nationalistic, and likely to look to Europe; the East tends to look to closer relations with Russia. Ukraine's past and its large diaspora (some three million) have seen episodes of radical ethnic nationalism. But ethnic nationalism within Ukraine's politics in recent years has been much more muted and liberal. As Krawchenko (1993, p. 86) points out, there is "virtually no interethnic conflict in Ukraine" (see also Birch and Wilson, 1999).[2] Yet

---

[1] For an argument that the negative aspects of Ukraine's past can be overcome, see Wise and Brown, 1999.

[2] The main exception to this statement is the conflict between Crimea (predominantly Russian) and Kyiv in the early 1990s. Crimea had been a part of Russia until 1954, and many Crimeans were irredentist, wanting to return to the pre-1954 situation. Support from Moscow was limited, however, and, once Crimea was granted autonomous status within Ukraine, the tensions largely dissipated. According to Krawchenko

Samuel Huntington in *The Clash of Civilizations and the Remaking of World Order* (1996) makes much of the cultural divisions in Ukraine, treating them in terms of the major fault-line between Western and Orthodox civilizations, thus a likely venue for future strife, indeed war. Such dire predictions have yet to be realized. In fact, Ukraine has witnessed remarkably little political convulsion of any real significance since 1991, certainly much less than its post-Soviet neighbors in Russia, Georgia, Moldova, or even Belarus. Post-communist Ukraine has been relatively free of violence.

This freedom from instability, ethnic conflict, and violence has been achieved in the face of some real identity problems since the collapse of the Soviet Union. When part of the Soviet Union, Ukraine held a special status among the fifteen republics. Along with Belarus, it had a seat in the United Nations, and, if only formally, the world's fourth largest nuclear arsenal.[3] This significant status was of course in the context of the Soviet Union as a whole. The Chernobyl incident (April 1986) raised only short-lived political consciousness and questioning of Moscow's hegemony. By the mid-1990s, Ukrainians were divided on whether or not it even made sense to have their own sovereign state (Karatnycky, 1995, p. 118).

Digging a little deeper, Ukraine has had a long history of shifting boundaries and subordination. With only brief interludes in 1918–20 and 1941–3, Eastern Ukraine had by 1991 been under Russian and then Soviet rule for over 300 years. Western Ukraine had been subdivided on numerous occasions (e.g., following the second partition of Poland in 1793, and in the aftermath of the 1921 treaty of Riga), with different parts having been ruled variously by Russia, the Austro-Hungarian Empire, and, in the interwar period, Poland (with small areas under Czechoslovak and Romanian control), until incorporation into the Soviet Union in 1939–40.[4] Thus Ukraine has no "normal" national boundaries in the past to serve as a reference point.

Nor does Ukraine have anything much in terms of historical anchors for the development of democratic or constitutional government, let alone any enduring legacy that could be drawn upon as a source of inspiration for post-communist political change. Only Galicia in the West could make any serious claims to experience with democracy, before and after the First World War. President Havel in Czechia can appeal to Tomáš Masaryk in terms of *both* national identity *and* democratic values. President Leonid Kravchuk, first president of the new Ukraine, referred in his 1991 campaign to Mykhailo Hrushevsky (independent Ukraine's first president in

(1993), the primary social divide in Ukraine is not ethnic but along rural–urban lines.

[3] We are here treating the four component parts of the Soviet nuclear arsenal separately.

[4] The Germans took control of some parts of Ukraine in the early 1940s, but these were taken back by the Soviets by 1944. For a more detailed analysis, see Subtelny, 1998, pp. 453–80.

1918), who was a nation-builder but not a democrat.[5] This stress on creating a dominant national identity in the early years of post-communist democratization led Krawchenko (1993, p. 86) to conclude that "the national movement in Ukraine is the democratic movement."

Yet the picture is really more complex in that a nationalist movement, Rukh, held its constituent congress in September 1989, and, under another name, secured almost one-quarter of the seats in the legislature in the 1990 elections. But much of its agenda was then taken over by leading communists, many of whose democratic *and* nationalist credentials were questionable. The communist sequestering of the nationalist agenda (even if for pragmatic survival reasons) helps to explain why there was relatively little organized nationalist or liberal democratic opposition to the Soviet regime come 1991. As in Belarus, the Ukrainian Communist Party hierarchy was firmly aligned with the more conservative wing of the Soviet regime (see Prizel, 1997, pp. 337–8). Although the Ukrainian Communist Party was formally banned following the failed coup in Moscow and Ukraine's declaration of independence in August 1991 (the ban was lifted in 1993), many of its leaders continued to play major political roles. Given the weakness of other political parties, when the Soviet Union collapsed in December 1991 it was not especially hard for this hierarchy to cling to power. Indeed, independence provided the former communist leadership with an opportunity to consolidate power, because it no longer had to contend with the winds of *perestroika* and *glasnost* blowing from Moscow.

This does not mean that this leadership welcomed the loss of control from Moscow, because such control was intrinsic to Soviet ideology, as well as being a prop for its own power. The ex-communist leadership therefore had to adjust to being left to face the majority clamoring for confirmation of the August declaration of independence (and voting for it in a December 1991 referendum). Rather than ride a nationalist wave, these ex-communists sought instead to highlight the problems that arrived with sovereignty, and to lay the blame for Ukraine's post-1991 difficulties at the door of pro-capitalist democrats, while blocking economic reforms that would have moved Ukraine more effectively to a market economy. (On the period from the late 1980s to the early 1990s, see Kuzio and Wilson, 1994.)

Independent Ukraine moved very slowly in the direction of political and economic reform. Its political leadership, with approval from much of the

---

[5] Formally, Hrushevsky was president for only a few hours in April 1918, when he was replaced in a coup (see Shulhyn, 1963, esp. p. 745). However, he was the head of the Rada (parliament) for several months in 1917–18, and was widely seen as *the* leader of newly independent Ukraine. Hrushevsky's focus was understandable in that Ukraine's sovereignty was far more precarious than that of the new Czechoslovak state.

opposition, seemed far more interested in establishing and consolidating a Ukrainian state, with democratization and marketization not especially high on the agenda. Indeed, many of the ex-communists had a clear interest in seeing such reforms prove ineffective. Kravchuk had been a Communist Party leader in Ukraine prior to 1991.[6] He lost an election in 1994 to Leonid Kuchma, though Kuchma himself had close connections to "the party of power" (Prizel, 1997, p. 355), having served for a period as Kravchuk's prime minister. Yet aside from belated and halting moves in the direction of economic reform, this change of leadership signaled no major departure in policy direction. On the other hand, this was at least a change of leadership resulting from an election – the first time this had happened in the history of Ukraine.

Parliamentary elections were also held in 1994, contested by a large number of parties, many of which were concentrated in particular regions. The elections were conducted under the requirement that, to be elected, a candidate had to secure the support of over 50 percent of registered voters, either in the first round or in a runoff between the top two candidates in a constituency. The results were hardly conclusive. Many constituencies could not elect a representative under this system, and the largest bloc in parliament consisted of nominal independents, though many of these were allied with the Communist Party of Ukraine, which was therefore in practice the dominant force. Thus the parliamentary and presidential elections of 1994 did not undermine the political and economic power of the former members of the *nomenklatura* who had managed to negotiate the transition on terms favorable to themselves.

After 1994, Ukraine began to move more clearly in the direction of economic reform designed to improve the conditions for economic growth through guarantees to private property, cuts in taxes and expenditure, tax reform, and currency stabilization. But significant differences between the president and parliament, and within parliament, meant that the reforms in fact proceeded along a stony path – and sometimes even retreated for a while back down that path. By the end of the 1990s, according to World Bank statistics, Ukraine's per capita GDP was only one-third of that in Russia or Belarus. Despite dramatic economic decline, Ukraine's growth rates were still negative, whereas Russia's had become marginally positive. Moreover, such reforms as *were* implemented enriched some but impoverished many more; the 1990s witnessed rapidly growing inequality. Economic reform finally began to look as though it might become more substantial, with the approval of a five-year reform package in April 2000.

[6] Kravchuk had been second secretary of the Communist Party, then "speaker" of the Ukrainian Supreme Soviet.

Following one of the few unambiguously positive reforms to the political institutional framework, the 1998 parliamentary elections were conducted under a different electoral system, adopted in September 1997. The absolute majority system with its requirement of at least 50 percent turnout among registered voters was replaced by one in which half the members were elected from single-member constituencies and half from party lists under proportional representation.[7] The latter was intended to promote the role of parties (on the sorry state of parties prior to the reform, see Wilson and Bilous, 1993). Former members of the *nomenklatura* still managed to win a substantial number of seats. Between them, a left grouping composed of Communists, Socialists, Rurals, Progressive Socialists, and several smaller parties won 177 of the 450 seats in the Verkhovna Rada. The various centrist and right parties (including greens, nationalists, the more liberal–nationalist Rukh, and social democrats) together won 157 seats. An additional 116 single-member constituency seats were won by independents not likely to ally themselves with the communists (Birch and Wilson, 1999, esp. p. 281). Thus parliament was characterized by a three-way split not conducive to decisive action in any direction, and this result effectively impeded the process of economic reform.

These deep divisions perhaps help to explain why Kuchma was reelected president in 1999. While his record was hardly outstanding, he did stand up to parliament on occasions, and it was unclear that anyone else would be more effective. Like their Russian neighbors the following year, a majority of Ukrainian voters apparently wanted strong leadership, not constant bickering in parliament.

Ukrainian discourses of democracy

We identified four Ukrainian discourses: Social Democracy, Communist Nostalgia, Prosperous Contentment, and Liberal Capitalism. The second and third of these discourses are mirror images of one another. One of the factors was bipolar; that is, it featured substantial numbers of subjects loading heavily at both positive and negative ends. Such bipolarity indicates sharp division. This is our factor B; the notation we will use for the Communist Nostalgia end of it is B+, for the Prosperous Contentment end B−.[8] It should be remembered that B+ and B− do not indicate variations on B, rather direct opposites. To interpret factor B−, the signs for each of the statement scores on factor B in table 7.1 should be reversed. (In the narratives, numbers in parentheses refer to the statements from the first table.)

---

[7] The new mixed system is thus similar to that in many other post-communist countries.

[8] Again, the positive and negative symbols are of purely notational significance; they do not imply any judgment (positive or negative) about the content of discourses B+ and B−.

Table 7.1. *Statement scores on three factors for Ukraine*

Factor A is Social Democracy.
Factor B+ is Communist Nostalgia.
Factor B− is Prosperous Contentment, such that a negative score for a statement indicates *agreement* with the statement.
Factor C is Liberal Capitalism.

	Factor		
Statement	A	B	C
1 Democracy means freedom of speech.	+5	−1	+1
2 Democracy allows one to express one's thoughts freely.	+3	−3	−5
3 Democracy is the power of the people.	+6	−4	0
4 Democracy is based on the middle class; if the middle class is absent, this cannot be a democratic country.	+2	−4	+2
5 All societal levels should be represented in parliamentary organs.	−2	0	−1
6 In a democratic society, deception by the government is restricted by a free press.	+1	−1	0
7 Democracy presumes great participation in the process of decision-making.	+4	0	−1
8 The basis of democracy is the personal economic independence of the individual. A person can have self-respect when he knows that he has this independence.	0	−5	+3
9 Democracy doesn't allow a country to fall into neglect.	−1	0	−3
10 Some forms of direct democracy can include protection against the tyranny of the majority.	0	0	+2
11 Power starts from responsibility, which our politics has lacked.	−2	+3	+1
12 Politicians care about their own interests first, and then about the people.	+1	+5	+5
13 A democracy is consensus toward certain issues.	0	+1	−2
14 A fully realized democratic system includes three conditions: political equality, nontyranny, and deliberation.	0	+1	0
15 A country is democratic when every layer of society has social security.	+1	+1	+1
16 In a democratic country, everyone should have an equal chance.	0	+1	+1
17 Natural rights served as the basis for democracy to develop.	−1	+1	−4
18 Democracy combined with some forms of liberty threatens equality and therefore, finally, democracy itself.	−5	+3	−4

Table 7.1. (*cont.*)

Statement	Factor		
	A	B	C
19 The democratic process is to some extent complicated in federal systems.	−4	+2	−3
20 It was the national movement which became the catalyst of the political struggle to destroy the communist system.	+2	+2	−5
21 In a democratic society, majority rule is the guiding principle of the system.	+3	−1	0
22 All directions in our declining region are decided by the political elite of converted communists, who seek a basis for further rule over the impoverished and discontented masses.	−1	+3	+2
23 Continuing to reorient and adjust itself, the former *nomenklatura* preserves in its hands control over the state apparatus in the majority of republics of the former Soviet Union.	−1	+2	+6
24 Communists refurbished into democrats rule over Ukraine.	+3	+2	+4
25 The institution of representation in any democratic society can prevent a possible conflict between political equality and deliberation.	−2	+1	−1
26 Material insecurity pushes people toward illegal activity.	−5	0	−1
27 For politicians of all orientations, the struggle for power has become more important than escaping from economic depression.	+3	+4	+5
28 Money is the most important thing everywhere, including in elections.	−3	+4	+3
29 No democratic reform is possible without economic reform.	−3	−2	+6
30 To be democratic, the nation or state should be sovereign.	+4	−4	−1
31 Rich people have money and all the privileges here, but the poor have nothing.	+5	+6	−3
32 One group of people in our society has more rights, though officially everybody has equal rights.	+1	+3	+1
33 Ideal democracy is a fallacy.	+6	0	+1
34 Democracy is not the best imaginable form of governance, but it seems to be the best possible.	0	−5	−1
35 The people expressed their everlasting desire for an independent state during the referendum, but did not understand how difficult it is to create such a state. Everybody believed that independence would make life better, but in reality this has not happened.	+2	−1	+2

Table 7.1. (*cont.*)

Statement	Factor A	B	C
36 There is no order in the collective farm, where collective property exists.	−2	−2	+3
37 Civil society is an indispensable part of democratic society.	+3	−3	−2
38 A democratic society protects one's right to education.	−3	−1	−5
39 It is likely that we will change not into a legally based state, but into a clan-based state.	−2	0	+4
40 Theoretically a woman can become president of Ukraine, but in practice it would not be allowed.	−3	+4	−3
41 Democracy is preferred by the vast majority.	+2	+4	+4
42 Communist society was moral in some aspects, but it was a means to reach immoral goals.	+1	−2	+1
43 For democracy to be valuable, it should be widely accepted in society.	0	−3	−2
44 It is a shame that everybody looks only for his own profit.	+2	+5	−6
45 Money and power mean more than equality in all so-called democratic systems.	−5	+6	−1
46 The oppression of the human personality in totalitarian society cannot be accepted, even if something good was in that society.	0	−3	0
47 Our people used to live in circumstances of limited freedom, and do not know how to use this increased freedom now.	−4	+3	−1
48 The worst problem in our society is the lack of coordination between the three branches of power (namely legal, law-making, and executive).	−6	+2	−3
49 At the heart of the development strategy should be the Ukrainian national idea, the spiritual and moral quintessence of national self-consciousness. Other ethnic groups in Ukraine share this historical fate.	+1	−1	−2
50 All the treasures of the state should serve the people, not one group of people. Unfortunately this is not the case now.	−1	+5	−4
51 Exterminating capitalism in Russia, the Bolsheviks killed tens of millions of people in order to change economic life to socialism. Our society should now go back to capitalism.	−1	−6	+5
52 The Ukrainian state should not be built on a cosmopolitan basis.	−4	+2	−6

Table 7.1. (*cont.*)

| Statement | Factor | | |
	A	B	C
53 A person bears power for just a small time designated for them to be on Earth. The rest of the time one is just the same citizen as all the rest. That is why he must think while he is in power.	+5	+1	0
54 It is elites who must steer the state, but everybody has the possibility to make their way into the elite.	−3	−2	+2
55 National minorities must have rights equal with those of the basic national groups.	+2	−2	+1
56 The mass media must be independent in the ideal democratic country.	−1	0	+3
57 We must proceed from collectivism to individualism, to the way of thinking of a market society. Each person should work for himself or herself, and struggle for self-survival.	−1	−6	+4
58 Only rich people should come to power; they will not steal from the state because they already have everything.	−6	−3	0
59 Democratic reform in Ukraine has to be based on the cultural heritage of Ukrainian society.	+1	−2	−4
60 The Ukrainian national idea should stimulate the growing economic and cultural potential of the Ukrainian people.	+1	−4	−2
61 To launch the process of deliberalization, society should move to a more direct, more majoritarian democracy.	−4	+1	−2
62 The rights of minorities should be preserved.	+4	−1	0
63 All have the same rights; the rest depends on what one can achieve with one's personal talent.	+4	−1	+2
64 It is important to know two languages in a bilingual country.	−2	−5	+3

Ukraine factor A: Social Democracy

Democracy in the ideal sense may be impossible to achieve (33), but we should still pursue democracy here and now in terms of the participation and power of the people, expressed through majority rule (3, 7, 21). We should not fear democracy and liberty (18). Democracy does not have to wait for economic reform (29), for people know how to use their freedom already (47). Thus there is no need to make economic excuses for a lack of democratic behavior (26). Inequality is a problem in Ukraine, as the rich have too much and the poor not enough (31). People should not just look for their own profit (44). But in a democracy it is not just the rich who can or should come to power, for elections cannot be bought with money, and there can be a measure of political equality (28, 45, 58). While we can be skeptical about the motivations of politicians, especially those communists turned into "democrats" who still rule Ukraine (24, 27), the fact that in a democracy they will have to return to being citizens one day means that they have to take into account the interests of citizens (53). Democracy requires a cosmopolitan civil society combined with a sovereign state (37, 52). A democratic system involves protection for the rights of minorities, especially national minorities (4, 55), and freedom of speech (1, 2). Everyone should have equal rights, but beyond that it is up to individuals to make the most of the opportunities available to them (63).

The term "social democracy" is a popular self-description for politicians and parties in Ukraine, which means perhaps that the term is somewhat imprecise. Some small parties have "social democratic" in their title, and the liberal–nationalist Rukh party (the second most significant party in the 1990s, after the Communists) has some social democratic elements. We label factor A "Social Democracy" because of its weak support for market individualism (57), hesitancy about profit-seeking behavior, and commitment to material redistribution, though this commitment may itself be contingent upon the degree of inequality characterizing post-communist Ukraine. Otherwise, this discourse subscribes to most of the norms of liberal democracy, including equality of opportunity. Social Democracy here even adopts a liberal skepticism concerning the motivations of politicians – though this again may be contingent on the kinds of politicians in power in Ukraine. The individuals loading heavily on our Social Democracy factor are a very mixed bag in terms of their political self-descriptions, including liberals, conservatives (conservative here meaning resistant to marketization and liberalization), socialists, social democrats, and no affiliation (see table 7.2). This sheer variety suggests that Social Democracy is indeed the "broad view" in Ukraine, consistent perhaps with the weakly developed parts of the party system.

Ukraine factor B+: Communist Nostalgia

Democracy seems to be what most people now want, but this so-called democracy we have now has led to inequality that threatens the whole idea of democracy (18, 34, 41) – for what we have now is a system in which the rich have grown richer and the poor have grown poorer, and the rich control government for their own benefit (28, 31, 45, 50). People do not know how to use this so-called freedom; all they care about now is their own profit (44, 47). There was nothing much wrong with collectivism and communist society (42, 46), and it should not be replaced with capitalism (51, 57). Unfortunately some of the communist elite have now converted themselves into so-called democrats so that they can

Table 7.2. *Subject loadings on factors for Ukraine*

	Factor		
Subject and political self-description	A	B	C
1 M, teacher, moderate	65*	−15	19
2 M, worker, liberal	67*	−10	29
3 F, police officer, conservative	33*	−5	46*
4 F, tax police, moderate conservative	49*	−2	23
5 F, public service worker, liberal	72*	9	−5
6 M, accountant, liberal	70*	−1	5
7 F, technician, liberal democrat	72*	1	−1
8 M, nurse, liberal	10	0	33*
9 M, doctor, democrat	41*	2	7
10 F, worker, liberal	6	2	22
11 F, teacher, democrat	46*	−26	48*
12 F, clerk, conservative	53*	8	8
13 M, student, democrat	13	1	32*
14 M, army officer, neo-conservative	10	−5	54*
15 M, unemployed, democrat	−7	−5	52*
16 M, worker, liberal	42*	−12	10
17 F, student, democratic-liberal	41*	−16	−6
18 M, public service, democrat	46*	−29	18
19 F, bank clerk, moderate liberal	19	23	50*
20 F, worker, moderate liberal	41*	−37*	21
21 M, retired military, communist	16	57*	18
22 M, self-employed, no interest	−18	−13	71*
23 F, housewife, indifferent	−5	−24	50*
24 M, programmer, indifferent	18	1	52*
25 M, bus driver, socialist	50*	14	16
26 F, actress, democracy	35*	−30	24
27 F, journalist, national-democrat	33*	−52*	−26
28 M, student, liberal democrat	3	−57*	24
29 M, student, liberal nationalist	39*	−20	−5
30 M, church minister, none	53*	−4	4
31 F, student, democrat	33*	−51*	15
32 M, police officer, pro-government	41*	−52*	−41*
33 M, retired, communist/pro-Soviet Union	31	59*	30
34 M, businessperson, pro-democrat	23	−56*	23
35 F, teacher, social democrat	56*	11	0
36 F, bookkeeper, independent	−17	−2	43*
37 F, peasant, indifferent	25	41*	20
38 M, salesperson, democrat/supports the market	−6	−71*	14
39 F, account manager, liberal	31	−64*	15
40 F, worker, communist/socialist	36*	−3	30

*Denotes a loading significant at the .01 level.

continue to rule (22, 23, 24). Politicians are irresponsible and do not care about the people as they should, only about their own wealth and power (11, 12, 27). They would never allow a woman to become president (40). They cannot even coordinate across the different branches of government (48). We do not need Ukrainian nationalism (59, 60) and there is no need to be bilingual (64). The most desirable system is communist, neither nationalist nor cosmopolitan (52).

The Communist Nostalgia of factor B+ is straightforward in its condemnation of the present and concomitant approval of the Soviet past. It is not hostile to democracy as such, if democracy is interpreted Soviet-style as "socialist democracy." But this discourse clearly has no time for the so-called democracy that characterizes post-communist Ukraine. It is especially bitter about the betrayal of the former members of the Soviet-era elite who prospered from the transition by consolidating their own political power and making sure that wealth and control of the economy flowed into their own hands as well. Communist Nostalgia is clearly a discourse of those who did not prosper from the transition. Those loading heavily upon it include a retired military communist, a retired pro-Soviet Union communist, and a peasant claiming indifference to politics (see table 7.2). The problem for adherents of this discourse is that they have nowhere much to go in terms of the configuration of Ukrainian party politics. Their obvious home is the Communist Party of Ukraine, but this party's leadership is complicit in the very status quo that Communist Nostalgia condemns.

Ukraine factor B—: Prosperous Contentment

Things are pretty good in Ukraine compared to the way they used to be, because we have put communism behind us and are moving to a capitalist and democratic society (22, 23, 24, 51). Everyone is benefiting (50), and people know how to use their freedom (47). Our politicians are responsible and care about the people (11, 12, 27). There is no need to be concerned about inequality of wealth and its effect on politics, and it is fine if the rich come to power (28, 31, 45, 58). Democracy is the best possible form of government (34); it is about the power of the people, and especially the middle class (3, 4). It is based on personal economic independence and economic reform (8, 29), and involves freedom of expression (2). The only problem is that not everyone wants it, and it needs to be more widely accepted (41, 43). Profit-seeking is fine, and we must move to individualism and market competition (44, 57). Our Ukrainian heritage can stimulate both economic and political development, but Ukraine should also have a cosmopolitan aspect (52, 59, 60), and people should learn more than one language (64).

The Prosperous Contentment of factor B— is clearly the discourse of those benefiting under the existing political and economic arrangements. Table 7.2 shows that the subjects loading most highly upon it are a salesperson who claims to support democracy and the market, a "liberal" account manager, a "pro-democratic" businessperson, a pro-government police officer, two students, and a national-democratic journalist. What is perhaps surprising is that Prosperous Contentment equates the existing economic and political arrangements with capitalism and democracy. To an outsider this equation might seem odd, given the slow pace of reform of the centrally planned economy and the persistent authoritarian elements in government (though the absence of public provision of welfare might back a tenuous connection to "capitalism"). The adherents of this discourse are also willing to generalize their own experience of prosperity to that of the whole population, which is even more startling given the context of economic decline. It would be easy to criticize Prosperous Contentment as a dream world, but generalization of the experience of oneself and one's acquaintances to the larger society is by no means unique to this factor or this country. Such an orientation is functional for the people who subscribe to it – at least in terms of removing the likelihood of a guilty conscience. It is also functional in terms of securing support for the existing regime, though it is unclear that the support given by Prosperous Contentment takes the form of considered commitment rather than instrumental calculation.

Bipolarity and its connotation of sharp polarization between opposed points of view are rare in Q factor analysis; among the other countries in this study, we find it only in Belarus. But whereas in Belarus the opposition is between enthusiastic presidential authoritarians and liberal democrats, in Ukraine it appears to be between two different kinds of successor to the Soviet regime. Communist Nostalgia clearly wants to turn the clock back, and resents those former communists who took advantage of the demise of the Soviet Union to enrich themselves and consolidate their power in the new system. Indeed, its vituperation is reserved for these former comrades; any criticism of liberals, nationalists, or Western-style capitalists is muted by comparison. Prosperous Contentment is in part the discourse of those former communists who made sure that when the clock was turned forward they would be the ones to benefit.

Ukraine factor C: Liberal Capitalism

Democracy is mostly about economics, and the economic independence of in-dividuals is its foundation (8), so no democratic reform is possible until there is economic reform (29). Collective property is terrible (36). Profit-seeking, ma-terialistic behavior is fine, so long as it proceeds under proper legal conditions, which unfortunately are absent in Ukraine (44, 57, 63). We should not worry about inequality of wealth (31). People know how to use freedom (47). But as things are in Ukraine, former communists still rule (23, 24), politicians care only about their own power and interests (12, 27), and we might even lapse into a clan-based state (39). We need to put murderous Bolshevism behind us, and move to a capitalist system (51). Our political and economic systems should be cosmopolitan, and nationalism should not get in the way of this (42, 52, 59, 60); people should learn more than one language (64). Things like freedom of speech, equality, a free press, participation, minority rights, the right to education, and majority rule are not especially important (1, 6, 7, 21, 38, 50), though the mass media should be independent (56). There is no need to worry about democracy's negative effects (18).

Factor C's Liberal Capitalism is discontented when it comes to the post-communist situation in Ukraine, but for the opposite reason to Communist Nostalgia. Whereas the latter believes capitalist development has gone too far, Liberal Capitalism believes it has not gone far enough, bemoaning the degree to which Ukraine clings to old political and economic habits. Thus Liberal Capitalism condemns the communist past in much stronger terms than it condemns the post-communist present. In some ways, Liberal Capitalism is the least interested of the four discourses in democracy. It is much more energized by the need to establish private property and a capitalist economic system. If these economic features connote democracy, then Liberal Capitalism has no objections; but it sees little intrinsic value in political participation and majority rule, or for that matter in the political rights and freedoms normally associated with liberal democracy. This is why we name factor C Liberal Capitalism rather than Liberal Democracy. Its commitments to liberal democracy are weak to absent; indeed, it could be consistent with the kind of authoritarian liberalism which, as we saw in chapter 1, some observers believe to be the most effective way of managing marketization in post-communist societies.

Problems and prospects in Ukraine

As in the other Slavic states of the former Soviet Union, democratization in Ukraine has had to cope with simultaneous attempts to consolidate an integrative national identity and a full set of new political institutions. There remains considerable disagreement within the political elite about the appropriate powers and relationships of the various branches of the state, which in turn weakens the state as a whole. By 2000 President Kuchma and parliament were still struggling over the division of powers, with the former seeking constitutional changes to enhance the power of the presidency over the legislature (Wilson, 1997, esp. p. 67, described the existing arrangements as a "president–parliamentary" system). This met with criticisms from the Council of Europe, and charges that the Ukrainian president was imitating his Belarusian counterpart. Although the constitutional court had rejected as unconstitutional Kuchma's call for a referendum similar to that organized by Lukashenka in 1996, it had – confusingly – allowed a number of other referendum questions that would have amounted to much the same.

A referendum was held in April 2000, approving a bicameral arrangement for parliament, reduction in size of the current house from 450 to 300, and weakening of parliamentary immunity. These measures can be interpreted as designed to make parliament more answerable and effective, rather than paving the way to presidential control. In our concluding discussion of Russia we recognized the role of effective state leadership in constructing democratic institutions, though a lot depends on the discursive field in which such actions occur. In Ukraine, this sort of state leadership could connect positively with the discourse of Social Democracy, but a very different kind of statism could result from any link to the discourse of Communist Nostalgia. As economistic discourses, it is hard to know what to make of Prosperous Contentment and Liberal Capitalism in these terms, though neither has overt sympathy with authoritarianism.

Our results indicate that the discursive configuration of Ukraine when it comes to democracy is quite complex. Of the four discourses, only one, Communist Nostalgia, is openly hostile to liberal democracy, and its supporters seem to have no clear party political home. On the other hand, only one of the four, Social Democracy, seems to have any strong commitment to liberal democratic norms. Both Prosperous Contentment and Liberal Capitalism put the pursuit of prosperity before democracy, though they differ as to whether that pursuit can be effective under the existing regime.

If we compare Ukraine with Belarus and Russia, its prospects for democratization might seem more auspicious, for in both Belarus and Russia we find authoritarian discourses that can be related quite readily to powerful political forces (in Belarus, to an authoritarian presidency); there are no such discourses in Ukraine. Ukraine's economic decline in many ways exceeds that of Russia, but it is less easily associated by any of these discourses (except Communist Nostalgia) with a reformist government. In short, the *idea* of democracy seems not to elicit quite the negative sentiments in Ukraine that it does in Russia; and the democrats themselves, notably those associated with the Social Democracy discourse, have less reason to feel chastened than their Russian counterparts. At the time of our study, it was probably easier to believe in a positive democratic future in Ukraine than in Russia; Ukraine in the 1990s was of course spared the kinds of political convulsions Russia experienced, and it was comparatively free of demagogues. When it comes to the economy, it is probably easier to believe in capitalism than it is in Russia, for Ukraine has also suffered somewhat less from mafia control of the economy and the associated violence and lawlessness. Ukraine is also relatively free of ethnic nationalism, though there have been some incidents (for example) where Polish and Russian graves in Western Ukraine were vandalized, and some discrimination by Russians against Ukrainians and Tatars in Crimea. Our discourses all reveal a fairly cosmopolitan and tolerant outlook, reflecting the fact that any nationalism found in contemporary Ukraine takes a fairly moderate and liberal form, not an authoritarian and exclusive one.

The fact that nationalism and associated ethnolinguistic divisions seem not to energize Ukrainians suggests too that Ukraine can accommodate the differences between its East and West that we discussed at the beginning of this chapter. Our results confirm that there are important divisions between East and West. We conducted interviews in the Chortkiv region of Western Ukraine, and in the capital, Kyiv, which mixes the influences of East and West. Of the subjects listed in table 7.2, numbers 1–20 come from the Chortkiv region, numbers 21–40 from the Kyiv region. What is striking is that those subjects loading significantly on both the positive and negative ends of our bipolar factor B come *only* from Kyiv. That is, the split between Communist Nostalgia and Prosperous Contentment does not exist in Western Ukraine, because neither discourse has any adherents there. Given that Communist Nostalgia and Prosperous Contentment represent two sets of successors to the Soviet-era regime, their absence in the West is consistent with the perception that the East is more communist, while the West looks more to liberal democracy and Europe. This perception is corroborated by the results of the 1998 parliamentary elections; the "democratic" parties did especially well in the West. The only two discourses present among our Western Ukraine subjects were Social Democracy and Liberal Capitalism; these represent a fairly conventional left–right split in West European terms. All four discourses were present in the capital, reflecting its mixture of East and West.

Unfortunately, we conducted no interviews in the true East, so that we cannot be sure about the degree to which Social Democracy and Liberal Capitalism are weak or even absent there. But we suspect they are not completely absent in the East, because that would make Eastern Ukraine more devoid of liberal democratic discourse than Russia, which is implausible.

At the beginning of the 1990s, many Ukrainians revealed that they could be very active citizens (on the sheer energy of mass movements at the end of the communist era in Ukraine, see Krawchenko, 1993, pp. 77–9). Along with the results of our discourse analysis, this suggests Ukrainians are ready for something better, or at least different, than their elites generally offered to them in the 1990s (the political stability delivered by elites notwithstanding).[9] Quite what that something may be is an open question, receiving very

---

[9] For another positive assessment, see Karatnycky, 1995.

different answers from our four discourses. But only one of them, Communist Nostalgia, wants to turn the clock back – and even this discourse is not overtly authoritarian. Political-economic reform in Ukraine does not have to contend with popular support for authoritarianism, with ethnic division, or with disillusion about democracy. It does have to contend with an economy that underperforms even by the standards of former Soviet Union countries.

PART IV

Transition torn by war

Yugoslavia aside, the three countries we group in part IV were those most torn by war in the 1990s. The relationship between war, state-building, and democratic development is a complex one; many states were forged in the experience or threat of war, and the implication of total war for democratic development is not necessarily negative (as the experience of the Federal Republic of Germany suggests). Still, in the context of extraction from communism, a successfully prosecuted war (as in Armenia) might be positive when it comes to state-building, but negative for democracy if the passions aroused threaten to undermine the legitimacy of governments. An unsuccessful war, as in Georgia, can easily carry over into civil chaos. In Armenia, Moldova, and Georgia alike, military mobilization, at least in the short run, constituted a necessity that trumped democratic procedures; and resources were diverted to the war effort that could otherwise have been used in economic development. War is also not generally conducive to foreign investment in a country. Given all the other problems that these three countries shared with the other successor states of the Soviet Union discussed in part III, it is perhaps remarkable that they all exited the decade with governments installed by competitive election, however tenuous the accomplishment.

8

Armenia

Like many other countries analyzed in this book, Armenia had little experience with democracy prior to the 1990s. It has also experienced identity problems relating to its frequently changing boundaries over the centuries and to its relationships with other states. As Offe (1991) has argued, creating a new political system is much more difficult for a country whose boundaries are still contested.

Armenia was partitioned in the seventeenth century, with the western part (basically Anatolia) coming under Turkish (Ottoman) control, the eastern part under Persia's. The latter part was annexed by the Russian Empire in 1828, becoming a province. In 1917, it joined Georgia and Azerbaijan in an anti-Bolshevik federation; but this soon collapsed, and Armenia declared its independence in 1918. A brief democratic experiment ended in September 1920 when Turkey (now under Ataturk) attacked Armenia, countered by Russian troops. By November 1920, a new Soviet Republic of Armenia had been created. Armenia lost additional territory to Azerbaijan in the 1920s, which led to trouble in the 1990s.[1]

Identity problems also arise in connection with religion. The Armenians were the first nation officially to adopt Christianity; in 2001, the country celebrates the 1700th anniversary of this. But Armenia is surrounded on three sides by Muslim countries – Azerbaijan to the east, Iran to the south, and Turkey to the west. Its northern neighbor, Georgia, is Christian, but of the Orthodox variety, whereas Armenia is Apostolic.

Despite these problems, when it comes to conditions generally thought to be conducive to democratization, Armenia's balance sheet contains positives

[1] For more detail on Armenian history, see Lang, 1970; Suny, 1993.

as well as negatives. On the positive side, by the time the Soviet Union collapsed, Armenia was relatively highly developed in industrial and educational terms, at least in comparison with the rest of the Soviet Union. Its population was ethnically homogeneous, around 90 percent Armenian. In this respect, it might appear that there were few difficulties related to the establishment of Armenia's "stateness," despite its brief and disastrous experience of independence. Further, there was a large and prosperous Armenian diaspora in the West, especially the United States, which showed a willingness to renew political and financial connections with independent Armenia (see Dudwick, 1997, pp. 492–3).

On the other hand, independence for Armenia came at the height of a conflict with neighboring Azerbaijan over the region of Nagorno-Karabakh, which undermined the solidity of Armenia's stateness. The enclave had been transferred by Stalin to Azerbaijan's jurisdiction in 1923, yet the population of Nagorno-Karabakh in the late 1980s was still approximately 70 percent Armenian (Hunter, 1993, p. 246). Armenia's claim to this part of Azerbaijan, at first within the structure of the Soviet Union, was supported by a February 1988 vote by the Nagorno-Karabakh Supreme Soviet to secede from Azerbaijan and rejoin Armenia, plus huge street demonstrations within Armenia, which in turn provoked Soviet repression. Violence between Azeris and Armenians in both republics began in that year, escalating with the decay of Soviet authority and culminating in war between the two states. A ceasefire was negotiated in 1994. Armenia won the war, but at considerable cost; some 13,000 people had by 1993 lost their lives in the conflict (Gitelman, 1994, p. 245). There were large flows of refugees in both directions, and Azerbaijan and Turkey were able to enforce an economic blockade against Armenia. The rail link to the north through Azerbaijan was cut; the alternative route through Georgia was severed by the conflict in Abkhazia. Oil and gas supplies too were cut off. With hostile Turkey to the west, Armenia had two neighbors that were enemies, and a third (Georgia) with which it had little in common and which had plenty of problems of its own. The Armenian economy, already devastated by a 1988 earthquake that had left some 25,000 dead and numerous towns and villages destroyed, was in dire straits, and a dose of economic shock therapy in 1992 produced only further economic collapse and inflation. The mid-1990s saw some economic recovery, but from a low starting point. By then the country was plagued by corruption and poverty. Between 600,000 and 1,000,000 people emigrated from Armenia in the 1990s (Suny, 2000, p. 726). While emigration increased the scope for potential finance from the Armenian diaspora, the scale of the exodus led to skill shortages within the country, and an undermining of national self-confidence (on the problems of establishing stateness when there is a substantial diaspora population, see Brubaker, 1996).

The space for political mobilization accompanying decline in Soviet authority was occupied in Armenia by nationalism, beginning in earnest in 1988 (see Rutland, 1994, for a chronology). This nationalism was not directed against the Soviet Union; and, following independence in 1991, Armenia soon established an alliance with Russia, which made obvious geopolitical sense in light of the actual or potential enemies that almost surround Armenia. Nationalist mobilization concerned only territorial conflict with Azerbaijan. The leading nationalist politician, Levon Ter-Petrosian, was elected chair of the Armenian parliament in 1990, then president in 1991, in a system that became strongly presidential.

By the standards of Armenian nationalism, Ter-Petrosian was a relative moderate. Much of his opposition came from the more extreme Armenian Pan-National Movement, formed in 1989, which had many allies in the Armenian diaspora. In December 1994, Ter-Petrosian closed down the nationalist Dashnak party (the Armenian Revolutionary Federation), by then the largest opposition party, on the (plausible) grounds of its links with both drug-trafficking and terrorism (Dudwick, 1997, p. 492) – the latter corroborated in the view of some observers on October 28, 1999, by the assassination of the prime minister, the speaker, and six others in the parliamentary chamber by people with alleged ties to Dashnak.

But Ter-Petrosian himself hardly proved a model democrat. His regime engaged in repression of the opposition beyond the extreme nationalists and in intimidation of the media. His controversial reelection in September 1996 was followed by large demonstrations that supported the accusations of electoral fraud made by defeated opposition candidate Vazgen Manukian, who claimed to have received 60 percent as opposed to the 41 percent with which he was officially credited (compared with Ter-Petrosian's official 52 percent).

In February 1998 Ter-Petrosian was forced to resign, in what has been described as a velvet coup (*Transitions*, 5 [3] [1998], p. 7), after his willingness to be flexible toward Azerbaijan on the Nagorno-Karabakh issue caused the defection of a large section of his Armenian National Party members of parliament, as well as several members of his cabinet. The subsequent presidential election was won by the nationalist Robert Kocharian, with 59 percent of the vote to 41 percent for the ex-communist Karen Demirchian.

But this result *per se* hardly signaled the arrival of more authentic democracy in Armenia. The Organization for Security and Cooperation in Europe and the Council of Europe had again identified irregularities in the first round of the presidential election. Kocharian for his part had earlier been the president of Nagorno-Karabakh, and was considered far more hawkish vis-à-vis Azerbaijan than his predecessor. This seemed to mean trouble for democratization because even the most democratic countries tend to become more centralized and authoritarian in times of crisis and war. There was also a question about the constitutionality of Kocharian running for the presidency. Under the Armenian constitution, presidential candidates must have lived in Armenia for at least ten years. As just mentioned, Kocharian had spent much of the 1990s in Nagorno-Karabakh (the chair of the Central Electoral Commission considered Kocharian's candidacy valid).

The new president actually proved quite willing to sit down with his Azeri counterpart – sometimes under the auspices of either the Commonwealth of Independent States or the OSCE – to discuss the Nagorno-Karabakh issue. Although the status of the enclave had still not been resolved as of mid-2000, both sides were attempting to negotiate with, rather than kill, each other.

President Kocharian has also tolerated political parties opposed to him. Upon Ter-Petrosian's resignation, the Ministry of Justice legalized the Dashnak party; shortly afterwards, this judgment was endorsed by Kocharian, who then appointed two Dashnak members to his administration.[2] Apparently, the new president could distinguish between the illegal acts of some members of Dashnak and the party's right to exist. Dashnak has been represented in parliament since the May 1999 elections. Moreover, various parties both inside and outside parliament have on occasion seriously challenged the president (e.g., in January 1999, regarding the parliamentary immunity of a former minister of the interior), but have not suffered as a result.

Of even greater significance is the fact that Kocharian announced the establishment in May 1998 of a commission to consider amending the constitution in a way that would *reduce* the powers of the presidency. He also indicated that such major constitutional changes could be made only if endorsed in a nationwide referendum.

Finally, it is testimony to the extent to which the president and government were serious in their fight against tax evasion, corruption, and organized crime – and hence serious in their commitment to both the rule of law and a cleaner and more efficient form of capitalism – that one of the most popular interpretations of the October 1999 assassinations in parliament is that they were carried out by people connected to the underworld who were seeking revenge for the clampdown.[3] A number of senior officials have been charged with corruption since Kocharian became prime minister in March 1997.

---

[2] At the same time as Dashnak was legalized, two of its leading activists were released from prison – one of whom then described the political atmosphere in Armenia as "excellent" and "healthy" (see *Transitions*, 5 [3] [1998], p. 7).

[3] This was by no means the only suggested motive. Another is that extremist nationalists were deeply dismayed at the way the president and government were negotiating with the Azeris about the future of Nagorno-Karabakh. It is, of course, quite possible that there were several motives.

Under him, Armenia has meted out some of the toughest sentences for corruption in the post-communist world. Perhaps the best example is of a former minister of light industry, who was found guilty in September 1998 of embezzlement and sentenced to eight years' imprisonment plus a fine of some US$500,000.

Some developments under Kocharian were less conducive to democratization. In November 1999 Kocharian appointed the younger brother (Aram Sarkisian) of the recently assassinated prime minister (Vazgen Sarkisian) as the new premier – making it appear that Armenian "clan" politics was still alive and well. Charges of "clanism" have been one of the most frequent criticisms of Armenian politics for many years (and were voiced by participants in our study). In any event, Sarkisian the younger was dismissed by the president in May 2000.

One might also raise questions about democracy in a country in which parliament can be stormed and leading politicians killed or injured.[4] But this testifies more to slack security than to a weak commitment to democracy. There was no mass unrest following the murders, and the killers were soon arrested (though subsequently released pending further investigations). Moreover, the assassinations did not clearly constitute a coup attempt.[5] Countries such as the United States and Sweden have of course also seen political assassinations.

Hesitant Armenian discourses of democracy

The experience of our discussion groups, meeting in early 1997, carried out to generate statements about democracy, indicate that Armenia faces some genuine problems when it comes to the speech and expression intrinsic to most conceptions of democracy. When the tape recorder was switched on, individuals initially showed great reluctance to say anything. When they did speak, participants at first all tried to use Russian rather than Armenian, on the grounds that the procedure looked like an "official" one, therefore requiring an "official" language. In several cases individuals began by asking the researcher exactly what he wanted them to say. The only heated discussion that ensued in the six groups took place in a village near Yerevan; the topic was inspired by the theme of our discussion groups, but the argument only began once the tape recorder was turned off.

---

[4] The reference is not merely to the October 1999 assassinations; there were several more incidents in the late 1990s.

[5] The assassins did claim that the government had permitted an undemocratic system to develop and corruption to flourish. But, as we have indicated, there is substantial evidence to counter this claim.

The individual Q sort interviews were carried out in August and September 1997 – thus while Ter-Petrosian was still president – in Yerevan, Gumri, and Vandzor. Factor analysis produced three identifiable discourses, which we label "Impossible Social Democracy," "Timocracy," and "Legalistic Paternalism." (In the narratives, numbers in parentheses refer to the statements from the first table.)

Armenia factor A: Impossible Social Democracy

Democracy does mean something good, in both theory and practice, and it is a goal that it would be nice to strive for (4, 12). It would be good to have an active democratic state that looked after the social welfare of its citizens and promoted economic development (53, 55, 59, 61). I have always thought this, even under the Soviet system (24). Democracy means freedom of expression, responsible and democratic leaders with good political education, a law-governed society, and equality before the law (8, 43, 44, 54, 58, 64). Unfortunately we do not have democracy in Armenia (17). What we have instead are clan relationships and patronage (25), officials who place themselves above the law (22), leadership that has lost the faith of the people (26), an undemocratic opposition (27), and media that deliver only state propaganda (38). Ordinary individuals have no political influence (23). There is no rule of law or constitutional government (34, 46). Unfortunately I do not think that any of this can be changed, so we are not on the road to democracy (21). Certainly the strong hands of the president will not bring us democracy (56). It is not Armenia's lack of natural resources that is the obstacle to democracy (20), but the way our politics and society are organized.

This first Armenian discourse is social democratic, combining commitments to liberal freedoms and constitutional government with an active, interventionist state that promotes economic development and secures social justice. But as our title suggests, there is no sense that this sort of government can be achieved in Armenia. The status quo is condemned as undemocratic, corrupt, and repressive. The problem is seen not in terms of a transient presidential authoritarianism, but rather in terms of the deeper structure of Armenian politics and society. The opposition is condemned as well as the regime, and the patronage accompanying clan relationships is seen as a major obstacle to democratization. Officialdom in general is seen as corrupt and undemocratic. In conventional Western terms, Impossible Social Democracy is the most clearly democratic of the three Armenian discourses, but it is thoroughly pessimistic concerning the likelihood of its ideals being achieved in political practice. Our second discourse, to which we now turn, is not quite so alienated from the status quo, but has a unique and peculiar view of what democracy might entail.

Table 8.1. *Statement scores on three factors for Armenia*

Factor A is Impossible Social Democracy.
Factor B is Timocracy.
Factor C is Legalistic Paternalism.

		Factor	
Statement	A	B	C
1 Democracy is a civilized way of revolution. Before, a king conquered people, beheaded them, then governed. Now this is not possible.	−2	+6	+1
2 The role of propaganda is to teach people how to be good citizens and to give information.	−1	−6	+1
3 The state is a means to achieve social welfare.	0	−2	+1
4 In fact, democracy is theoretically absurd.	−6	0	+3
5 Freedom of the mass media does not mean to say whatever they want to say: i.e., to push anti-state propaganda, pornography.	+1	+2	−5
6 Democracy is the desire of everyone to have his/her voice heard.	−2	+3	0
7 You can express yourself as much as you want, as long as it does not threaten the leadership.	+1	−2	0
8 Democracy is impossible unless people are free to express their will.	+5	+4	−2
9 Communism was created as a cover to tell people to obey.	0	−2	−2
10 To declare that the establishment of democracy requires much time is similar to the idea that the path to communism was a long one.	−2	+2	+1
11 Of course there is a need for a strong social program, but this does not mean that the government should provide every member of the population with a job.	0	+2	0
12 Democracy is not necessarily an ultimate goal.	−5	0	+6
13 Democracy is anarchy if it means government by the people. That is very dangerous. Democracy is acceptable if it is understood as the rule of law.	−2	−5	+5
14 Everyone should be rich and not poor. Equality comes from this premise.	−1	−1	−1
15 Power is above the law.	−2	+2	−3
16 People's rule does not mean that the majority should rule the minority.	+1	+5	0
17 Armenia is between authoritarianism and democracy; both a "strong hand" and democratic leverages are necessary.	−4	−4	+5

Table 8.1. (*cont.*)

| Statement | Factor | | |
	A	B	C
18 Western democracy will not fit within a framework of Armenian reality.	0	+3	+3
19 Democracy in practice depends upon the national character.	+2	0	−1
20 Armenia lacks natural resources and this is an obstacle for democracy.	−6	+1	−4
21 I believe that we shall overcome this situation and follow the democratic road.	−3	+1	+2
22 People cannot prosecute officials for violation of the law.	+6	+5	−6
23 I think that a single person is able to influence the democratic process.	−5	−1	−3
24 I never thought about democracy during Soviet times. At that time I thought that everything was all right.	−5	+3	+2
25 Clan relationships and patronage will always maintain their role in Armenia.	+4	−1	0
26 The people have lost their faith in the leadership.	+5	+6	−2
27 Our opposition is not democratic.	+3	+1	−5
28 The financial situation affects democracy. When people have no money they have no time to think of democracy.	+2	+3	−1
29 People try to trick others to get power. So, life is a struggle.	+1	0	−6
30 When the population takes part in governance of the country, one can talk about democracy. In Armenia only a tiny minority rules everybody.	+2	+4	+3
31 We have an extremely polarized society − on the one extreme are the rich, on the other are the poor. In such a situation democracy is hardly possible.	+1	−3	0
32 The future of democracy depends on economic development.	+2	+1	−1
33 Whatever the West has achieved, we will never achieve; as a system of government ours is different.	−1	+1	+1
34 What is the law? There is no law. Even if there were laws one would violate them.	−3	0	−4
35 The inviolability of property does not exist. One person can appropriate it. States in which this is the case are usually weak.	0	−3	0

Table 8.1. (*cont.*)

Statement	Factor		
	A	B	C
36 Our president is a typical oriental ruler.	−3	−1	−4
37 Government by one person is dangerous.	+2	−1	+4
38 Our television is controlled by the state, which promotes state propaganda.	+4	0	−1
39 I could not have changed anything by my participation in the elections because they were falsified.	0	−6	+3
40 With personal participation one can promote democracy.	−1	+1	+1
41 We did hope that things would change and the leadership would do something.	0	−2	+2
42 The leadership of the democratic movement should have resisted the temptations of power.	0	+2	−3
43 It is possible to take actions of violence against government if it violates the law.	−4	−1	+2
44 In all societies the elite is undemocratic.	−3	0	+1
45 Equality is absurd.	+4	+5	+2
46 It is natural to have laws and a constitution in authoritarian systems, whereas in real life they do not function.	+3	−3	+3
47 Unfortunately in Armenia we have rule of the minority over the majority.	+2	−1	−1
48 The Armenian Church was always more democratic than the Catholic. This fact will probably allow us to reach democracy easily.	−3	+2	−2
49 One general law is necessary to govern over people. Otherwise, anarchy will triumph.	−1	+1	+4
50 The transition from totalitarianism to democracy should be made in legal ways.	+1	+4	+2
51 Democracy exists for a limited circle of people.	−1	−1	−2
52 Democracy is a good thing when it is supported financially.	+1	+1	−5
53 It is necessary to strive from poverty to a normal living standard.	+4	−2	+4
54 It is preferable that only politically educated people are elected to parliament.	+3	−4	−3
55 The state must take care of its citizens.	+3	−5	+4
56 To secure democracy in Armenia we need the president to have strong hands.	−4	−3	−3

Table 8.1. (*cont.*)

| | Factor | | |
Statement	A	B	C
57 I am for democracy if it means the rule of law.	−1	−4	−1
58 The president should be responsible for his ministers' statements.	+3	0	+1
59 The society should take care of those unable to take care of themselves.	+5	−4	−1
60 Only those who have substantial wealth should govern the state, to avoid corruption.	−1	+4	−4
61 There should be a separation between state policy and the law.	−4	+3	−2
62 In democratic countries the power in parliament should be distributed between different political parties.	+1	−3	+5
63 Democracy is not for everybody; for example, American democracy is for Americans, Australian democracy is for Australians, etc.	−2	−2	0
64 Everybody must be equal before the law.	+6	−5	+6

Armenia factor B: Timocracy

In Soviet times I did not think much about democracy; everything seemed all right (24). But now I have decided democracy is fine as a form of governance, as a way to ensure peaceful transition of power (1, 13). In a democratic system everyone can have their say, so free speech is important and government propaganda is absent (2, 6, 8). The population can take part in democratic government (30), but that does not mean the majority should rule (16). The wealthy should govern, because they will not be corrupted (60). Wealth matters more than political education in determining who is most fit to govern (54). So democracy can exist in a society polarized between rich and poor (31). To pursue equality is pointless and absurd, for society will always be unequal (45, 64). So the state should not redistribute wealth and provide programs for the poor (11, 55, 59). Armenia at the moment is not very democratic; people have no faith in the tiny minority that rules (26, 30), officials are above the law (22). But elections can make a difference (39). We do not need a strong president on the one hand or sharing of power between political parties on the other (17, 56, 62). We need to move in legal ways from totalitarianism to democracy (50).

Timocracy – government by the best and richest – resembles Impossible Social Democracy in its endorsement of the basic symbol of democracy and in its perception that Armenia is not very democratic. But the similarities go no further. Timocracy is a discourse of those come newly to democracy, who admit that under the Soviet system they saw no need for any change. This discourse believes in government by the best and wealthiest, and so is thoroughly elitist. It is not necessarily a discourse *of* the wealthy, as a glance at the occupational characteristics of its supporters in table 8.2 should make clear. But it is a discourse of those who think that wealth, and so inequality, are fine things – or at least that they are the way things are and as such should be accepted – thus opposing any attempt by government to redistribute wealth. Having experienced only corrupt political elites, Timocracy's remedy is to hand government to a supposedly uncorrupt economic elite. Thus it is opposed to majority rule – even if it does favor elections and freedom of political expression. From a Western liberal democratic perspective it would be easy to dismiss Timocracy as an incoherent and inconsistent point of view: one that proclaims a commitment to democracy and citizen participation, while specifying that a particular economic class must rule. It is perhaps understandable that a society without any experience of anything but rule on the part of well-defined elites should be home to such a discourse, which sees the main political problem only in terms of getting the right elite into power. Yet other countries we have studied with equally little exposure to alternatives to elite rule have developed discourses that are more skeptical of rule by any elite, no matter how well defined.

Armenia factor C: Legalistic Paternalism

Democracy if it means government by the people is dangerous, and is not a goal we should seek (4, 12, 13). More important is the rule of law (13). If officials violate the law, they should be prosecuted – there should be no power above the law, before which everyone is equal, and which everyone should obey (15, 22, 34, 49, 64). The Western model of democracy does not fit Armenia, for here we still need a strong hand (17, 18) – bearing in mind that government by one person alone can be dangerous, so that does not mean presidential government (37). It is more important to work together rather than compete and struggle against each other (29). At the moment the wrong people are in power (41). Election results were falsified so our votes did not count (39). So the laws and constitution we have do not in reality function (46). Power needs to be shared by the democratic opposition parties (27, 62). The mass media need to be free to criticize the government (5). Once we get the right people in power, we can move toward a state that actively promotes economic development and takes care of the people (53, 55). It is not the educated or the wealthy who should rule, but those who care most about the people (54, 60).

Our third Armenian discourse, Legalistic Paternalism, believes strongly in the rule of law. Yet the discourse is neither liberal (except in its advocacy of media freedom) nor democratic. It is not liberal because law is seen as

Table 8.2. *Subject loadings on factors for Armenia*

Subject	Factor A	B	C
1 M, engineer, democrat, age 29	9	0	10
2 M, unemployed, semi-nationalist, age 43	−8	12	17
3 F, salesperson, neutral, age 32	6	37*	7
4 M, post-graduate, pro-government, age 29	−12	20	−2
5 F, student, nationalist, age 18	−12	−1	7
6 F, housekeeper, neutral, age 58	0	−13	39*
7 F, salesperson, apolitical, age 22	46*	23	51*
8 M, engineer, opposition/conservative, age 45	6	50*	−8
9 M, construction manager, democrat-liberal, age 48	−4	−5	25
10 F, bank official, libertarian, age 48	−13	11	34*
11 F, government employee, liberal, age 25	−1	−34*	43*
12 F, housekeeper, neutral, age 50	18	46*	−16
13 M, business owner, traditionalist, age 36	5	−4	32*
14 M, student, democrat, age 19	4	28	11
15 F, doctor, democrat, age 33	9	−29	20
16 F, teacher, nationalist-democrat, age 42	7	46*	8
17 M, doctor, neutral, age 53	8	29	−3
18 M, student, conservative, age 21	43*	8	17
19 F, government employee, supports government, age 36	2	8	28
20 F, engineer, right-wing, age 29	16	6	−3
21 M, professional, democrat, age 57	55*	10	23
22 F, clergy, no interest, age 43	50*	17	−1
23 F, worker, indifferent, age 35	61*	−14	5
24 F, clergy, no political preference, age 48	60*	−9	−6
25 F, government official, indifferent, age 27	22	−15	26
26 F, nurse, democratic views, age 43	46*	−33*	13
27 F, worker, neutral, age 48	57*	−12	−2
28 F, clergy, democrat, age 53	38*	9	−11
29 M, science worker, no political preference, age 57	38*	−25	24
30 M, student, indifferent, age 23	27	9	18
31 F, economist, neutral, age 29	20	1	33*
32 F, unemployed, indifferent, age 32	22	−15	26
33 F, sociologist, neutral/indifferent, age 22	54*	−1	−4
34 M, student, views not available, age 22	56*	10	−17
35 F, housewife, determined democrat, age 62	52*	5	6
36 M, artist-designer, pacifist, age 27	16	2	9
37 M, clergy, centrist, age 25	37*	−7	4
38 M, military officer, liberal, age 29	42*	−3	7
39 M, businessperson, democratically inclined, age 27	51*	11	8
40 M, United Nations employee, liberal, age 40	44*	10	17

*Denotes a loading significant at the .01 level.

existing to keep government officials and citizens alike on the straight and narrow, as an instrument of rule. Law is not seen in terms of providing people with any protection against what government leadership might do, let alone any space for a free market, which Legalistic Paternalism rejects. Indeed, the whole point of law is to enforce the desires of leadership. Despite this attitude, the third discourse (like the first two) is inconsistent with the kind of presidential authoritarianism that has dominated post-communist Armenia, because it believes that the key to successful and effective leadership is having the "right people" in the plural in power. This discourse explicitly rejects concentration of power in the hands of the president. Still, Legalistic Paternalism is elitist, though less specific than Timocracy on the proper composition of the elite, beyond pointing to the moral qualities and caring motivations required of it. This is where paternalism enters: government should take care of the people. Echoes of Soviet notions of the role of government are not hard to discern here. Legalistic Paternalism rejects Western models of democracy, and any notion of rule by the people. The discourse believes in cooperation rather than competition in both economics and politics, and in this it resembles corporatist notions about government. The status quo in Armenia is condemned not because it is undemocratic, but because it is unlawful and ineffectual; the current regime does not care sufficiently for its citizens.

Prospects

On the face of it, the constellation of discourses in Armenia provides few resources for those interested in democratic transition and consolidation. But to accentuate the positive, it is perhaps surprising how little nationalism figures in these Armenian discourses, given the importance of nationalist parties and mobilizations in post-communist Armenia. Yet perhaps this is because nationalism is simply taken for granted, and so is not really an issue when it comes to what democracy might mean within Armenia. There are no ethnic minorities of any size, so the composition of the *demos* and relative rights of ethnic minorities and majorities are not issues. Thus nationalism arises as a policy issue, but not as something intrinsic to how the polity should be constructed.

An optimist might perceive that the key to Armenian democratization would be for our first discourse to treat social democracy as a possibility rather than an impossibility, though that would probably begin to happen only with a loosening of repression; as indicated earlier, there were some signs of this by 2000. From the perspective of those interested in conventional paths to democracy, the only other positive result is that all three discourses reject the kind of semi-authoritarian presidency that has dominated politics much of the time in post-communist Armenia, and away from which Kocharian has taken limited steps. All three discourses condemn this situation, though only Impossible Social Democracy grounds that condemnation in a view of what democracy should be. Timocracy pays lip service to democracy, but would replace the presidential system by the rule of economic elites. Legalistic Paternalism too wants strong, elite-led government.

However, to return to a theme developed in our concluding discussion of Russia, it is conceivable that the path to democracy in Armenia might be starting with the desire for a stronger and less corrupt state that all three discourses emphasize (if in somewhat different ways). Just as in Russia, we can at least imagine a stronger political leadership that is also committed to democratic development akin to the Juan Carlos model.[6] In fact, this path is easier to envisage for Armenia because its identity problems, while real enough, are less acute than Russia's or Ukraine's. By 2000 the economy had seen (very modest) improvement (with energy supplies looking more secure and relatively radical reforms taking effect). Political parties were consolidating into a few fairly distinctive groupings.[7] While our discourses contain much that is disconcerting from any democratic point of view (and dangers lurk in groups such as the paramilitary Yerkrapah), positive political leadership could well find synergy with the few green shoots we have identified.

[6] The consolidation of democracy in Spain is often associated with the successful handling of the storming of the Cortes (parliament) in 1981. The October 1999 events in Armenia might have constituted a similar turning point, but such questionable historical analogies might stretch a point too far.

[7] For a cautiously upbeat assessment even before Kocharian came to power, see Halbach, 1997, esp. p. 109.

9

Georgia

Georgia issued one of the first challenges to the integrity of the Soviet Union in the Gorbachev era. By 1988 there were clear signs that this small (population c. 5.5 million) Transcaucasian state could soon demand independence. Many Georgians saw their situation as similar to that of the Baltic states – viz. that they had been forcibly annexed by the Soviets, albeit much earlier (1921). Georgia declared its independence in April 1991, earlier than most former Soviet republics.

But breaking the ties with the Soviet Union proved problematic. Russia was unhappy about this. Georgians themselves were deeply divided about the type of country they wanted, as symbolized by divided attitudes toward the most famous Georgian of the twentieth century, Djugashvili – known to the world as Stalin. Here was yet another country with identity problems that complicated the transition to post-communism.[1]

Before, during, and immediately after the collapse of the Soviet Union, Georgia was visited by most of the horrors that could afflict a post-communist society. Georgia was an ethnically diverse state, with relatively small but geographically concentrated minorities: Abkhazians in Abkhazia, Ossetians in South Ossetia, Armenians in the south, Azeris in the southeast. Such concentrations can lead to autonomist, secessionist, or irredentist demands. Some 70 percent of the population was ethnically Georgian. The impending collapse of the Soviet Union was heralded by the rise of extreme authoritarian nationalism in Georgia. The Round Table–Free Georgia coalition that won the October 1990 election under the leadership of

---

[1] Compounded perhaps by folk memories of a geographically much larger and more powerful Georgia (especially in the eleventh and twelfth centuries).

Zviad Gamsakhurdia did so on a platform that seemed fairly liberal in terms of human rights, the rule of law, and freedom of the press and association (see Nelson and Amonashvili, 1992). Yet liberalization on the surface was accompanied by crude attempts to impose a Georgian identity on the state, and suppression of national minorities to the point of population transfer (elsewhere called ethnic cleansing – see Bell-Fialkoff, 1993). Not surprisingly, war broke out in Abkhazia in 1993, where Russian support eventually secured a rebel victory. South Ossetia too became effectively independent under Russian protection.

Gamsakhurdia appeared to have wide popular support. In the May 1991 election for the presidency, he received 87 percent of the vote – a remarkable proportion in a fair (but not entirely free, given attacks on the opposition) election. But his opponents were with some justification soon calling him a fascist dictator. By January 1992, Gamsakhurdia had been ousted, overthrown after fighting in Tbilisi and other cities, in which his opponents were supported by the military. The military leadership then, in March 1992, invited Eduard Shevardnadze, former Soviet foreign minister and noted advocate of *glasnost* and *perestroika*, to assume the leadership of the state council. Though a senior communist, Shevardnadze when Georgia's first secretary (1972–85) had acquired a reputation as a relatively fair and tolerant leader; his closeness to Gorbachev and good standing with Western governments enhanced this image. With some irony, the far more democratic Shevardnadze therefore succeeded the popular and elected Gamsakhurdia as a result of the use of force.

Civil war continued into 1993, with Gamsakhurdia continuing to claim he was Georgia's rightful leader. He died in January 1994, probably by his own hand, and the situation began to stabilize somewhat. However, elements of traditional "warlordism" and continued support for Gamsakhurdist ideas undermined the power and authority of the Shevardnadze regime.

Thus early post-communist Georgia featured ethnic warfare, traditional clanism, secession, a refugee problem, the interference of a great power (Russia), civil war, assassination, rising crime, economic collapse, and authoritarian populism. A form of economic shock therapy was introduced in late 1994, but this proved more shocking than therapeutic, and Georgia's economic path too looked rocky.

With the adoption of a new constitution in 1995, which proclaimed Georgia a presidential republic, it looked quite possible that the country was set to become a dictatorship. But since some Georgians were also criticizing Shevardnadze for conceding too much to the Russians over territorial integrity, the country looked likely to be a *troubled* dictatorship.[2] None of

---

[2] Georgia was the last country to join the Commonwealth of Independent States. While Shevardnadze hoped for economic and strategic advantages, many Georgians believed that

this augured well for the prospects for liberalization, effective economic reform, or democratization, and it is hardly surprising that so many observers dismissed Georgia's democratic prospects.

Nor was it possible to dig more deeply into Georgia's history to recover foundations upon which contemporary democrats could build. The country had been under Russian control almost continuously since the beginning of the nineteenth century, having been a sovereign republic only in 1918–21.[3] A brief experiment in democracy at that stage was cut short by the Red Army and forcible incorporation into what was soon to become the Soviet Union. However, as Georgian scholar Ghia Nodia (1995) argues, Georgians could still relate to democracy by seeing it as the system adopted by Europeans. As members of a country that had adopted Christianity in the fourth century and had spent centuries fighting off Islam, many Georgians saw affinity with the West. This self-image had been strengthened during the nineteenth century by the writer Ilia Chavchavadze. But the West was in fact a long way away; this, plus decades of Soviet censorship, meant that Georgian understanding of Western conceptions of democracy remained extremely underdeveloped. (Standard works in English on Georgian history and identity include Lang, 1962 and Suny, 1989.)

Given this background, one would not perhaps expect a great deal of Georgian discourses of democracy. Yet our possibly surprising results suggest that Georgia is not necessarily doomed to a recurrence of its miserable experiences in the early post-communist years. Our individual interviews were carried out in mid-1997, by which time Georgia's various political conflicts were much reduced in intensity, though economically the country remained in dire straits, with signs of only a very limited turnaround.

Georgian discourses of authority and democracy

Factor analysis of our individual Q sorts produced three discourses, which we label Democratic Enthusiasm, Presidential Statism, and Firm Constitutionalism. (In the narratives, numbers in parentheses refer to the statements from the first table.)

Georgia factor A: Democratic Enthusiasm

We are moving toward real democracy in Georgia (11, 57), and we do not have to wait for economic development to do this (8, 9). Democracy means the rule

joining was a high price to pay for a country that had only just managed to shake off the Russian yoke.

[3] Many Georgians in the early nineteenth century were apparently ambivalent about coming under Russian control; at least Russia was a powerful, Orthodox country that could protect them against the neighboring Islamic countries they had been fighting for centuries.

Table 9.1. *Statement scores on three factors for Georgia*

Factor A is Democratic Enthusiasm.
Factor B is Presidential Statism.
Factor C is Firm Constitutionalism.

Statement	Factor		
	A	B	C
1 Democracy is the supremacy of law.	+4	−3	+6
2 Democracy implies the protection of human rights.	+2	+4	−1
3 There is no answer to the question "what is democracy?"	−1	−3	−6
4 Democracy is the government of the majority.	−1	+5	−4
5 There is no absolute democracy.	−1	−5	+4
6 Democracy is the most difficult model of society.	−3	0	−2
7 Democracy is understood in different ways by the representatives of different religions.	−1	−1	−4
8 At this stage of transition we cannot expect more democracy.	−5	−5	+2
9 In a hungry society democracy is meaningless.	−4	+2	0
10 Democratic principles are less implemented in rural areas.	−6	−2	−2
11 We are far from a real democracy.	−5	−4	+3
12 The still undeveloped political party system is an obstacle for the development of democracy in Georgia.	−3	+2	0
13 Democracy needs to exist in the genetic makeup of the nation.	−3	−6	−5
14 Democratic principles should be taught from childhood.	+4	−3	0
15 An independent court, not influenced by the government, should exist in a democracy.	−2	+6	+5
16 Democracy should not be transformed anarchy.	−2	+1	+1
17 Democracy is the supremacy of law.	−2	+1	+3
18 Democracy is freedom of the mass media.	+4	0	−2
19 Democracy is not the aim of but the means for establishment of the state governed by the rule of law.	−2	+1	0
20 Democracy is the expression of the people's will by elections.	+5	−4	+1
21 The initial stage of democracy requires dictatorship, as in the case of Chile.	−1	−3	−5
22 Financial groups are dependent on the government.	+1	+4	−3
23 The public lacks the knowledge of laws.	−2	+1	0
24 People have no possibility to protect and exercise their rights.	0	+3	+1
25 There are some threats that the presidential system in Georgia will be transformed into authoritarian rule.	+2	−6	−1
26 Parliament is one of the islands of democracy in comparison with other state institutions.	−6	−4	−1
27 Free elections of the president and parliament are one of the main guarantees of democracy in Georgia.	0	+2	+3

Table 9.1. (*cont.*)

	Factor		
Statement	A	B	C
28 The newly established Constitutional Court should promote the protection of human rights and the establishment of legal order.	0	+3	+5
29 People should be ready for democracy.	+1	−3	+2
30 The government should be controlled by the people.	+1	−2	−2
31 The will of the people should be reflected in the constitution.	+2	+1	+3
32 National minorities should feel themselves to be equal citizens of Georgia.	0	−1	+2
33 Democracy means nonviolence.	+6	+1	+4
34 Democracy means respect for the opinions of others.	+1	+2	0
35 One of the basic principles of democracy is trust of the state.	−3	+3	−3
36 Democracy means responsible mass media.	−1	+3	0
37 Government officials speak and act in different ways.	+1	−2	−4
38 People from the communist period are accustomed to violating laws.	−4	+2	−2
39 It is difficult to change the mentality of the older generation.	0	0	−3
40 Political parties act just for their own interests.	−3	+5	+1
41 A large part of the political elite remained the same, with the same communist mentality.	−2	0	−3
42 It is inadmissible to force the implementation of democracy.	0	0	+4
43 The communist legacy still accompanies not only the government but also the whole society.	−1	+2	−5
44 Ethnic conflicts create great obstacles for the development of democracy.	+3	−1	+3
45 Government should promote the establishment of democratic institutions.	+1	+4	+2
46 First of all the state itself should protect the laws.	+5	+6	+1
47 The transition should first of all take place in the mind of the people.	+3	−4	0
48 The anti-corruption campaign should be started from the highest level of officials.	+3	0	+1
49 Democracy means equality before the law.	+3	−1	+6
50 Democracy means a plural society.	+1	+1	−1
51 Democracy means the protection of minorities.	0	+4	−1
52 Democracy requires the development of a civil society.	0	−2	−1
53 Free mass media (especially television) require a strong economic base.	+2	−1	+1

Table 9.1. (*cont.*)

| | Factor | | |
Statement	A	B	C
54 Democracy and morality are indivisible.	+5	−1	−2
55 Democracy requires the development of the nongovernmental sector.	+4	−2	+1
56 Democracy is dependent on normal functioning of a judicial system.	+2	+5	+5
57 Democracy is a sham, in which the clever minority cheats the less clever majority.	−5	+1	−3
58 Democracy is not accessible for poor people.	−4	−1	−6
59 Democracy is the primary tool for preventing the use of force against those who think differently.	+3	−1	+2
60 Democracy is the reevaluation of our past.	−4	0	+4
61 There should be no authoritarian rule of government.	+6	−5	+2
62 For democracy it is necessary to implement the principle of checks and balances.	−1	+3	−4
63 Human rights should prevail over the state's rights.	+2	−2	−1
64 Democracy should prevent the tyranny of the majority.	+1	0	−1

of law, equality before the law, respect for human rights, free media, elections, and peaceful resolution of conflicts among those who think differently (1, 2, 18, 20, 33, 46, 49, 59, 63). Democracy and morality are indivisible (54). There is no place here for authoritarian government (61). There remains much to be done: we need to develop a strong nongovernmental sector (55), root out corruption (48), and convince people of the desirability of democracy (14, 47). And there are some dangers: the presidential system could lead to authoritarianism, parliament is not very democratic (25, 26), and democracy is threatened by ethnic conflict and nationalism (13, 44). Still, everyone has access to democracy in all parts of the country (10, 58), we have removed the communist mentality from the elite and ordinary people (38, 41), and the party system seems to be working (12).

Our first Georgian discourse, Democratic Enthusiasm, defines democracy in fairly conventional liberal terms; and, recent history notwithstanding, believes that such a liberal democracy could indeed be pursued in Georgia – if not easily achieved. This discourse is not naive; it is alive to the threats that ethnic conflict, corruption, and the degree of centralization of political power in the hands of the presidency pose to democracy. It is noteworthy that this discourse could maintain its optimism about democracy in light of all that Georgia has experienced. On the other hand, those experiences do not have to be interpreted as failures of democracy as such. They can be seen as resulting from failure to move properly in the direction of constitutional

Table 9.2. *Subject loadings on factors for Georgia*

Subject	Factor		
	A	B	C
1 M, engineer, not a party member	69*	20	31
2 M, bank manager, not a party member	63*	18	25
3 F, accountant, not a party member	70*	11	13
4 M, worker, not a party member	58*	23	33*
5 M, driver, not a party member	50*	−18	26
6 M, historian, not a party member	53*	16	19
7 F, student, not a party member	25	32*	40*
8 M, engineer, member of government party	31	29	4
9 F, peasant, not a party member	34*	24	19
10 F, doctor, not a party member	76*	−2	18
11 F, unemployed, not a party member	83*	−2	18
12 M, student, not a party member	81*	−7	21
13 M, student, opposition party member	83*	0	18
14 M, driver, not a party member	79*	−4	12
15 M, computer engineer, not a party member	86*	0	16
16 M, lawyer, opposition party member	86*	5	14
17 F, teacher, not a party member	52*	13	5
18 F, worker, not a party member	38*	36*	37*
19 M, businessperson, not a party member	51*	16	29
20 M, student, not a party member	25	34*	18
21 F, teacher, not a party member	36*	21	5
22 M, engineer, not a party member	−15	60*	3
23 M, mathematician, not a party member	−8	57*	8
24 M, doctor, member of government party	35*	26	55*
25 M, businessperson, opposition party member	45*	10	45*
26 M, state lawyer, not a party member	24	9	33*
27 M, private lawyer, not a party member	3	53*	30
28 F, philosopher, not a party member	58*	4	25
29 M, student, not a party member	45*	8	41*
30 F, engineer, not a party member	14	31	38*
31 M, economist, opposition party member	8	17	15
32 M, peasant, not a party member	16	52*	56*
33 M, unemployed, not a party member	58*	−8	1
34 M, businessperson, not a party member	7	51*	10
35 M, secretary in state office, member of government party	−7	61*	0
36 F, state lawyer, not a party member	16	36*	39*
37 F, engineer, opposition party member	24	42*	44*
38 M, unemployed, not a party member	1	32*	14
39 M, peasant, not a party member	−1	34*	9
40 M, teacher, not a party member	17	36*	42*

*Denotes a loading significant at the .01 level.

government and peaceful conflict resolution, as when a freely elected president pursued authoritarian, populist, and aggressively nationalistic policies.

Georgia factor B: Presidential Statism

Democracy requires first and foremost a strong presidency that embodies the will of the majority (4, 25), along with the protection of human rights (including minority rights) through an independent court system (2, 15, 28, 51, 56). The state itself needs to be strong and authoritative, to promote this system actively (45, 46, 61); there is no conflict between a strong state and human rights (63). So true democracy in this sense is now attainable, and we can move toward it (5, 8, 11). We do not have to wait for the principles to become established first of all in the mind of the people (47). Once this kind of authority is established, people should trust the state and the mass media should not cause too much trouble (35, 36). Elections are not so important for expression of the people's will, and parliament is not an effective democratic institution (20, 26). Our political parties are selfish and an obstacle to democracy (12, 40). People are now ready for democracy, though there are some problems: those with experience of communism are accustomed to violating laws (38), and people need greater opportunity to exercise their rights (24).

During the 1990s, center stage in Georgian politics was dominated by two powerful figures, Gamsakhurdia and Shevardnadze. For all their differences, both presided over regimes that emphasized their own individual dominance. Shevardnadze was, formally, first leader of the state council, then chair of parliament, then prime minister, then president. Our second Georgian discourse, Presidential Statism, treats this dominance as a proper state of affairs. The president, representing the majority, should be supreme. Parliament and parties are treated with scorn; they should yield before presidential power. Beyond this emphasis on presidential power, this discourse appears at first sight to contain a number of contradictions, or at least uneasy juxtapositions. A commitment to checks and balances sits uneasily with acceptance of authoritarian rule. Democracy is seen as involving protection of human rights, in part through an independent court system, but there is no recognition of the need for the supremacy of law, and human rights are likely to fare poorly in the face of the kind of authoritarian state favored by this discourse. This contradiction might be resolved if human rights are treated as entitlements to goods, rather than the standard liberal notion of protections against government and against others. But it is not hard to see how such a discourse could be drawn upon to legitimate authoritarian rule, despite the fact that it does not explicitly favor dictatorial government.

Georgia factor C: Firm Constitutionalism

We can answer the question of what democracy means, and we should move toward it (3, 29, 57). In a democratic society, everyone is equal before the law, which is why a well-functioning and independent judicial system is essential (15, 49, 56), so that conflicts can be resolved without violence (33). Democracy is for everyone, rich and poor alike (7, 10, 58). The establishment of a legal order is the basis of democracy, and the constitutional court can promote that (1, 28). Democracy is based on a strong constitution reflecting the will of the people, so there is no need for checks and balances (17, 31, 62). This is not the same as majority rule, which is not an essential feature of democracy (4). Free elections do have a role to play (27), but they are not as important as the rule of law and strong constitution. In Georgia we are a long way from true democracy, but realistically we cannot expect more democracy at this stage of our transition (5, 8, 11). This does not mean the transition should be authoritarian, for democracy cannot be forced upon people (21, 42, 61). We have all put communism and its mentality safely behind us (38, 39, 41, 43, 60), though now ethnic conflicts cause problems for the development of democracy (44). Today we can usually trust government officials to be honest with us, though we should not place unconditional trust in the benevolence of the state and its officials (35, 37).

Firm Constitutionalism shares Presidential Statism's hostility to parliament and parties, but not its enthusiasm for centralizing power in the hands of the executive. Rather, as our name for it implies, firm authority is to be vested in the impersonal hands of a constitution, administered by the courts. There is no sympathy for the idea of checks and balances between different components of government. But this emphasis on legalism and the courts is not for the sake of human rights, about which this discourse cares little. Rather, it is for the sake of social order. This is a very legalistic view of democracy, which emphasizes the rule of law above all else – including elections, which are not seen as central to democracy. Firm Constitutionalism can be understood as a reaction against the lawlessness (on the part even of democratically elected leaders) that pervaded Georgia and its politics in the 1990s.

A negative reading of our second and third discourses would see each of them as searching desperately for a source of order in a chaotic world: the second finds that source in a strong presidency, the third in a strong legal system. Both reveal little faith in the ordinary give-and-take of politics; one can see how both might in the end legitimate authoritarian government. A more positive reading of these two discourses would point out that neither represents unreconstructed authoritarianism of the sort found in some of the other countries we have studied. Neither is really disaffected from the post-communist status quo, neither seeks a return to the order of the communist years, and both seek to make the best of the present while retaining an in-principle commitment to democracy.

Democratic prospects and problems in Georgia

Any dangers associated with the second and third discourses notwithstanding, the overall pattern that emerges from these three discourses in many ways belies Georgia's disastrous experiences in the early to mid-1990s. Oddly enough, though, this pattern is in some ways quite consistent with Georgia's post-communist history. Gamsakhurdia and his opponents alike resorted to extraconstitutional and sometimes violent means to pursue their ends. But at the same time they espoused platforms – and when in office pursued policies – that had distinctly liberal democratic components. So in Gamsakhurdia's case, even as he was consolidating presidential power, imposing a Georgian ethnic identity on the state, oppressing even his ethnically Georgian opponents, and feeding propaganda to the media, his government was also passing laws to set up an independent judiciary, guarantee freedoms of the press and of association, and give parliament the right to scrutinize executive actions (Jones, 1997, pp. 515–16). His successor, Shevardnadze, represents a somewhat different mix of undoubted democratic commitments and occasional (perhaps reluctant) resort to extralegal powers and actions.

In the concluding discussions of both Russia and Armenia we argued that the key to post-communist democratization in countries lacking an active civil society, democratic practice, and supportive discourses could lie through stronger state leadership committed to democratic principles. In this light, does not Eduard Shevardnadze represent exactly the kind of figure that is needed? And do not Georgia's second and third discourses, with their desire for a strong and uncorrupted state, represent exactly the kind of discourses that could support this route to democracy?

There is no doubting Shevardnadze's personal democratic commitments. If his leadership has not (yet) produced the kinds of results that might be envisaged in such a route – though there were positive movements in this direction in the late 1990s – it should be remembered that this route also requires a strong state capable of formulating and implementing laws and policies, not just a strong leader. This is perhaps what Georgia still lacks. However, given its disastrous post-communist beginnings, continuing ethnic conflicts, and persistent economic slump (compounded by the effects of the 1998 Russian economic crisis and a severe drought in 2000), Georgia under Shevardnadze has in many ways overperformed when it comes to democratic transition – and our discourses reflect this. Our findings are in line with those of, for example, Stephen Jones's recent assessment, considerably more upbeat than his own earlier analyses (cf. Jones, 1993 and Jones, 2000; for another positive evaluation see Halbach, 1997). One of the main reasons for Jones's revised assessment is that there are clear signs of a nascent civil society, even though the new nongovernmental organizations and "embryonic" pressure groups remain weak, both organizationally and financially.[4] If Georgia were to witness a simultaneous strengthening of both the state (one committed to democracy) *and* civil society, its democratic future would look very encouraging.

Beyond desires for a strong and uncorrupted state, the three discourses provide some further resources for those interested in Georgian democratization – most straightforwardly, in the Democratic Enthusiasm of the first discourse. There is little support in any of them for the kind of ethnic nationalism that produced catastrophic results for Georgia in the early 1990s – and which has been largely repudiated by the Shevardnadze regime, though that regime has tried to retain the unity of the Georgian state in the face of regional rebellion. None of them explicitly favors authoritarianism, even though authoritarian possibilities lurk in the second and third discourses.

Come 2000, the Georgian electorate continued to give strong support to Shevardnadze's form of democratization, though the economic situation remained dire. In the October 1999 elections, the "presidential" party (Citizens' Union of Georgia) secured 42 percent of the votes and 130 of the 227 seats actually filled in the unicameral parliament (an improvement on their performance in the November 1995 elections). The "Gamsakhurdist" All-Georgian Union for Revival trailed with 25 percent of the vote. Shevardnadze was reelected president for a second term in April 2000, on an anti-corruption ticket, with a support level of nearly 80 percent of votes cast. Georgian politics was stabilizing, and its leader was highly popular without being a dictator (in contrast to Lukashenka in Belarus). Moreover, while the relationship with Abkhazia had still not been resolved, it was in a *relatively* peaceful condition.

Unfortunately, though, none of the discourses seems to recognize the need for a flourishing civil society as an aspect of democratic government, Jones's recent findings notwithstanding. In short, Georgia's constellation of discourses is amenable to both positive and negative readings – just like Georgia's own political prospects. It would be naive to consider the country's short- to medium-term democratization prospects with more than cautious optimism. Georgia could become, if not quite the Switzerland of the Caucasus, a society that moves in a more peaceful and constitutional direction; but the experience of the early 1990s shows the availability of some grim alternatives, against which these discourses of democracy do not provide complete protection.

---

[4] Another positive development mentioned by Jones (2000, p. 73) is the reform of the judiciary that began in 1997.

10

Moldova

Perhaps even more than other countries in the post-communist world, Moldova is beset by difficulties caused by the definition of both nation and state. Like Belarus and Ukraine, Moldova is apparently uncertain about whether it would rather be a sovereign state or part of a revamped Soviet Union (the largest party in parliament, the communists, favors closer relations with the CIS). But many people in post-communist Moldova believe that a greater Romania might be their "natural" home.

While there was a kingdom of Moldova in the Middle Ages, its boundaries do not coincide with present-day Moldova; the former was much larger, and included much of today's Romania. The region has a complex history of shifting boundaries and divisions, most of it spent under Turkish or Russian rule. In the interwar period, much of Moldova was part of Romania. The Soviet Union established a separate Autonomous Soviet Socialist Republic (ASSR) of Moldova in 1924 (formally under Ukraine) on the left bank of the River Dniestr, in an area that first came under Russian control in 1792. The Romanian part was annexed and linked to the existing ASSR to form a constituent republic of the Soviet Union in 1940, in the aftermath of the Molotov–Ribbentrop pact. This situation was consolidated in 1944. Moldova (or Moldavia as it was known at that time)[1] became thoroughly integrated into the Soviet Union, even though – along with the three Baltic states – it was a relative newcomer.

---

[1] To endorse the point about overlap and traditional close ties between Moldova and Romania, note that Romania still has an area called Moldavia.

Although Romania was part of the Soviet bloc, its leadership became increasingly independent of Moscow from the early 1960s, and so for almost three decades Moldova was politically distant from its western neighbor. Come the demise of the Soviet Union, nationalists were unsure whether to seek to join Romania, with whom most Moldovans shared a common language and much common history, or to pursue independence. The majority of the population eventually opted for independence. Even then, Moldovans argued about whether to call their language Moldovan or Romanian. In joining the CIS, Moldova showed far less desire to distance itself from Russia and the former Soviet Union than did the Baltic states, despite their common experience of interwar independence. Although most Moldovans appear to have accepted independence, demonstrations in the Moldovan capital in 1995 in favor of union with Romania (see Campbell, 1996) testify to a continuing identity crisis. (On the complexities of Moldovan identity politics, see King, 2000.) Moldova has almost no democratic experiences in its deep history on which to draw.

To those who regard ethnic nationalism and its associated conflicts as the most serious impediment to post-communist democratization and economic reform, Moldova's ethnic mix looks likely to create serious problems, and indeed ethnic warfare did break out in 1992. Within its present boundaries, only 64 percent of the population is Moldovan. The two largest minorities are Ukrainians (14 percent) and Russians (13 percent). Among the remaining 9 percent is a minority of Gagauz, of Christian Turkish origin, concentrated in the south.

Beginning in 1989, Moldovan and Romanian nationalism attained expression through the organization of the Moldovan Popular Front. The Front became increasingly important on the nationalist side, winning the elections to the Moldovan Supreme Soviet held in March 1990 in alliance with Reform Communists. This alliance soon fell apart, leaving the nationalists – counting among their leadership a dominant faction of pan-Romanian extremists – in control (Crowther, 1997b, p. 293). In September 1990 both the Trans-Dniestr region (which is around 40 percent Moldovan, 28 percent Ukrainian, and 25 percent Russian, but predominantly Russian-speaking, and having been part of the Moldovan ASSR established in the 1920s) and the Gagauzia region declared their independence from Moldova within the Soviet Union. The nationalist majority in the Moldovan Supreme Soviet refused to recognize this secession. While the secessionists welcomed the attempted coup in Moscow in August 1991, the nationalist majority in Chisinau (the Moldovan capital) responded with an immediate declaration of independence, claiming sovereignty over the entire disputed territory. War began in 1992, with the Trans-Dniestrians receiving substantial support from Russia, especially via the Russian army stationed in

Trans-Dniestr.[2] The war ended with a ceasefire in July 1992, with the Trans-
Dniestrians in control of their territory but no political agreement in sight.
It was not until May 1997 that the Moldovan government and the self-
proclaimed Trans-Dniestrian Moldovan Republic signed a "memorandum
of agreement" that symbolized at least a *modus vivendi* (see Garnett and
Lebenson, 1998), despite continuing differences and simmering tensions.
Meanwhile, the Gagauz issue was eventually resolved – more peacefully –
with substantial autonomy granted to the Gagauz region.

In light of Huntington's (1996) thesis about the clash of civilizations, it is
noteworthy that the ethnic conflict which led to war was an internal affair
of the "Orthodox" civilization, while the one which was resolved peacefully
was between members of the Orthodox civilization and a group anomalous
in Huntington's terms, inasmuch as it is ethnically Islamic (Turkish) but
culturally and religiously Christian.

Come the 1990s Moldova was still a largely agrarian and underdeveloped
economy, and, just as in Ukraine and Belarus, its Communist Party leadership had resisted *perestroika* and *glasnost*. As we have seen, the politics of
the early post-communist years was dominated by ethnic and nationalist
issues, with extremists in control on all sides. Moldova therefore saw little in the way of effective administration or attention to economic issues
(Crowther, 1997b, p. 300). The nationalist extremists of the Popular Front
did, however, lose some ground in June 1992 with the installation of a new
government.

Given this background of ethnic strife and economic underdevelopment,
it is perhaps surprising that in February 1994 Moldova managed to hold a
reasonably free and fair parliamentary election that marginalized extreme
nationalists, with the Popular Front receiving only 7.5 percent of the vote.
Some 43 percent of the vote and an absolute majority of seats were gained
by the Democratic Agrarian Party. The second-largest grouping was the
Russophone Socialist Party/Edinstvo bloc (Crowther, 1997a, p. 326). Both
groupings were dominated by reform communists. As in other countries
in Southeastern Europe in which much of the population was rural, parties prospered that did not promise to move too quickly toward a radically
different system. Nevertheless, the pragmatic new government immediately
set about accelerating privatization and associated economic reform. In
1998 parliamentary elections, the Agrarians won no seats, while a revitalized Party of Communists that drew votes across all ethnic groups became
the largest party with 30.1 percent of votes and 40 percent of seats (King,
2000, p. 162). An uneasy alliance of nationalists and centrists installed a

[2] Fish (1999, p. 812) argues that the Trans-Dniestr issue is not about ethnic conflict but
turf wars ("gangster separatism"). Concerns about corruption and crime do indeed figure
prominently in both factors we identify.

technocratic government to keep the Communists out of power (ibid., p. 163).

The most striking feature of post-communist democratization in Moldova is that it has happened at all, given the inauspicious mix of ethnic, nationalist, and identity issues faced in the early 1990s. Perhaps more remarkable still is that by the mid-1990s Moldova hosted a multiparty system in which nationalist parties and politicians were not dominant. Yet as we shall now see, our discourses of democracy in Moldova reveal that the country's hold on democracy and democratization may be a little insecure.

Moldovan discourses of democracy and authoritarianism

Our factor analysis of the Q sorts for forty Moldovan subjects, based on interviews carried out in late 1997, produced two discourses, which we label Socialist Authoritarianism and Democratic Development. (In the narratives, numbers in parentheses refer to the statements from the first table.)

Moldova factor A: Socialist Authoritarianism

This is a corrupt, pretend democracy, a pretext for power grabs by so-called democrats who control the government but are really mafia and bandits (10, 31, 42, 43). This enables thieves to get rich while honest workers hardly eat and can find nothing in the shops; democracy has made us poor (1, 20, 24, 25, 57). Politicians are no help; they all make promises they cannot keep (47). Luckily people can see through these promises; you can trust ordinary people more than a government that works badly (8, 14, 16, 19). In the end we need order rather than democracy, to fight corruption and turn the economic situation around (23, 30, 41, 46). We do not need opposition or protection for minorities (45, 55). However bad things are, protest strikes only make matters worse, so there is no point to them (4, 5, 6). Things were not so bad in the old system, and we especially need a return to the social provisions that the state used to make for people (4, 21, 33).

Socialist Authoritarianism is among the most emphatic of the discourses we have found in the different countries in rejecting liberal democratic principles. From the point of view of democracy, its only saving grace is its egalitarian faith in ordinary people as opposed to the government, drawing a strong distinction between ordinary people on the one hand and political-economic elites on the other. However, this faith does not support any model of participatory politics. Socialist Authoritarianism is also relatively unmoved by ethnic nationalism, though neither is it especially sensitive to the rights of ethnic minorities. Indeed, it sees ethnic factors playing little importance in public life. Moldovan Socialist Authoritarianism rejects even the idea of democracy as a basic symbol, which is quite

Table 10.1. *Statement scores on two factors for Moldova*

Factor A is Socialist Authoritarianism.
Factor B is Democratic Development.

	Factor	
Statement	A	B
1 If you don't have anything to eat, how can you talk about democracy? To the people it doesn't make any difference.	+4	−1
2 As for elections, well the goal was: let's make some changes, in order to see what will happen.	−1	−4
3 What does the street protest or strike do to the state? Nothing. So what if they are gathering and shouting slogans?	−4	−2
4 The state should protect the children, the old people: before if a woman was pregnant, she was paid for up to three years; she received medicine for free. Nowadays nobody cares about these kinds of things.	+5	+1
5 If you're unhappy about the state not paying your wages and pensions, block the railway nearby, at least for a day!	−5	−1
6 Strikes make no sense if you just stop working. They make sense only when you block the roads, the railways, the entire economic system.	−6	−1
7 Here in Moldova there is no tradition of fighting for your rights. Moldovans are very conservative.	−1	+2
8 Governments have been ruling very badly. This does not mean that the people are not working well.	+4	+2
9 The people have started to get involved but the process is very slow.	0	+1
10 The current government consists of some mafia, some bandits.	+4	−2
11 You cannot create democracy with a person who has no culture, who is not open.	−2	+1
12 The most natural system of government is enlightened despotism. It is perhaps dangerous, but no more dangerous than democracy. Democracy brought Hitler to power.	−1	−6
13 Democracy cannot stop a Hitler from getting into power.	0	0
14 You can convince people of whatever you want.	−4	−3
15 The fundamental problem of democracy is: why do we deny the right to vote to a clever teenager of fifteen and grant it to a drunkard of twenty-five?	−2	−3
16 The clever must have the right to vote.	−5	−5
17 Democracy should let the best rule.	+1	+5
18 The Gagauz minority should have no influence on the foreign policy of the Republic of Moldova.	+1	0

Table 10.1. (*cont.*)

	Factor	
Statement	A	B
19 Here, the Russians vote for Russians and Moldovans for Moldovans, whether the candidates are fascists, communists, or democrats.	−5	−3
20 Democracy means theft: it robbed me, it made me poor.	+3	−6
21 Today is not a good situation. When Andropov [leader of the Soviet Union, 1982−4] was the ruler, there was order; nobody could go shopping during working hours.	+2	−4
22 There will be no peace in this country as long as the population votes not according to doctrine or economic programs, but according to kinship and ethnicity.	−2	+2
23 I don't know much about democracy; here we need order, not as today, with everybody acting as he or she pleases.	+2	−3
24 Nowadays the thieves get rich and those who work honestly have barely anything to eat.	+6	0
25 Now with this democracy one can't find anything in the shops; everything is at the marketplace, at the illegal merchants; before for this, one would go to jail.	+4	−5
26 What kind of democracy is this one, with the former rulers of collective farms in parliament? If we had some women there, things could move faster.	−3	0
27 The West has its own interests, economic interests. They are talking about democracy. Why are they not talking about democracy in China?	0	0
28 Before we did not know anything about what was happening in the world, we were proud of living in the Soviet Union and I was very sorry for the Italian children who used to go to school carrying their own chairs.	0	0
29 The people are responsible for the acts of the governing elite, because the people have elected them.	+2	+6
30 With a regime that would institute order and discipline, this country would flourish within three years.	+2	−2
31 Democracy was a pretext so that new people could get into power positions.	+3	−3
32 Here, in Moldova, we don't have the state that we should have.	+2	+1
33 The state should protect its citizens.	+3	+5
34 There is no adequate legislation; our laws are badly conceived.	+1	+4
35 Even where there are laws, they are not applicable. For Moldovans a law is enacted and obeyed for a maximum of one day.	0	+1

Table 10.1. (*cont.*)

Statement	Factor A	B
36 In our country instead of striving to get a good law, it is preferable to be in touch with the minister.	−1	+1
37 Compared with the enlightened despot, democracy often allows checks and corrections.	+3	−1
38 In any society there is an organized, active minority and a majority who trusts it. This is a natural political system.	−2	+1
39 To destroy the self-government of the villages, their autonomy, it was enough to organize mass deportations and arrests to get rid of the conscious active minority.	−3	+3
40 I don't know if one can talk about liberty in a poor, underdeveloped country.	−1	+1
41 It does not matter through what kinds of methods the leader got to power — dictatorial means, democratic or nondemocratic elections — what really matters is how he is organizing the country and what sort of goals he has.	+2	−5
42 Here, we don't have democracy. It's just makebelieve. The rulers are just pretending to be what they are not; it is simply corruption up to the highest level.	+5	+3
43 All these pretended democrats are stealing, breaking the country; they are milking it.	+5	−1
44 Democracy is somehow related to human rights, but the problem in our country is not about this.	−1	−2
45 Any democratic state should ensure protection for political society, for the opposition. In our country the opposition is maintained just pro forma.	−3	+2
46 Even the fight against corruption must be by democratic means; otherwise there is no democracy but dictatorship or something else.	−4	+4
47 Here populism is very developed; everybody makes promises but does not keep them.	+6	+3
48 I cannot go on the radio to complain that there is no heat in my flat; I could have problems with the authorities.	−3	−4
49 They cannot say that everything is all right when most people are becoming worse off.	−1	0
50 Perhaps our children will learn what democracy is; *we* were educated in the communist spirit.	−2	−1
51 There should be a real concern about democracy and its procedures at the top level, not just empty imitation of Western institutions.	0	+3
52 We still lack a real political class, who could take the destiny of the country in its hands.	+1	+6

Table 10.1. (*cont.*)

	Factor	
Statement	A	B
53 There is nothing wrong with communist ideals, as long as they are not interfering with human dignity and freedom.	0	−2
54 It is difficult to start something new with the old people. Here the former presidents of collective farms are members of parliament and they are thinking just as before.	−2	+5
55 There cannot be democracy without majority concern for minority protection.	−3	−2
56 The self-government of the many is democracy.	0	+2
57 Very few are getting rich in a market economy, but many are better off than those who lived a decent life under a planned one.	−6	−1
58 We should not forget that we have our own economic way of development and our specific institutions, that the new wave of democratization should cope with and not destroy.	−1	−1
59 If those who are running our factories are motivated not by the interest of the unit, but by their private interest, we're not going to see the light soon.	+3	+2
60 There are too many men and not enough women at the top level. Democracy also means equal chances for women.	+1	+4
61 In a democratic country the citizens take into consideration concepts such as virtue and shame.	+1	0
62 When a class or ethnic group is pretending to represent the whole population, there is not going to be an impressive outcome; everybody should have a word to say.	+1	+4
63 We must strive to work better, because only by working hard can our country attain a decent place among neighboring nations.	−4	−4
64 Nobody should oppress anybody, and the legitimacy of rule should rest on free acceptance of the rulers by the ruled.	+1	+3

rare. It is highly disaffected from the post-communist status quo, regarding post-communist elites with contempt. Presumably this contempt extends to the reform communists who were in power in the late 1990s when our study was undertaken (though not necessarily to the subsequently reconstituted Party of Communists). Socialist Authoritarianism has a more positive view of the Communist past than the post-communist present, and sees little opportunity for redeeming the present, given its hostility to privatization and the market economy in general. This discourse seeks a more orderly situation, with greater social discipline. Its hostility to disruptive protests such as strikes and demonstrations – even while allowing that these can be effective against a regime the discourse despises – highlights the stress on order and discipline.

Moldova factor B: Democratic Development

In Moldova we have no true democracy (42). There is corruption, laws are often badly conceived, politicians make promises they cannot keep, and unfortunately people often vote by kinship and ethnicity (22, 34, 42, 47). The state should do a better job in protecting its citizens (33). We still lack a political class that could take the destiny of the country into its hands (52). Those people in power who were part of the old regime still think in the old ways (54). The people cannot deny responsibility for these problems, for they elected the government (29). Even in Moldova there is some democracy; it is not just a cover for power grabs (31). We should strive to make democracy work rather than allow it to be replaced by despotism and oppression (12, 23, 30, 41, 64), and we should put our trust in the people (8, 14, 16). Real democracy lets the best of them rule (17). Democracy means self-government, a flourishing opposition, and equal chances for different age groups, ethnic groups, and women (45, 56, 60, 62). The fight against corruption needs to be organized by democratic means (46). The last thing we need is a return to the old, repressive system (21, 39). There are many problems, especially economic ones, but we should not blame democracy for these (20, 25). So let us move forward to making democracy work.

Our second discourse seems only marginally happier with the post-communist status quo than the first, but for opposite reasons: there is not enough "post-" in post-communism. Democratic Development believes Moldova is still controlled by political elites schooled in the communist era, who continue to think in basically the same old ways, and run a corrupt system. But despite its condemnation of the lack of true democracy in post-communist Moldova, this discourse believes there are glimmers of hope for real democratic control in the country. This real democracy would involve equal opportunity that led in the end to rule by the best of the people. Democratic Development's democratic commitments are more evident than its liberal ones. Little provision would need to be made for minority rights (55), though the discourse does believe that members of all ethnic groups should have equal chances. Thus Democratic Development believes there is a democratic project worth pursuing; though there is little evident optimism concerning the prospects for success, especially given the feeling that the Moldovan people are not up to the task of making democracy work.

This Moldovan discourse of Democratic Development bears some resemblance to the Chastened Democracy discourse we found in Russia. Both reject the communist past; both combine a commitment to the ideals of liberal democracy and progress toward these ideals with cynicism about the

Table 10.2. *Subject loadings on factors for Moldova*

Subject and political self-description	Factor	
	A	B
1 F, housekeeper, democrat	15	44*
2 M, driver, no affiliation	40*	49*
3 F, student, apolitical	−10	60*
4 M, student, apolitical	9	26
5 M, driver, apolitical	73*	−2
6 M, student, apolitical	27	54*
7 F, researcher, apolitical	5	68*
8 F, researcher, apolitical	21	57*
9 F, Ministry of Transport expert, apolitical	3	81*
10 F, retired professor, apolitical	59*	−8
11 F, ? (employment not known), apolitical	12	53*
12 M, disabled person, apolitical	12	48*
13 F, housekeeper, apolitical	−9	−9
14 F, worker, social democrat	−8	3
15 M, mechanical engineer, apolitical	47*	36*
16 F, accountant, apolitical	24	41*
17 F, housekeeper, no affiliation	0	9
18 M, worker, apolitical	75*	−15
19 F, nurse, apolitical	−1	43*
20 M, teacher, Christian democrat	−4	45*
21 F, public clerk, apolitical	−1	46*
22 F, pensioner, none	70*	9
23 M, prosecutor, independent	30	57*
24 F, shop assistant, apolitical	42*	4
25 F, nurse, apolitical	63*	13
26 M, professor, ex-communist	37*	40*
27 M, pensioner, apolitical	54*	36*
28 M, doctor, no affiliation	36*	45*
29 F, kindergarten teacher, no affiliation	69*	30
30 F, professor, no affiliation	4	80*
31 F, technician, apolitical	69*	3
32 M, shop assistant, apolitical	31	22
33 M, farmer, apolitical	64*	16
34 M, engineer, apolitical	29	41*
35 M, kindergarten teacher, apolitical	66*	33*
36 M, farmer, left	58*	−28
37 F, shop assistant, no affiliation	89*	5
38 M, farmer, apolitical	9	53*
39 M, driver, apolitical	67*	17
40 F, doctor, apolitical	−10	49*

*Denotes a loading significant at the .01 level.

reality of post-communist political development, even the clear gains that have been made from the perspective of liberal democracy.

Moldova's tenuous democratization

Overall, our results suggest little reason to be especially positive about more authentic democratic development in Moldova (in this, they suggest different conclusions from the upbeat ones of Crowther, 1997a, p. 337). Analysts subscribing to a minimalist or electoralist model of democracy might not be worried; for, as demonstrated again in 1998, Moldova does seem to be able to conduct competitive elections the results of which are respected. For all the struggles within parliament, and between parliament and the president, both sides had by the turn of the century continued to respect the decisions of the constitutional court (see Anon., 2000). Bearing in mind that Moldovan GDP was by the end of the 1990s only about half of what it had been at the start of the decade – having received another major setback in late 1998 with the Russian economic crisis – the new democracy appears *relatively* robust.

All this said, the struggle *is* an uphill one. Although our results confirm that ethnic nationalism is waning in Moldova, this development does not open the door to easy democratic development. The post-communist status quo lacks support from both those who look for a return to the order and discipline of the communist era and those who favor a more liberal and democratic future. In this light, Moldovan democratization remains both a highly limited and highly tenuous accomplishment.

The changing coalitions since 1998, plus President Lucinschi's apparently failed attempts (primarily via a referendum in May 1999) to convert the political system to a presidential one in which parliament would have little say, testify to the continuing fragility of this fledgling democracy even in terms of formal institutions.[3] It is also possible that Moldova will move even closer to Russia if Romania is ever admitted to the European Union; given the ambiguous developments in its huge neighbor since Yeltsin's demise, the implications of this for Moldova's democratization project are difficult to predict. It is in this highly uncertain and unpropitious context that the discourse of Democratic Development rejects not only the current regime, but also the competing discourse that wants to turn back the clock. However, to the extent that this discourse can make its presence felt, there may still be democratic history to be made, and it is premature to deny this possibility.

To those who might think we have contradicted the arguments we made in the chapters on Russia, Ukraine, Armenia, and Georgia about the role

---

[3] Almost two-thirds of those who voted favored increasing the president's powers; but turnout was below the 60 percent minimum required to validate a result.

strong leadership can play in democratizing states, we point out that such leadership must itself be firmly committed to democratization. Lucinschi is a former Moldovan Communist Party first secretary (1989–91) – but we have already allowed that communists do sometimes change their spots. Our concern, therefore, is based more on the fact that even the communists within parliament criticized what they saw as Lucinschi's attempts via the referendum to move the country *away* from democracy. Lucinschi did reluctantly sign a law in July 2000 turning Moldova into a parliamentary republic. Quite what this means for Moldovan democracy is difficult to say at this stage, since the law went against the spirit of the May 1999 referendum, requiring that presidents should in the future be elected by parliament, not the electorate. In Moldova's case, all that is clear is that there is still fierce debate as much *about* the rules as *under* them. Talk of either a strong leadership committed to democracy, or of a consolidating democracy, would therefore be premature.

PART V

Late developers

The three countries considered in part V – Slovakia, Romania, and Bulgaria – were, as of the mid-1990s, regarded by many observers as hopelessly mired in lingering authoritarianism and consigned to a future dominated by ethnic nationalism, having failed to build upon starts made in 1989. In the case of Romania and Bulgaria, this was attributed to their Balkan location and history. Such judgments had to be revised rather quickly in that all three then managed to dispose of quasi-authoritarian governments by electoral means. Thus by the end of the decade they appeared ready to move from a transformation stage (i.e., still dealing with extraction from the past) to a more forward-looking consolidation stage in political development.

11

Slovakia

WITH STEFAN AUER AND ANTOANETA DIMITROVA

From Czechoslovakia to Slovakia

Slovakia's post-communist transition has followed a winding path. When still part of Czechoslovakia in the early 1990s, it was categorized with Poland and Hungary as on the fast track to reform. Its separation from Czechia was accompanied by the emergence of a more authoritarian government that quickly turned Slovakia into the black sheep of this Visegrad family, its route to the European Union blocked by failure to meet the EU's criteria for democracy. Thus Slovakia was left out of the first round of both NATO expansion to the east and the EU's negotiations with potential new members. The new Slovak state faced many challenges, and some deep internal divisions. Yet by the end of the 1990s, Slovakia seemed set fair once again.

The independent Slovak state dates to January 1993, resulting formally from the vote on November 25, 1992, of the Federal Assembly of Czechoslovakia to legislate the "Velvet Divorce" from Czechia. The Divorce did perhaps have deeper roots. The creation of Czechoslovakia in 1918 out of the ruins of the Austro-Hungarian Empire was not entirely happy. Interwar Czechoslovakia was a parliamentary democracy and, apart from East Germany, the most prosperous and industrialized of the countries that were to become part of the Soviet bloc. However, the level of industrialization was much greater in the Czech lands than in Slovakia. During the Second World War, the Czech lands and Slovakia were separated, with a puppet fascist regime running Slovakia. The two parts were reunited after the war, and consigned to the Soviet sphere of influence at Yalta. Stalin hoped that Czechoslovakia would be the one country in Eastern Europe where the communists would come to power legitimately, through the ballot box. Though initially plausible, this did not happen, so a communist takeover had to be engineered in a coup in February 1948, which extinguished liberal democracy (Tigrid, 1975).

Czechoslovakia had one of the more Stalinist regimes until the 1960s, and dissent was harshly suppressed. But major change came in 1968, with the radical liberalization known as the "Prague Spring" (see Skilling, 1976), which recaptured some of the legacy of the interwar liberal democracy. Yet the early 1960s had seen something of a Bratislava Spring. As Karl-Peter Schwarz (1993, p. 191) points out, "in the early sixties there was much more open discussion within the party organizations, editorial offices, and the universities in Slovakia than in the Czech Lands." And the main leader of the Prague Spring was the Slovak reform communist Alexander Dubček.[1] Still, some writers argue that Slovaks saw 1968 as a nationalist opportunity rather than a democratic one (Wolchik, 1992, p. 137; J. Brown, 1994, p. 54).

The Prague Spring was brutally suppressed by the Warsaw Pact in August 1968, and soon Czechoslovakia was again among the more repressive East European states, with a highly orthodox communist regime. A (nonviolent) purge of the party was implemented under the label of "normalization" (see Rupnik, 1981). Led by the most reactionary part of the Czech and Slovak communist elites, the Czechoslovak regime did not reform itself in the slightest until its sudden and rapid collapse in November 1989. One concrete result of 1968 was a formal federalization of the country, symbolically important for some Slovaks. The granting of greater autonomy to Slovakia was the only political reform permitted by the hard-line new leadership under Husák.[2]

There had, then, been a few indications over the decades that some Slovaks had wanted either separation from the Czechs, or greater autonomy within Czechoslovakia. However, many others did *not* want to separate from their Czech neighbors.[3] The Divorce can actually be explained adequately in terms of events beginning in late 1989, which would tend to confirm Fish's (1999) thesis about the importance of "political constructivist" factors (i.e., elite struggles and choices) over political, cultural, or even rational-choice ones. The Divorce has roots – albeit indirectly – in the character of the Velvet Revolution in 1989. The brief round-table talks between the outgoing communist

[1] Dubček certainly supported all but the most radical proposals for reform. But much of the initial impetus for reform came from critical intellectuals.

[2] It can be argued that this was the sole concession to the reformers precisely because it was intended as a sop, and considered by the leadership to be of little consequence. After all, it had no obvious implications for communist rule; the Soviet Union was also a federal state. The fact that both the outgoing leader (Dubček) and Husák himself were Slovaks may also have been a factor.

[3] Even Stanislav Kirschbaum, who is a passionate advocate of Slovak national identity, acknowledges (1995, p. 275) that many Slovaks were "not necessarily uncomfortable" with being part of Czechoslovakia.

government and the civic opposition in November 1989 provided for a transfer of power, but made no reference to constitutional questions. Thus the
communist-era constitution, which provided for mutual veto of the Czech
and Slovak prime ministers, was left in place. Three years of complex constitutional politics followed, as Havel and the other leaders of Civic Forum
appeared to be in no great hurry to establish a new federal constitution.
In this context, the very different outlooks of the market-liberal Klaus government in the Czech lands and the more statist Mečiar government in
Slovakia meant that separation of the two entities suited the agendas of
both prime ministers and their parties. In the communist period, as before
in the interwar era, the level of modernization and industrialization was
generally much higher in the Czech lands, while in Slovakia a more partial
modernization took place. This contrast may help to explain some differences between the two countries in post-separation electoral behavior (and
perhaps also the more prominent rural–urban electoral divide in Slovakia).
(For one of the very few full-length histories of Slovakia in English, see
Kirschbaum, 1995.)

The separation could be free from violence due to a clear ethnic dividing
line and the absence of any disputed territory. Its peaceful character also reflected the lack of antagonism between the two parts of the former federation.
In fact, and in line with our argument about the dangers of overemphasizing
deterministic historical factors, public opinion surveys at the time showed
that most of the population of both Czechia and Slovakia did not support
the separation (Wolchik, 1995, esp. pp. 234–40). The separation was driven
by elites, not by any nationalistic masses.

Post-Divorce: populism, nationalism, and beyond

With no prior history of a Slovak state, save for the Nazi puppet regime between 1939 and 1945, Slovakia shared with Ukraine, Belarus, and Moldova
the problem of establishing statehood in the early years of post-communist
and post-Divorce transition. Unsurprisingly under the circumstances, nationalist politics came to play an important role, which on the face of it was
likely to prove destructive when it came to Slovakia's prospects for democratization, liberalization, and marketization. Our results lend some support
to such warnings, but also reveal some more positive features in Slovakia's
discourses of democracy, including notably a discourse of Developing Pluralism that has little time for ethnic nationalism.

At the moment of transition in 1989, Slovakia developed a counterpart
to the Czech Civic Forum in the form of Public Against Violence, but this
party soon fragmented. The dominant figure in Slovak politics in the decade
after 1989 became the populist nationalist Vladimír Mečiar, who led the

Table 11.2. (*cont.*)

	Factor	
Subject	A	B
41 M, civil engineer, no affiliation	2	31
42 F, graphic designer, SDK coalition	50*	5
43 M, student, SDK or SOP	18	40*

*Denotes a loading significant at the .01 level.
HZDS   Movement for Democratic Slovakia (populist)
MDK   Hungarian Democratic Coalition
SDK   Slovak Democratic Coalition (opposition to HZDS) composed of:
       DS   Democratic Party (conservative)
       KDH   Christian Democratic Party
       SDL   Party of the Democratic Left (reformed communist/social
             democratic)
SNS   Slovak National Party (extreme right nationalist)
SOP   Party for Civic Understanding (new party created to challenge both HZDS
       and established opposition)

stresses the agency of the citizenry rather than elites in the democratization project. The resources of the Developing Pluralism factor should not be turned aside so casually, especially in light of the fact that, even in the midst of the abuses of power by government before 1998, some observers could claim that "Slovakia has an extremely lively civil society and unusually active public participation in political debates" (Kaldor and Vejvoda, 1997, p. 80). According to the European Commission, in 1997 Slovakia had 12,000 registered nongovernmental organizations, despite a restrictive law concerning their foundation (European Commission, 1997, p. 18). Campaigns organized by some of these NGOs, such as the "Rock the Vote" campaign aiming to attract young voters before the September 1998 general elections, were evidence of the broad political mobilization of the supporters of the Developing Pluralism discourse.

The dominant role played by Mečiar and the HZDS party up until their defeat in the 1998 election notwithstanding, our Developing Pluralism discourse confirms that there is another side to politics in Slovakia, represented, as Tétrault and Teske (1997, p. 139) suggest, by "the political opposition, judicial institutions and processes, and an active citizenry, all of which display democratic credentials comparable to their counterparts in the NATO and EU states." However, the continuing popularity of the HZDS in the 1998 elections, in which, recall, it remained the largest single party (with some

27 percent of the vote), suggests that the "active citizenry" and its "demo-cratic credentials" are not all that they might be. Such positive assertions about these credentials are at best misleading, perhaps false, as are those of analysts such as Szomolányi who believe the blame for Slovakia's democratic failures lie primarily with political elites. Some of the blame has to be shared by the citizenry, as we shall now reveal in our second discourse.

Slovakia factor B: Unitary Populism

Our communist past had some good points, but our future is even brighter (33, 34). Those who criticize Slovakia make me angry; we need to strengthen our national pride (56). People here are not fearful and suppressed (31, 48); they are capable of thinking for themselves and not falling victim to politicians' fraud (28, 47). Slovakia has developed the principle of self-government (23). Ideally, all the people would want the same thing, but in practice there are differences of opinions (9, 59). However, in the end the majority must rule (even though the majority can err), and the government that was elected by the people must be allowed to govern (2, 45, 63). The opposition should not create conflicts but in-stead help the nation (63). Minorities should also recognize that the government must govern, and stop complaining that they are not represented (24). The media should stop complaining that they are being pressurized (26). Journalists should not be allowed to write stupid things (51). People should not complain about the state taking taxes from them (8). Everyone, including national minorities, is protected because in a democracy the laws guarantee their equality and their rights (16, 50). A constitution rules, not force (52). Democracy means freedom, so that I can be left alone as long as I do not harass others (1, 39). But there are people who misuse democracy and freedom, especially people who use positions of power for their own gain – politicians must not be allowed to ignore the law (25, 41, 60). Whoever has money has power (13, 36).

In our second factor, Unitary Populism, we can discern many elements of the authoritarian style of the Mečiar regime. All of the subjects who identified themselves as supporters of Mečiar's HZDS and the far-right SNS produced significant loadings on this factor (see table 11.2). Unitary Pop-ulism does claim to believe in democracy, but it is democracy of a decidedly illiberal and anti-pluralist sort. Unitary Populism, as our name for it im-plies, believes in a unitary conception of the public interest as defined by the will of the majority and its implementation by government. The idea that there might be legitimate dissent from this unitary notion is rejected, as is the possibility that people might reasonably disagree about the content of the public interest. The discourse is unitary, too, in its seeming inability to distinguish between the state and the party or coalition in power, under-standable perhaps in light of the fact that, when our interviews were carried out, Slovakia had essentially had only one prime minister.[6] Our interviews were conducted in 1998 before the Mečiar government was ousted; those subscribing to this discourse presumably experienced a rude awakening. Indeed, the result of these elections in a way constituted a falsification of a key part of Unitary Populism.

Unitary Populism's commitments to constitutional government, under which minorities are protected, seem rhetorical in light of the refusal to accept the legitimacy of criticism from ethnic minorities, and the casual attitude to freedom of the press and the legitimacy of opposition. Such aspects are consistent with Szomolányi's observation that, ever since the split of Czechoslovakia, citizens have been "informally divided into categories of 'good Slovaks' and 'bad Slovaks' – the latter being ethnic Slovaks who were against the division of the former Czechoslovakia and the independent statehood of the Slovak republic" (1997, p. 27).

The positive remembrance of the communist past is also somewhat ominous when it comes to this discourse's constitutionalist credentials. The discourse is populist in its faith in the good sense of the people, and its stress that politicians must not be able to use their offices to enrich themselves. Unitary Populism does not proclaim the desirability of oppression of ethnic minorities, but it clearly trumpets Slovak nationalism – consistent with its unitary notion of the public interest.

Prospects

As we saw at the outset, most observers of the prospects for authentic democracy in contemporary Slovakia have been divided into two camps. The more negative puts Slovakia in the group of countries in which ethnic nationalism and traditions of subjugation guarantee a bleak future in which the only movement likely or possible is in an authoritarian direction. But, in terms of deep history and "cultural traditions," it should be remembered that Slovakia was *also* part of the relatively successful Czechoslovak state of the interwar years, its subsequent fascist interlude notwithstanding. The more positive view claims that the fault lies only with elites who have behaved badly, that the citizenry itself is more committed to liberal and democratic principles. Our results show that both camps are wrong, because both tend to treat Slovak political culture as a single entity. The negative camp's dire predictions are called into question by the presence of the Developing Pluralism discourse. The positive camp is wrong to blame only the elites. The

---

[6] The term "essentially" is used because Mečiar was in fact replaced by Jozef Moravčik for a few months in 1994; but the latter was little more than a caretaker prime minister.

presence of Unitary Populism shows that misbehaving elites can call upon a supportive discourse among the citizenry.

Our results also falsify the maps of those who put Slovakia on the wrong side of a dividing line in CEE. If there is a dividing line, it runs right through Slovakia – not in any neat geographical sense,[7] but rather in terms of a sharp division between one discourse committed to civic, democratic, and constitutional norms, and another which sees democracy in more unitary, populist, nationalist, and oppressive terms. A great deal turns on the relative weight of these two discourses of democracy in Slovakia.

---

[7] Though, as we indicated above, there is something of a rural–urban divide in voting patterns.

12

Romania

WITH BOGDAN CHIRITOIU

Of the former members of the Soviet bloc, Romania was the last domino to fall in 1989, differing from its predecessors primarily in the violence associated with its transition. Prior to December 1989, there had been virtually nothing in the way of organized protest against or overt opposition to the communist regime. This was despite an attack during the 1980s on the cultural and political identity of the Hungarian minority in Transylvania. However, it was among this minority that the first serious challenges to the communist regime were made. Anti-regime protests, led by a Hungarian priest, began on December 16 in the city of Timişoara. Despite receiving a violent response, they spread to Bucharest, and to the majority Romanian population by December 21. The following day President Ceauşescu attempted to flee his capital. Ceauşescu had believed he could remain in power, especially with the aid of the Securitate secret police. But segments of the Communist Party and the Securitate, with the support of the army, defected from the regime to depose Ceauşescu, who was executed on Christmas Day after a secret and speedy trial that paid little attention to legal niceties (see Ratesh, 1991; Rady, 1992).

These events were not in and of themselves a clear transition away from communism, though the new leadership tried to emphasize its discontinuities with the communist era. As in Bulgaria, what took place at the top was more of a coup on the part of a section of the old regime, or at best a "revolution from above." In Romania, the communists in question expanded their membership to form the National Salvation Front, which subsequently dominated Romanian politics in the early and mid-1990s. The Front's leader, Ion Iliescu, was elected president in 1990, and the Front also won the first parliamentary elections, governing with the support of two radical nationalist parties, the Romania National Unity Party and the Greater Romania Party. The constitution adopted in 1991 was based on the French semi-presidential model, though differing significantly in that the Romanian president cannot dissolve parliament.

The Iliescu regime was reluctant to jettison all the trappings of its pre-decessor. In particular, it exerted substantial control over the media, and reconstituted the secret police in the form of the Romanian Information Service (not quite as fearsome as the Securitate). The regime did not feel obliged to play by constitutional rules, and in this sense compares badly with Bulgaria. In June 1990, Iliescu called in miners from the Jiu Valley to disperse demonstrators in Bucharest demanding more authentic liberalization and democracy, and publicly thanked them after they had used violence to silence the protestors. Between 1990 and 1999 the miners arrived in Bucharest a total of six times. (To a considerably lesser extent, the miners had established a rep-utation as being highly politicized even in the communist era.)[1] Economic reform proceeded very slowly, and the Iliescu regime did little to stem eco-nomic decline. Radical nationalists were part of the governing coalition until 1996. Iliescu himself explicitly denied that institutionalized opposition was a necessary component of democracy. Still, opposition parties were able to operate, if not as freely as in other Central and East European countries. And the Front itself soon revealed its own factional pluralism, culminating in a split in 1992 into two parties. The larger of these, associated with President Iliescu, named itself the Party of Social Democracy in Romania (PDSR).[2] The smaller, led by former Prime Minister Petre Roman into opposition, became the Democratic Party, eventually moving in a more liberal direction (on these developments, see Gallagher, 1995b). Iliescu eventually attempted to break a constitutional rule forbidding one person seeking a third term as president.

The uninspiring manner of Romania's extrication from communism and the lingering authoritarianism of the first post-communist regime provided plenty of grist to the mills of those who classified Romania as on the wrong side of the dividing line in CEE. To Huntington (1996), it is a matter of most of Romania belonging in the Orthodox civilization. For Vachudová and Snyder (1997), the problem is the same as in Bulgaria and Yugoslavia: poli-tics is dominated by ex-communists turned into ethnic nationalists, who can deliver only populism and authoritarianism (see also Dellenbrant, 1994).[3]

[1] Notably during the Jiu Valley strike of 1977.
[2] A much smaller party takes the Romanian acronym PSDR: the Romanian Social Democratic Party, a member of the Socialist International allied with Roman's Democratic Party, not with Iliescu's PDSR.
[3] One of the problems with this representation is that it does not recognize that nationalism had become a salient feature of the communist era, too. Romanian communist nationalism

Stereotypes about primordial Balkan ethnic conflicts and Byzantine influences inhibiting democracy complete the picture.[4] There was indeed some localized violence between Hungarians and Romanians in 1990, and vigilante actions against Gypsies[5] in rural areas have occasionally been taken. Yet most such conflict in Romania since 1990 has been negotiated peacefully, with ethnic issues between the Hungarians and Romanians, at least, having all but disappeared from the political agenda since the Hungarian–Romanian treaty of September 1996 (Pippidi, 1999, p. 145).

The dire prognostications received a further setback with the results of the presidential and parliamentary elections held in November 1996. Iliescu and his PDSR were defeated by an alliance between Roman's Democratic Party, the Democratic Convention – itself a coalition the dominant member of which was the National Peasant Christian Democratic Party (NPCDP) – and the Hungarian Democratic Union of Romania (HDUR), representing the 7 percent Hungarian minority concentrated in Transylvania. The presence in this alliance and subsequent government of an ethnic minority's party, which Pippidi (1999, p. 136) sees as the first step toward consociational democracy in Romania, calls into question analyses that consign the countries of Southeastern Europe to an authoritarian if not violent future dominated by ethnic nationalism. Further, this party comes from the other side of Huntington's civilizational divide; he draws the eastern boundary of West European civilization through Romania, separating Hungarian and Catholic Transylvania from the Orthodox majority in the remainder of Romania. (Huntington ignores the fact that Transylvania has a large Romanian and so Orthodox majority.)

Significantly, the election results were accepted by the outgoing regime, so that Romania finally looked more secure on its road to post-communist democratic transition. But to the consternation of some observers, the largest party in the governing coalition, the NPCDP, had proclaimed in its platform that it wished to restore the interwar constitution, complete with monarchy. The NPCDP had voted against the 1991 constitution (in part because it

under Ceaușescu had since the 1960s been directed against Hungarians; see Verdery, 1991, esp. pp. 116–34.

[4] Thus Ágh, 1999, p. 277, writes, "historically, as well as in the present situation, all Balkan states are latecomers in both nation-building and democratisation." This generalization would be more plausible if it were not that Ágh draws a sharp distinction between Central European and Balkan states. For a reference to Byzantine influences on Romanian politics, albeit primarily with reference to the later communist era, see Tismaneanu, 1999, p. 156. Some analysts have, however, refuted notions of a fundamental divide in CEE, providing both nuanced and relatively optimistic accounts of Romanian politics – see, e.g., Mihut, 1994.

[5] In this chapter alone we use the term "Gypsy" rather than "Roma" to avoid confusion with "Romanian."

contained insufficient guarantees for private property), as had the HDUR (the latter because the first article in the constitution proclaims Romania a national state). Thus, to use the distinction made by Elster, Offe, and Preuss (1998, p. 247), two of the main governing parties appear not to be committed to politics *within* constitutional rules as distinct from politics *about* constitutional rules. It is of course the former that can within limits (see chapter 1) be seen as one of the hallmarks of a consolidated democracy. In this aspect, Romania would seem to compare badly with Bulgaria, where constitutional rules have been accepted by all the significant political parties. Thus, the extent to which the 1996 election constitutes a landmark on the road to democracy would depend on the capacity of the Democratic Party to renounce its authoritarian roots in the National Salvation Front, the NPCDP to look to the future rather than to a failed past, and the HDUR both to present and to accept negotiable demands when it comes to the interests of the Hungarian minority.

At the time of writing, the indications are that the parties of the governing coalition have indeed moved in these directions. After the 1996 election, the NPCDP played down the monarchy issue. While the formal commitment was retained, it began to take on a character similar to that which Clause Four (committing the party to workers' control) long had in the constitution of the British Labour Party: a symbol that could not be jettisoned, but which nobody believed could be put into practice. Thus none of the governing parties took any steps toward amending the constitution after 1996. Indeed, several leading politicians have indicated that they do not wish to provoke instability at a time when Romania is anxious to join the European Union (formal negotiations on membership began in early 2000).

Economic reform, too, gathered pace after the 1996 election, with International Monetary Fund prompting and assistance, especially in terms of privatization and the reduction of state subsidies. Macroeconomic policy throughout the 1990s oscillated between periods of IMF-approved stabilization when economic output fell, and periods of relaxation when inflation took off. Manufacturing output fell throughout, and at the end of the 1990s Romania was still experiencing annual falls in its GDP: −6.6 percent and −5.5 percent in 1997 and 1998 respectively.[6]

Romania's deeper history might appear less than inspirational in terms of the provision of cultural memories to which democrats might appeal. The country was created in 1859 by the unification of the Ottoman principalities of Moldavia and Wallachia, which eventually became the Kingdom of Romania. Although this was a constitutional monarchy, its democratic

---

[6] It should, however, be noted that Romania has experienced positive growth in some years of the 1990s – notably 1995 and 1996. Limited positive growth (c. 1.5 percent) was also predicted for 2000.

elements were very limited; the monarch had substantial authority and the people few protections against the power of government. After the First World War Romania doubled its size and population with the addition of Bessarabia (now in Moldova) from Russia, and Transylvania and Bukovina from the Austro-Hungarian Empire, the latter leaving a substantial (now 7 percent) Hungarian minority in Romania. Interwar Romania remained a constitutional monarchy, but became a full-blown authoritarian regime in 1938, and a fascist one, aligned with Germany, during the Second World War. (On the prewar history, see Fischer-Galati, 1991; on the fascist period, see Nagy-Talavera, 1967.) The communist regime that was installed after the war was unremittingly Stalinist at home, though, particularly after the coming to power of Ceaușescu in 1965, Romania pursued the most independent foreign policy within the Soviet bloc, to applause from the West. Ceaușescu encouraged Romanian nationalism, which was even at times directed against Russia. He insulated Romania from Gorbachev-era reform currents, and no moves were taken in the direction of economic and political reform prior to 1989. The country was the most totalitarian in the Soviet bloc in the 1970s and 1980s. The Securitate kept a firm lid on dissent, such that there was no real organized opposition to the old regime prior to its downfall, only isolated individual dissidents. The regime had strong sultanistic features, for with time control passed from the *nomenklatura* to Ceaușescu, his family, and their associates, who enriched themselves at the country's expense. This was the era of so-called socialism in one family (see Flers, 1984). Come 1989, Romania was one of the poorest countries in Europe, and so it remains. (On the communist era, see Ionescu, 1964; Gilberg, 1990. For statistics on the Romanian economy, see *BCE* online.[7])

Despite the seemingly uninspirational character of the deeper history when it comes to the prospects for democracy, it conditions the pattern of party politics in Romania more profoundly than in any other post-communist country. The NPCDP and its partner in the Democratic Convention, the smaller National Liberal Party, both claim to be direct heirs to precommunist parties, while the Party of Social Democracy is dominated by politicians who made their start in the communist regime.

We classify Romania as a late starter, though not necessarily a chronic laggard, because the early 1990s really did reveal substantial continuities with the old regime. After the 1996 election a more authentic and liberal democracy looked to be on the cards, and the number of nongovernmental organizations has increased markedly since then (though by any standards Romanian civil society remains weak). By the criteria of minimalist scholars and observers of transition at least, Romania had shown that it could hold

---

[7] Business Central Europe Online, http://www.bcemag.com.

reasonably free elections, with any unfairness caused by the authoritarian dispositions of the outgoing Iliescu regime proving unable to prevent an opposition victory.

Our results will show that question marks remain concerning democracy in Romania, though these have little to do with nationalism and ethnic conflict.

Romanian discourses of democracy

Our discussion groups and interviews were carried out in 1997–8, and so followed soon after the landmark 1996 elections that had brought the three-party alliance to power. Through factor analysis of Q sorts for thirty-one subjects (interviewed in Bucharest, Cluj, and Iasi; five subjects were Romanians interviewed outside the country), we identified three discourses of democracy in Romania. We name these factors Liberal Democracy, Civic Fundamentalism, and Deferential Collectivism. We are confident that Liberal Democracy and Civic Fundamentalism represent discourses with an important presence in post-communist Romania. We are somewhat less confident about making the same claim for Deferential Collectivism. The reason is that shortcomings in securing variety in subject selection meant that we had to relax the standards of internal coherence, breadth, and distinctiveness of support among the subjects that we normally apply when it comes to deciding whether or not to report a factor. These shortcomings in subject selection meant that we were less certain than usual that the readily identified factors (in this case, the first two) really did constitute a reasonably comprehensive discursive map for the country. In other words, we have to squeeze the data harder for Romania than for the other countries in this study. The Romanian factor of Deferential Collectivism represents the only such lapse in all our countries. There is also an interpretive judgment involved here; without this third factor, the Romanian results appear almost too good to be true. (In the narratives, numbers in parentheses refer to the statements from the first table.)

Romania factor A: Liberal Democracy

Democratic politics can be informed by moral values (51), but this does not mean that there is a single truth, be it an ideology or religion (42). In a multinational and multicultural democracy, tolerance of those with different beliefs is vital (44, 55). Compromise is necessary between people with different beliefs, and pragmatism rather than ideology must guide political action (58, 59). While there is no need to expect consensus on values, consensus on the rules of democracy itself is vital (11). Democracy can survive only if people support it (30). Democracy also

Table 12.1. *Statement scores on three factors for Romania*

Factor A is Liberal Democracy.
Factor B is Civic Fundamentalism.
Factor C is Deferential Collectivism.

Statement	Factor		
	A	B	C
1 Democracy means the right of the people to choose how society develops.	−1	+1	−2
2 Democracy means the separation of powers and a multiparty system.	+6	+5	+6
3 Democracy means changing the government by the people's vote.	+3	+1	+5
4 Democracy does not mean absence of state authority.	+4	+2	+4
5 Democracy means an unwritten social contract in which, through voting, ordinary citizens bestow their confidence on leaders in order for the latter to solve their problems.	+1	+1	+3
6 Regardless of the democratic or nondemocratic character of a regime, the individual is only the tool of political power.	−3	−6	−1
7 Democracy is mobilizing in order to achieve something for yourself.	−2	0	0
8 Democracy entails that the majority does whatever it wishes.	−6	−3	−3
9 If democracy breaks down in Romania, I will leave the country.	−1	−3	+1
10 Today in Romania most people do not care about democracy; they are too concerned with economic conditions.	0	0	+2
11 A democratic regime can survive without a consensus regarding values, but not without a consensus concerning the basic rules of the political game.	+5	−2	−1
12 In order to have a democracy, you must force people to recognize their own interests.	−3	−2	0
13 Our type of bureaucracy is incompatible with democracy.	0	+4	+1
14 The main idea of communism is doing away with all kinds of inequalities in society. Therefore equality is better accomplished in communism than in democracy.	−4	−5	+1
15 Democracy can be part of any political system, except the totalitarian one.	+2	−1	−1
16 The higher the number of parties, the more democratic the system is.	−4	−2	0
17 Our democracy today is built on the principles of the French Revolution: equality, liberty, fraternity.	−2	−5	0
18 The Scandinavian countries are examples of real democracies.	+1	−1	+1
19 Real politics runs on information and money.	+2	+3	+2
20 The Romanian democratic process is nothing but a sham.	−4	0	−2

Table 12.1. (*cont.*)

	Factor		
Statement	A	B	C
21 In our democracy the duties of citizens cease after the payment of taxes.	+2	−6	−1
22 During communism everyone worked for others, while in a democracy everyone works for themselves.	−2	−1	−1
23 In an authentic democracy, civil society and power are fighting permanently.	−1	+5	0
24 Romanians misunderstand democracy.	0	+1	+1
25 Where respect among people is lacking, we cannot speak of democracy.	0	+6	−2
26 Democracy is meaningless for those who don't have power.	−3	−3	−3
27 Private property strengthens competition without which one cannot speak of democracy.	+3	+3	−4
28 In a society in which individuals cannot have private material autonomy, democracy can survive only by artificial means.	+1	−1	−5
29 We have rights, but we cannot enjoy them because we don't have a civic culture.	0	+4	−6
30 Democracy can prevail in a country only if the mentality of the people is adjusted to the already existing democratic institutions.	+3	+4	+6
31 The lack of democracy in Romania stems from the fact that good laws are not respected.	−2	+1	+5
32 Democracy works best with people who do not care too deeply.	−3	0	+2
33 Communism identifies democracy with anarchism or "anything goes," due to a false formulation of the need for order.	−1	−1	+4
34 Democracy in practice means only that the majority of the population is systematically manipulated by political elites.	−3	−5	+3
35 The overemphasized equality which prevailed under communism was detrimental to spiritual life due to censorship and repression of free thought and expression.	+1	+1	+3
36 Romania is currently democratic, but its democracy is of a very low quality.	+1	+2	−4
37 The democratic regime in Romania is the result only of international pressure and not of the popular will.	0	0	+2
38 Our politicians have learned communist politics. Really valuable politicians are lacking because they lack experience.	−1	+3	+1
39 Formerly, as a subject of the Romanian kingdom, I was living in a more democratic society than today.	−4	−1	−3
40 Because of democracy, people no longer work.	−6	−4	−2
41 People elect those who resemble them.	+1	−2	0

Table 12.1. (*cont.*)

Statement	Factor		
	A	B	C
42 One cannot be a good democrat if one does not fear God.	−5	+6	−1
43 Democracy is preserved even if political elites act against the general will, but in accordance with democratic principles.	+3	−2	0
44 Tolerance is a vital characteristic of democracy.	+4	+1	−1
45 People are not equal. Those who work and study hard become superior to those who do not, and consequently deserve more than they would get under communism.	+3	0	−2
46 In democracy the better argument has priority.	−2	+2	−3
47 Democracy is undermined by the existence of social classes and social inequalities.	−1	−2	−4
48 Local autonomy is essential for democracy, because problems can always be solved better in a decentralized way.	+4	+3	−5
49 What we ought to have in common is only the rules, not any other shared values.	−2	−1	−6
50 Multinationalism and multiculturalism should be characteristics of democracy.	+4	0	+5
51 Democracy must be subordinated to moral values.	+2	+1	+4
52 One of the features of democracy is that people do not have to agree on common goals.	−1	−3	+1
53 The most important thing in a democracy is that we all serve a common goal.	−1	−1	+3
54 Democracy entails that the majority does whatever it wishes.	−5	−4	+2
55 In a democracy, the most competent should be elected leaders.	0	+2	+2
56 In a democratic country, the state should provide social security for its citizens.	+1	+2	+1
57 One has to be democratic in one's own sentiments too.	+1	+3	0
58 Compromise is an essential feature of democracy.	+5	−4	−1
59 Pragmatism must guide any democratic political action.	+2	−3	+3
60 In our society, managers have great powers in deciding the fate of the institutions led by them and in determining the behavior of employees. Therefore, they should strive to set an example.	0	0	−2
61 Democracy must be a balance between respecting the rights of minorities and respecting the will of the majority.	+5	+5	−3
62 In a crisis, democracy should be given up in favor of more efficient methods of governance.	−5	−4	+4
63 There can be no democracy without a legal system set up in the interests of the free individual because otherwise there is no possibility for individuals to limit political power.	+6	+2	−4
64 Democracy requires that people are aware of their rights.	+2	+4	−5

Table 12.2. *Subject loadings on factors for Romania*

		Factor		
Subject		A	B	C
1	F, pensioner, moderate liberal	59*	51*	4
2	F, public relations manager, social democrat	63*	34*	−2
3	F, accountant, Christian Democrat	14	51*	28
4	F, retired, independent	0	38*	13
5	M, sports trainer, social democrat	37*	23	1
6	M, engineer (?), independent	4	21	0
7	M, student, liberal	52*	45*	6
8	M, retired, national-conservative	51*	39*	11
9	F, secretary, independent	34*	42*	1
10	M, manager, liberal	66*	24	−6
11	F, salesperson, liberal	69*	20	33*
12	F, researcher, social liberal	67*	23	−1
13	M, civil servant, independent	68*	−7	−4
14	F, academic, social liberal	40*	27	10
15	F, student, neutral	17	55*	12
16	M, student, no affiliation	16	25	0
17	M, professor, noncommitted	47*	52*	0
18	M, student, liberal democrat	37*	50*	−6
19	M, editor, ? (views not known)	6	−1	42*
20	F, foundation manager, ? (views not known)	34*	56*	7
21	M, designer, ? (views not known)	62*	26	0
22	F, student, liberal	−24	−58*	42*
23	M, teacher, ? (views not known)	57*	51*	−4
24	? (sex not known), engineer, ? (views not known)	59*	25	−1
25	F, retired journalist, liberal	41*	29	1
26	F, retired professor, ? (views not known)	46*	57*	6
27	F, economist, no affiliation	33*	71*	5
28	M, economist, no affiliation	31	46*	−2
29	M, archeologist, no affiliation	40*	9	18
30	M, journalist, liberal	57*	20	26
31	M, journalist, liberal	2	18	22

*Denotes a loading significant at the .01 level.

requires constitutional government. The rule of law is absolutely essential to limit political power and guarantee the freedom of individuals (63, 64). So the majority cannot do whatever it wishes, for minority rights also need to be respected (8, 54, 61). There must be a separation of powers and a multiparty system (2), though a large number of parties does not make the system any more democratic (16). Leaders must act in accordance with democratic rules and principles, so that, even if they are acting against public opinion, democracy is preserved (43). In Romania we are now moving slowly toward real democracy, though there is still a long way to go (20, 34, 36). We have put the undemocratic past of the Romanian kingdom and communism behind us (14, 39). Communism was supposed to give equality, but people are not equal, and those who study and work harder deserve to get ahead, unlike under communism (45). Private property strengthens competition and so democracy (27). Local autonomy is a good idea (48).

Our first Romanian discourse is fairly conventional in its liberal and democratic commitments – though its very existence might come as a surprise to many observers. The discourse is committed to the market economy, private property, individual rights, minority rights, equality of opportunity (but not of reward), constitutional government with a separation of powers, representative multiparty democracy, and a politics of compromise. The discourse is pluralistic in its approach to political values and actions. The accent is in the end on liberalism rather than democracy, for in tune with classical liberal thinking the discourse believes that public opinion can err, such that rule-abiding leadership can and should ignore public opinion when necessary. The Romanian discourse of Liberal Democracy looks to the future (and, one suspects, the West) rather than the precommunist past. Indeed, it explicitly rejects the interwar kingdom as a model (thus also rejecting one element of the platform of the NPCDP, the largest party in the governing coalition). Liberal democratic development is seen as a project on which Romania has embarked, but on which there is still a long way to go. Those loading on this factor would doubtless be pleased and reassured that Romania has now commenced accession negotiations with the EU.

It is not easy to map this discourse of Liberal Democracy onto the prevailing pattern of party politics in Romania. We suspect it cuts across the major parties, consistent with the perspective of Romanian analysts who speak of the existence of reformist and conservative factions present in all parties. This has no *necessary* negative consequences for the stability of party politics; significant discourses that cut across party affiliations can be found, for example, in the United States too (Dryzek and Berejikian, 1993).[8]

Romanian factor A is straightforward in its relation to conventional models of democracy, and in its similarity to discourses we have found in other countries. Our second and third Romanian discourses have no such parallels, be it in democratic theory or the kinds of discourses we have found elsewhere. They suggest that plenty of scope for learning about democracy remains in Romania.

---

[8] In chapter 16 we will, however, suggest that one way to secure party system stability is by alignment with a country's discursive field.

Romania factor B: Civic Fundamentalism

Romania is democratic, but not yet a high-quality democracy, for it does not fully represent the ideals of equality, liberty, and fraternity (17, 36). One problem is that the kind of bureaucracy we have in Romania is incompatible with democracy (13). Also, too many politicians learned their politics under communism, and so we lack politicians with the right kind of experience (38). They should not act against public opinion, even if they are obeying the rules (43). People must adjust their beliefs to democratic institutions (30, 57), but that is not enough. We also need stronger respect because, when respect among people is lacking, we cannot speak of democracy (25). A democratic system needs a consensus on values, not just the rules of the game (11). One cannot just believe anything and be a democrat; one cannot be a good democrat if one does not fear God (42). Thus we must unite toward common goals (52). In a democracy, the good arguments win (46). Compromise is not part of democracy; there should be no compromise between good and bad (58), no pragmatic search for the middle ground (59). And we need a stronger civic culture and civil society, without which we cannot enjoy our rights (23, 29). Individuals do not have to be manipulated by the politically powerful (6, 34). People need to be more aware of their rights (64), but also of their obligations; citizens have duties far beyond the payment of taxes (21, 23). The minority has rights too, so the majority cannot do whatever it wishes (54, 61). Democracy should be able to promote equality better than communism did (14). Democracy also requires the separation of powers, a multiparty system, private property that promotes competition, and local autonomy (2, 27, 48, 63).

Our second Romanian discourse, Civic Fundamentalism, appears to embody a paradox, reflected in our title for it, which seems like a contradiction in terms. On the one hand, it is committed to some of the same norms as Liberal Democracy: the separation of powers, constitutional government, private property, a multiparty system, liberty, and the rights of individuals and minorities. But a closer look reveals that Civic Fundamentalism is not especially liberal or pluralistic. The discourse is highly moralistic in its portrayal of a unitary public good which all must accept; there is no tolerance of compromise, for politics is seen in terms of right and wrong, black and white, rather than shades of gray. There is no middle ground to seek. Though Civic Fundamentalism rejects the communist past and is impatient with the pace of change away from communism, in this uncompromising aspect it reveals continuity with the terms of communist-era politics, if only as a mirror image.

The proclamation that one must believe in God to be a good democrat suggests that this is a Christian democratic discourse, and there is indeed some resemblance between Civic Fundamentalism and the positions taken by the National Peasant Christian Democratic Party. The wing of the NPCDP grouped around Victor Ciorbea, prime minister following the 1996 election until April 1998, is sometimes referred to by Romanians as their "Taliban," on the grounds of its moralistic approach to politics. We have already noted that the NPCDP regards itself as a successor to a precommunist party, and perhaps Civic Fundamentalism as a discourse is continuous with this backward-looking aspect of Romanian politics. Its uneasy juxtaposition of absolutism when it comes to the truth and democratic forms when it comes to procedures reflects part of the ethos of interwar Romanian politics.

Civic Fundamentalism bears some superficial similarities to the republican discourses we found in Poland and Czechia, notably in terms of its emphasis on civic virtues, the duties of citizens, and political equality. But, to Civic Fundamentalism, political truth is something that exists and should prevail, rather than something to be discovered through democratic debate, and so the discourse is not republican. This attitude begs the question of what is to be done about those who disagree with Civic Fundamentalism's notion of the truth – especially if these people should prevail on an important issue. It is easy to imagine a scenario in which a commitment to the perceived truth, or "public opinion" as conceptualized by Civic Fundamentalism, overrides a commitment to the procedures of constitutional democracy, one of the defining features of which is, of course, the willingness on the part of key participants to accept defeat under constitutional rules. This discourse is truly fundamentalist, with all the dangers to democracy this connotes.

Romania factor C: Deferential Collectivism

People in Romania now need to adjust to the fact that Romania has high-quality democratic institutions with a supporting culture (29, 30, 36). We have a multiparty system, and the separation of powers, and government can be changed by the people's vote (2, 3). Communism, which overemphasized equality and denigrated democracy, is now behind us (33, 35). The main problem today is that good laws are not respected (31). We need to let strong leaders solve our problems, and the state must be allowed to exercise authority (4, 5, 59). Local autonomy must not be allowed to obstruct state authority (48), nor should we worry too much about the need to balance minority rights against majority rule, though we should accept that Romania is a multicultural society (50, 61). Democracy is about the pursuit of the common interest, not individual rights, so we should not let the legal system get in the way by limiting the power of government (63, 64). The common interest is defined in terms of moral values, not just the rules of democracy, and democracy should serve this morality (49, 51). Indeed, in a crisis we may have to give up democracy in favor of more efficient methods of government (62). Democracy is based on morality, not on economics; private property and competition are not the foundation for democracy (10, 27, 28). On the other hand, nor is material equality (47).

Deferential Collectivism proclaims a commitment to the symbols and forms of democracy, but closer inspection shows that this commitment is paper-thin. Democracy serves the public interest, and is regarded as dispensable should crisis demand it. The collectivism of the discourse arises in connection with its hostility to markets, private property, and individual rights, and so to key principles of liberalism. As with Civic Fundamentalism, the public interest is defined in unitary terms, but otherwise the content of that public interest is not entirely clear. Any common goals do not involve the sort of material redistribution to which collectivists are normally committed. Deferential Collectivism rejects both the pursuit of material equality and an emphasis on market competition. Thus it is not easily placed on any conventional left–right spectrum. Deferential Collectivism is illiberal in its lack of regard for individual rights and the rule of law, as well as its attitude to market competition. Of the three Romanian discourses, this is the one happiest with the post-communist status quo. It is deferential in its attitude to political leadership and state authority, and perhaps that deference extends even to the definition of the public good. Thus there is such a thing as the common good, political leaders can pursue it, and partial interests and individual rights should not be allowed to get in the way. Deferential Collectivism does not appear to be especially nationalistic, perhaps because its unitary notion of politics cannot recognize conflict between nationalities within a country as a problem.

Prospects

Romania is undeniably a late starter in the post-communist democratization stakes, and this lateness is perhaps reflected in the configuration of the discourses we have identified. The good news for democrats is that all three of the discourses proclaim commitment to constitutional government. Moreover, ethnic nationalism, nostalgia for the communist past, and explicit support for authoritarianism all appear to be weak, thus contradicting a number of stereotypes about Romania. Ethnic nationalism might conceivably make itself felt in connection with the kind of uncomplicated and unitary view of the public interest that appears in our second and third discourses, Civic Fundamentalism and Deferential Collectivism. Support for a return to communism seems to have been banished more comprehensively, which is hardly surprising given Romania's dismal experience in the Ceauşescu era. The silver lining of this experience is that Romania lacks the kind of nostalgic, anti-democratic discourse found next door in Moldova. This contrast in turn suggests that simplistic ethnic determinist accounts of political culture are misplaced; the past does matter, but in terms of the political memories it supplies, not any cultural determinism.

But if we scratch the surface, we find that of our three Romanian discourses only Liberal Democracy has a commitment to constitutional democratic norms that could survive stormy weather. For Civic Fundamentalism, the storm would involve a government that strays from the straight and narrow in terms of the values the discourse supports. For Deferential Collectivism, the storm would more likely involve political or economic crisis; but even in the absence of such a crisis, this discourse wants political leadership and not the citizenry to play the dominant role. It is easy to imagine circumstances in which both sorts of storm coincide, such that two out of three discourses might withdraw their support for constitutional government.

While the authoritarian option receives no explicit support in our Romanian discourses, its banishment seems less secure than does that of nostalgia for the communist era. Deferential Collectivism appears prepared to accept its return in a crisis, and the politics of uncomplicated truth to which Civic Fundamentalism subscribes could easily take an authoritarian turn, of the sort seen as possible by observers such as Dellenbrant (1994, esp. p. 216). In this respect the configuration of discourses in Romania compares poorly with that in Bulgaria. In Bulgaria, constitutionalism receives more universal assent, and democratic politics under constitutional rules is more widely and securely recognized as the only game in town. This difference reflects perhaps the more ingrained tradition of constitutional government in Bulgaria prior to the communist era. On the other hand, Romania reveals little of the nationalism and isolationism we found in Bulgaria.

The configuration of discourses of democracy in Romania as analyzed in this chapter appears to be finely balanced. One suspects that the prospects for democracy in Romania turn less on the comparative strength of Liberal Democracy and its two competitors, more on the degree to which these two more problematic discourses can learn a little more about what any kind of democratic politics – be it liberal, republican, participatory, or elitist – has to entail. One can imagine Civic Fundamentalism undergoing transformation with time into a more republican discourse, in which political truth is seen as the product of debate, rather than something that exists in advance of debate. There would be no need for Civic Fundamentalism to abandon its moralistic ideas about the need to pursue the common good, just to accept that there might be competing notions of the good, which could be reconciled in public deliberation. Deferential Collectivism might in its turn learn to deepen what is currently a very superficial commitment to the symbols and forms of democracy, though such learning might well occur only to the extent that democracy in Romania can show an ability to negotiate crises and deliver the goods without any need for a more authoritarian alternative.

The democratic shortcomings of Civic Fundamentalism and Deferential Collectivism may stem from the fact that both are products of a country with extremely limited experience of compromise politics and its possibilities. That is, the problems associated with these discourses may simply be indicative of a lack of maturity when it comes to thinking about and within democracy. We have suggested that there is scope for transformation of these two discourses in a positive direction, but we can also imagine less positive futures. As the case of Russia demonstrates, if experience with notionally democratic forms coincides with rampant corruption, incivility, and economic decline, then that experience does not necessarily lead to greater support for the idea of democracy (liberal or otherwise). Hence, these two Romanian discourses could also change in directions far less conducive to greater democratic authenticity.

At the time of writing it appeared that ex-president Iliescu might be about to win reelection to the presidency and, if the PDSR also wins the parliamentary elections, a setback for democratization could be in store. But, as mentioned above, Romania's attempts to join the EU should counter Iliescu's questionable commitment to democracy. Moreover, the PDSR itself has in recent years committed to the EU project, and has been trying to present itself as a more moderate social democratic party – though this remains to be proven. The significance of the EU connection places substantial responsibility on "the West" – and drives home our point that treating countries such as Romania as "the other" is counterproductive when it comes to democratization as well as questionable in scholarly terms.

There would appear to remain a substantial need for democratic learning in Romania. Democracy is not yet clearly and finally the only game in town. However, our empirical analysis shows that nationalism, violent or otherwise, is not a key component of Romanian politics that will hamper democratization. In addition, we have demonstrated the existence of substantial discursive resources available for democratic learning in a citizenry more politically diverse than is often claimed.

13

Bulgaria

WITH ANTOANETA DIMITROVA

To the careful observer, of whom there have been too few, Bulgaria presents a democratization paradox.[1] Cursory assessments by those who appear not to have studied the country in depth have often tended to be negative, consigning Bulgaria to the long-term laggard category. Such assessments are influenced by the image of the Balkans as backward. Some writers with deeper knowledge of Central and Eastern Europe have reached the same conclusion. For example, Gati (1996, esp. pp. 169–71 and 193) expected Bulgaria to become ever more clearly a "semiauthoritarian regime."[2] Vachudová and Snyder (1997) argue that the dominance of "nationalist former communists" in Bulgaria (as well as in Slovakia and Romania) between 1989 and 1996 signaled that the Bulgarian transition was different in kind from those in CEE, installing a regime that allowed ethnic politics to prosper. Even Hellén, Berglund, and Aarebrot (1998), while generally more sensitive to the dangers of stereotyping and more upbeat about the prospects for democracy in most of CEE, argue that Romania and Bulgaria are mere transition democracies, in contrast to the clearly consolidating democracies of Poland, Czechia, and the three Baltic states. They attribute a North–South divide to "the resilience of authoritarian features in the Balkans," which in turn is strongly related to "the clientelistic heritage in that particular region" (Hellén, Berglund and

---

[1] As Linz and Stepan (1996, p. 333) note, the literature on Bulgarian transition is poor in comparison with that for other post-communist countries. For one of the area specialists who did see a real possibility of successful democratization at the outset of the Bulgarian post-communist phase, see Bell, 1991.

[2] Other commentators were more generous in their assessments, including Adam Przeworski (1991) and Stephen Holmes (1996).

Aarebrot, 1998, pp. 365–6).[3] Such depictions of backwardness are reinforced by the tendency of writers in CEE to use the concept of the Balkans as a constituting other (see Todorova, 1997).[4] All these assessments ignore the fact that Bulgaria had a liberal constitution as early as 1879 that established the formal trappings if not the full spirit of parliamentary government (Gallagher, 1995a, p. 339), and an economy that in the 1980s surpassed Poland and approached Hungary in terms of national income per capita. (For a good history of Bulgaria, see Crampton, 1997.)

In this chapter we analyze discourses about democracy inside Bulgaria rather than the very different discourse about democracy in Bulgaria that has developed outside the country. The Bulgarian discourses we identify turn out to be broadly supportive of democratization and constitutional government, but in a much less straightforward way than in the other countries that have been comparatively successful in negotiating post-communist transitions. In these other countries, reformist political elites can find discourses consistent with their efforts. This is not the case in Bulgaria, where discourses that support the idea of reform condemn the way it has in fact proceeded. It is not just elites who are so condemned, but also the citizenry, who allowed matters to take this course.

Bulgaria's transition was indeed different from those in Poland, East Germany, Czechoslovakia, and Hungary, but this has nothing to do with any supposed backwardness. Prior to 1989, there was little organized opposition to the communist regime, which was of the near-ideal Soviet type. Nationalist sentiment could not be directed in an anti-Soviet direction because many Bulgarians remembered that the very existence of their country is due to Russia's victory over the Ottoman Empire in 1878. Communist-era leaders would not permit any public criticism of the Soviet Union.[5] Bulgaria differs from many of the countries of CEE – though not Hungary – in that its transition was primarily elite-led. The year 1989 witnessed some protests,

---

[3] These three authors were themselves influenced by the Bulgarian contributor to their volume, Georgi Karasimeonov (1998, esp. p. 339), who argues along similar lines.

[4] One of the four anonymous readers of our original typescript implied that we had either invented the concept of Balkan backwardness, or else that it was no longer used. Anyone who agrees with this reader should see, e.g., Sowards, 1996; Ágh, 1999; Djordjevich, 1999; Carassava, 2000. For a full-length edited study of the concept of "backwardness" in Eastern Europe more generally, see Chirot 1989b. While Chirot's collection focuses on *economic* backwardness, both he and some of his collaborators consider the impact of economic underdevelopment on politics and society (see Chirot, 1989a; Stokes, 1989).

[5] Which is not to say that there were no criticisms. One of the present authors (Holmes) has been surprised on recent visits to Bulgaria at how few highly educated Bulgarians knew anything at all about the 1965 attempted coup, which was on one level an indication of dissatisfaction among people near the top with the senior leadership's sycophancy toward the Soviet leadership.

several of them organized by Eko-Glasnost. But as Schöpflin (1993, p. 233) observes, the mass demonstrations in November 1989 really only provided "an added fillip" to what was in effect a palace coup (Karasimeonov, 1998, p. 358) on November 10 in which long-time leader Todor Zhivkov was deposed. There were round-table talks between government and opposition, but these occurred *after* the coup. The Communist Party restyled itself the Bulgarian Socialist Party (BSP), and duly won the 1990 election. The BSP lost power to the Union of Democratic Forces (UDF) in 1991, regained power in 1994, then was heavily defeated by the UDF in the early election held immediately following the economic catastrophe of 1996–7. So although the moment of transition cannot be pinpointed to 1989, when Bulgaria featured less a "revolution from above" (Munck and Leff, 1997, p. 356) than a mere coup (Ganev, 1997, p. 126), by the late 1990s Bulgaria had a good claim to be well on the way to democratic politics under constitutional rule. Thus we classify Bulgaria as a late starter, rather than a chronic laggard. Bulgaria has also been spared the destructive ethnic conflicts of some of its neighbors, despite the legacy of the Zhivkov regime's "renaming" campaign against the 8 percent Turkish minority in the 1980s, under which Turks were forced to adopt Bulgarian names.[6] As we will demonstrate, nationalism does exist in Bulgaria; but its place in the constellation of political discourses helps explain why it does not take a destructive form.[7]

The most serious challenges to Bulgarian democratization have come not from ethnic or nationalist conflict, but from the failure of half-hearted economic reforms that precipitated a major crisis in the winter of 1996–7. The collapse of the banking system took away the savings of millions of people. According to the National Statistical Institute (NSI), inflation soared to 310 percent in 1996, approximately ten times the average rate for CEE (AFP reports, January 9, 1997). The Confederation of Independent Trades Unions in Bulgaria reported that average real income fell by 40 percent in April–September 1996. The failings of the BSP government of Zhan Videnov were cruelly exposed. Corruption was pervasive, especially in connection with the first stages of privatization. Political parties were often overshadowed by actors connected with members of government who used privileged access to information to enrich themselves. Excessive exports of grain in early 1996 led to shortages by the end of the year.

---

[6] This move provoked indignation among dissidents, human rights groups, and the intelligentsia in general, and was reversed after Zhivkov's fall. The consequences included the exodus of thousands of Turks, conflicts over their property on their return, and mistrust among communities that had previously coexisted peacefully.

[7] Another reason may be Bulgarian awareness of the effects of nationalism next door (former Yugoslavia); however, it is Bulgarians' own experiences that constitute the principal explanation.

In the autumn of 1996 the lack of progress in economic reform, the collapse of Bulgarian financial institutions, and the threat of hyperinflation led the International Monetary Fund (IMF) to suspend negotiations on a new loan agreement and propose instead a currency board to stabilize the financial system, an offer which was rejected by the Videnov government. Popular discontent with the government was registered in the October 1996 presidential election, won by opposition candidate Petar Stoyanov with 60 percent of the votes cast in the second round. The government resigned at the end of December 1996, with Videnov admitting that he lacked the trust of his own party as well as society as a whole.

This resignation failed to stem popular dissatisfaction, which now centered on the attempts of the BSP to form another government. Street demonstrations, especially in Sofia, reached a level unprecedented in Bulgaria between December 30, 1996, and February 4, 1997, when the BSP candidate Dobrev agreed to the demonstrators' demand for an early election. The election was held in April 1997, giving a majority to a coalition led by the UDF. The incoming government, led by Ivan Kostov, introduced a currency board in June 1997 and began the process of serious restructuring of the economy via price liberalization and accelerated privatization.[8] We conducted our Q sort interviews in the immediate aftermath of these events, in the summer of 1997, so the crisis atmosphere should be borne in mind when interpreting our results. Our discussion groups had been conducted in late 1996, as the economy collapsed, so not surprisingly these groups generated many disaffected and critical statements. What is perhaps surprising is that in the individual interviews these sentiments did not translate into any systematic rejection of liberalization and democratization – in direct contrast to (say) Russia.

To extend the metaphor of Elster, Offe, and Preuss (1998), we can say that, while the Bulgarian ship was being rebuilt at sea, it was subjected to gale-force winds of economic crisis. But Bulgarian democracy did not sink. Contrary to widely held expectations, the institutions of the new democracy were able to weather the economic storm (Ganev, 1997). If the institutional framework was the rigging of the ship, the discourses we identify represent what the crew was thinking during the storm.

Despite the initially controversial nature of the constitution passed in 1991 by a Grand National Assembly dominated by former communists, Bulgarian politicians have since respected both the letter and the spirit of this constitution, thus averting major institutional crises (Verheijen, 1995,

---

[8] The adoption of a currency board means that the quantity of leva in circulation is strictly matched to the National Bank's reserves; the value is pegged to foreign currencies, in particular the German mark; and government fiscal activity is curtailed.

p. 151). Why did political elites in Bulgaria adhere to the constitution while their counterparts in Russia, Belarus, Romania, Slovakia, and elsewhere felt at liberty to ignore or manipulate constitutional rules when it suited them? The answer may be that Bulgaria has a longer history of constitutional government (Dimitrov, Kabakchieva, and Kiossev, 1996). Reference to the provisions of the constitution helped to preserve social peace at several important junctures.

Unlike its 1879 predecessor, the 1991 constitution was hardly at the forefront of liberal democratic development.[9] But symbolically, both constitutions were signed in Turnovo, and the 1991 document contained several references to its predecessor. These historical connotations helped to secure respect and legitimacy for the 1991 constitution, putting Bulgaria at an advantage compared to countries such as Slovakia, Moldova, Belarus, and Ukraine, which have had to establish their statehood for the first time in the years since 1989.

The 1991 constitution established a Constitutional Court, which has since helped to maintain the separation of powers. Largely due to respect for the decisions of this court, ethnic politics remained subdued. The formation and registration of the Turkish-based Movement for Rights and Freedoms (MRF) was the first major ethnic test for post-communist Bulgaria, for Article 11 of the constitution forbade political parties organized on an ethnic or religious basis. The Constitutional Court's decision to uphold the registration of the MRF provided the Turkish minority with a conduit for expression of grievances and pursuit of their rights; the MRF consistently wins 7–8 percent of the vote in national elections. The decision created a context for renewed peaceful coexistence between Bulgarian and Turkish populations, and the MRF has several times played a crucial "kingmaker" role in providing or withholding support for governments – notably in the loss of a no-confidence vote by the UDF government of Filip Dimitrov in 1992, and the subsequent installation of a government headed by the independent technocrat Lyuben Berov. Along with the quick reversal of Zhivkov's renaming campaign, these developments confirm Bulgaria's avoidance of the ethnic nationalism that has bedeviled some other transitional countries (Mitev, 1997, p. 64).

We do not mean to imply that Bulgarian democracy in the 1990s was unblemished. Corruption was a major problem. The bureaucracy was subjected to constant purges which reflected the attempt of every government since 1989 to install its own political supporters at high and medium levels of the administration. This was initially a reaction to the interpenetration of

---

[9] The Communists also produced constitutions, in 1948 and 1971; but these were not even meant to be liberal democratic, so we exclude them from consideration.

state and party structures under communism, which made lustration seem attractive as a way to ensure that an administration separate from the structures of the former communist party was created. Unfortunately, Bulgaria has also suffered from the tendency present in other post-communist countries to turn the struggle for an impartial bureaucracy into a partisan contest for installing a new politicized administration. So far a change of government has always brought a new broom with which members and supporters of the defeated party would be swept from their administrative positions, even at levels where they would not have had any political function (see Kolarova, 1999, p. 159). This has often led to paralysis in decision-making, obstructing the implementation of laws, and generally impeding the development of an effective bureaucracy, one of the main conditions for a successful democratic consolidation (see Linz and Stepan, 1996, pp. 7, 11).

Despite these shortcomings, Bulgaria's success in negotiating both ethnic divisions and economic collapse in constitutional fashion is undeniable. Let us now turn to the content of the discourses of democracy we found in Bulgaria, which can help us to make sense of these developments.

Bulgarian discourses of democracy

We conducted forty interviews in a variety of locations: Sofia, Pleven, Pernik, Buchino, Jarema, Zheleznitza, Kjustendil, Blagoevgrad, Razgrad, and Varna. We followed the usual injunction to maximize variety in subject selection; and several interviewees were members of the Turkish minority. Factor analysis produced three discourses of democracy, which we label New Democratic Thinking, Democratic Nationalism, and Populist Isolationism. However, we should stress that New Democratic Thinking is very much the dominant theme. It took some effort to isolate the other two factors, and most of the individuals with a significant loading upon them also have a significant loading on New Democratic Thinking (see table 13.2). The number of consensus statements, receiving a similar ranking in all three discourses, is also striking (see table 13.1). With the usual caveat about the difficulty in generalizing to population proportions using Q methodology, we can tentatively characterize factor A as dominant. And as we shall now see, this factor and the configuration of discourses in which it is embedded are quite unique, having no counterparts in the other countries we studied. (In the narratives, numbers in parentheses refer to the statements from the first table.)

Bulgaria factor A: New Democratic Thinking

Democracy should exist above all in the way people think, in terms of civic commitment, tolerance, and respect for the rights of others (8). So the road to democracy can begin only if people change the way they think and adopt the

Table 13.1. *Statement scores on three factors for Bulgaria*

Factor A is New Democratic Thinking.
Factor B is Democratic Nationalism.
Factor C is Populist Isolationism.

Statement	Factor A	B	C
1 Each and every intervention from the international financial institutions only deepens the economic problems of Bulgaria.	−4	−2	+4
2 A real asset of the reform is the increased freedom of movement of people.	−2	+6	−1
3 People are free but do not know what to do with freedom.	+2	0	−2
4 The market should be the only mechanism allocating property rights.	+3	+1	+2
5 The political parties are in confrontation and make people quarrel.	−1	−1	+1
6 Democracy means respecting and observing the rights of every member of society.	+4	+4	+5
7 The form of democracy which has taken root here is deformed.	0	0	−5
8 Democracy requires a way of thinking including civic loyalty, tolerance, and acceptance of other perspectives of the world.	+5	+4	+4
9 With the exception of a very small intellectual part of our society, everyone else has a deformed view of democracy.	0	−5	−2
10 A multiparty system should operate according to democratic rules.	0	+3	−1
11 Democracy ensures that the decision the majority favors is adopted even if it not the correct one.	0	+3	+2
12 If you are hungry, thirsty, and freezing, you go onto the street and shout that there is no democracy.	−2	−2	0
13 Democracy is a matter of freedom and equilibrium in society and the regulating mechanisms that maintain this equilibrium.	+1	+2	−2
14 Democracy is a matter of basic instinct – no one will give up something good for something worse.	−2	+2	−2
15 In my family we want the same thing but we vote for different parties – I think one party will give it to me, my grandmother thinks the other will.	−2	−1	−3
16 We as a people have the mentality of slaves and the lack of freedom does not concern us.	0	−6	0
17 One of the main issues related to democracy is the issue of corruption which is everywhere.	+1	+5	+1
18 Those who were in possession of material wealth in the past are still in power now.	−1	−2	+3

Table 13.1. (*cont.*)

	Factor		
Statement	A	B	C
19 I am a nationalist and I am against someone calling themselves a Roma of Turkish origin or a Turk of Bulgarian origin.	−5	+4	+2
20 If the rulers of a nation are working for the benefit and interest of the nation, there can be no interethnic conflict.	+1	+2	+2
21 We are heavily dependent on the West and the West interferes in our affairs.	−1	+3	0
22 Bulgaria can be economically independent and exist without foreign assistance.	−3	0	+5
23 We are now at a turning point and may turn into a dictatorship, democracy, or anarchy.	−2	0	−1
24 Democracy really is not the best possible form of government, but there is no better one.	+3	−1	−2
25 We Bulgarians are used to acknowledging problems but not fighting against them.	+2	+2	−2
26 We have to fight to prove that we deserve democracy.	+1	0	+3
27 Many Bulgarians think that democracy means anarchy and permissiveness rather than freedom.	+1	−5	−1
28 Many say that the murders, robberies and break-ins are what constitute democracy.	−3	−4	−3
29 Former communists control strategic positions and manage the banking system incompetently.	−1	0	+3
30 At the moment we are getting ready for a new revolution.	−5	−3	−4
31 The Bulgarians are used to someone else doing their thinking for them.	+6	−5	+1
32 Democracy is a form of government which gives power to the people but our Bulgarian people seem to be avoiding taking this power.	+3	−1	+1
33 Democracy must include the possibility for movement of labor.	+1	+5	0
34 Democracy should provide a constitution that defends the interests of the people, instead of the interests of the parties of power.	+2	+3	+2
35 People in Bulgaria do not want to be free because they don't know what freedom means.	+3	−4	−1
36 Democracy means anarchy, the complete freedom of all to do whatever they want or need to.	−6	−3	−6
37 Democracy brought economic and social crisis.	−4	−2	+1
38 Democracy is rewarding everybody according to his merits and work, not according to hierarchy.	+2	−1	+4

Table 13.1. (*cont.*)

Statement	Factor		
	A	B	C
39 Democracy can be created only by people brought up in a democratic spirit.	+4	−2	0
40 Democracy can be preceded by an authoritarian regime, which should establish law and order and then give way to democracy.	−3	−3	−3
41 Democracy's market economy is only speculation and the black market.	−5	−2	−4
42 Law and order cannot be implemented by a democratic government, but only by an authoritarian regime.	−4	−6	−3
43 The way of thinking should be the first thing to change on the road to democracy.	+6	+1	+6
44 Democracy has to build itself; it cannot be imposed by certain individuals and foreign influence.	+2	+3	−1
45 Democracy cannot be built in a society where people are not ready to take risk and responsibility.	+5	+2	+1
46 In a democracy young people should be able to believe that their future depends on their abilities and performance.	+3	+6	+5
47 Economic and political stability are needed for the construction of democracy.	+5	+1	+2
48 Since Europe is moving forward, it cannot and will not tolerate an undemocratic Bulgaria.	+4	+2	−5
49 Equal treatment of people from various ethnic groups is a basic part of democracy.	+4	−3	−3
50 Democracy and nationalism are incompatible.	0	−4	−6
51 Nowadays there is no democracy, as they let criminals out. Everyone thinks they can do what they want under democracy.	0	−1	0
52 You can write anything you want in the papers, but democracy has made people afraid to walk the streets.	−2	0	+1
53 Today only tradesmen earn money, but it is not honest trade as they don't pay their taxes.	−1	0	−4
54 No one can earn enough money from honest labor nowadays.	−1	−3	−1
55 The misunderstood democracy is not the fault of the people; everything comes from above.	−3	+1	+1
56 If government imposes order, controls the traders, then there will be democracy.	+1	−1	0
57 A society in which pensioners dig in the rubbish bins for food cannot be democratic.	+2	+1	0

Table 13.1. (*cont.*)

	Factor		
Statement	A	B	C
58 Voting is not an important factor; elections have created a confrontation in society.	−4	−1	−5
59 Politicians in the National Assembly only quarrel and cannot solve the problems of the country.	−3	+1	+3
60 Those who don't vote have despaired of both parties.	−1	+1	+4
61 The situation in our country is the result of a global plan and policy from outside.	−1	+1	+3
62 Corruption is to be found in the highest echelons of power.	0	+4	+6
63 It is better to have dictatorship so that everything can be sorted out.	−6	−4	−4
64 Democracy is a chance to advance society, to make one's mark, not a populist dream about equality.	+1	+5	−1

democratic spirit, to take risks and responsibilities (39, 43, 45). The trouble is that, in Bulgaria, people are used to someone else doing their thinking for them; they do not know what freedom means, and are not ready to take power (3, 31, 32, 35, 55). We must move toward democracy and reject dictatorship, for there is no better form of government than democracy (24, 40, 42, 63). Bulgaria should look outward both politically and economically toward democratic Europe, and reject narrow nationalism (1, 19, 22, 48). We are moving slowly in the right direction, in terms of elections and responsible politicians (30, 58, 59). Economic and political stability are required if this process is to go further (47). This movement cannot be blamed for our economic problems (37). Democracy also means respect for the rights of all individuals, equal treatment of all ethnic groups, a market economy, and a constitution which protects the people (4, 6, 34, 41, 49). It is not anarchy and crime (28, 36)!

New Democratic Thinking is committed to both liberal and democratic principles (with its democratic commitments more pronounced than its liberal ones). It is outward-looking, and rejects ethnic nationalism. In these features, it is hardly unique, however much it runs against the grain of the stereotypes about "the" Balkan mentality (for one example of such stereotyping, see Gati, 1990). What is unique about New Democratic Thinking, and the reason we put "Thinking" in its title, is the degree to which it locates both problems and solutions concerning democratization in the realm of mass psychology. This discourse does not believe the Bulgarian people are up to the task of taking on responsibility and power and thereby becoming

Table 13.2. *Subject loadings on factors for Bulgaria*

		Factor	
Subject and political self-description	A	B	C
1 F, teacher, no affiliation	54*	64*	12
2 M, company manager, democrat	47*	65*	18
3 F, economist, rightist	42*	59*	24
4 M, engineer, socialist	36*	75*	12
5 M, engineer, democrat	66*	26	11
6 F, retired, socialist	4	6	37*
7 F, student, no affiliation	53*	46*	8
8 F, housewife, democrat	39*	65*	19
9 M, businessperson, nationalist	−14	66*	25
10 F, administrator, no affiliation	56*	36*	8
11 F, researcher, center-right/UDF	63*	50*	23
12 F, consultant, no affiliation	57*	20	20
13 M, computer specialist, Turkish/UDF	60*	47*	10
14 M, taxi driver, Turkish/MRF	51*	42*	4
15 M, unemployed, center-right	43*	50*	13
16 F, pharmacist, rightist	45*	59*	19
17 F, government employee, neutral	63*	38*	24
18 F, student, aspiring democrat	36*	48*	34*
19 F, retired, no affiliation	61*	37*	9
20 F, local government employee, no affiliation	64*	31	10
21 F, copywriter, no affiliation	67*	23	22
22 F, journalist, liberal	49*	59*	11
23 M, unemployed, nationalist	14	62*	21
24 M, engineer, neutral	58*	33*	21
25 M, businessperson, democrat	19	24	40*
26 F, shop assistant, no affiliation	23	25	49*
27 M, student, no affiliation	32*	65*	11
28 F, television director, apolitical	73*	21	6
29 M, editor, reluctant liberal	73*	22	17
30 M, company inspector, apolitical	69*	46*	11
31 M, chemical engineer, nationalist	37*	69*	10
32 M, bank security officer, democrat	49*	23	30
33 F, accountant, democrat	57*	33*	40*
34 M, building engineer, democrat	71*	15	17
35 M, artist, nonpolitical	48*	−12	6
36 F, peasant, apolitical	4	−34*	34*
37 F, farmworker, market democracy	12	21	54*
38 F, cook/pensioner, stays out of politics	34*	47*	23
39 M, technician, no interest	50*	46*	16
40 F, singer/pensioner, liberal democrat	50*	54*	27

*Denotes a loading significant at the .01 level.

the active citizenry that democracy requires. It is perhaps surprising that such attitudes persisted after mass demonstrations had unseated the BSP government in the winter of 1996–7.

This attitude is very peculiar indeed. For if we are right in our suggestion that New Democratic Thinking is in fact the dominant discourse in Bulgaria, then it appears that Bulgarians suffer from a chronic lack of self-confidence. Alternatively, they really are ready to take on the responsibilities of active citizenship – but are quite unaware that their neighbors down the street are too. This discourse seems to believe that Bulgarians do not know what democracy means and requires; but the other two discourses, as well as New Democratic Thinking itself, clearly do have strong conceptions of what democracy means. All three have democratic commitments which, while different in their character, ranging from liberal to populist, clearly fall within the range of conventional attitudes to democracy. There is a civic deficit in Bulgaria; but it is of a very odd sort.

These findings are in fact consistent with the analysis of the eminent Bulgarian social scientist Ivan Hadzhiiski, who, writing his "Optimistic Theory of the Bulgarian People" just before the Second World War, noted two contradictory tendencies in Bulgaria. The first assumes that Bulgarians' alleged "slave mentality" is inadequate to the task of establishing a democracy (as a result of five hundred years of Ottoman rule). The second is the actual existence of a strongly developed political conscience and love of liberty among Bulgarians (Hadzhiiski, 1997, pp. 33–5). Hadzhiiski believed that "Democracy has become a part of the conscience of the Bulgarian people as it was the condition for the formation of the Bulgarian nation, for its liberation and societal development" (ibid., p. 35).[10] Hadzhiiski's comments shed light on the unique and paradoxical elements of the New Democratic Thinking Discourse.

The New Democratic Thinking of factor A is reflexively incoherent. We would suggest that all it really needs is a mirror, such that its adherents would then understand that Bulgarians are indeed up to the task of consolidating and deepening democracy within their country. There is also perhaps a task here for more effective political leadership. Political elites in Bulgaria have been quite responsible in the post-1989 era in abiding by constitutional rules and conceding power gracefully when the occasion arose, but what is missing perhaps is the kind of "civic" and ethical leadership of the sort provided by Václav Havel in Czechia or (at least once) by the leaders of Solidarity in Poland. On the other hand, those subscribing to a minimalist model of democracy and democratization would see no problem here, on the grounds that Bulgaria has shown its consolidated democratic credentials

---

[10] The translation from the Bulgarian is by A. Dimitrova.

in a series of elections, such that it hardly matters what people think, there being no deeper or more authentic democracy to pursue.

New Democratic Thinking is quite consistent with the way the Bulgarian transition developed up until 1996, because that transition was indeed elite-led and regime-controlled (to use the terminology of Linz and Stepan, 1996, pp. 333–42), with little sign of popular mobilization. But rather than supporting these elitist aspects of the transformation, New Democratic Thinking bemoans them, hoping for both deeper democracy and more effective economic reform.

Bulgaria factor B: Democratic Nationalism

Ordinary people in Bulgaria do know what democracy means (9). It means respect for the rights of others, tolerance, freedom of movement, a constitution for the people, a multiparty system, and majority rule (2, 6, 8, 10, 11, 33, 34). Young people need to believe that their future depends on their own abilities and efforts, for democracy means getting ahead, not some dream about equality (46, 64). Democracy does not mean equal rights for all ethnic groups, for we should all be Bulgarians in this nation. I am a nationalist (19, 49, 50). We can trust the Bulgarian people, who have the capacity to think for themselves, who want to be free and know what freedom means, who understand that democracy is not the same as anarchy and crime (16, 27, 28, 31, 35, 36). We need to keep our distance from the West, which interferes too much in our affairs, and build our own democratic system (21, 44). We reject authoritarianism in the short and long term (30, 40, 42, 63). Here as elsewhere, democracy is associated with problems of corruption, and these need to be solved – but through democratic means (17, 62).

The Democratic Nationalism of factor B clearly has more faith in the capacities of the Bulgarian people to measure up to the requirements of democratic citizenship than does New Democratic Thinking. The existence of this factor suggests that ethnic nationalism does exist in Bulgaria, resonating with the nationalist rhetoric in party platforms, which even increased somewhat between the 1991 and 1994 elections (Mitev, 1997, pp. 64–83).[11] Not surprisingly, our three subjects who described themselves as nationalists had very high loadings on this factor (see table 13.2). However, this discourse's nationalism is coupled with an emphatic rejection of authoritarianism, and an affirmation of liberal rights and principles – except those pertaining to the rights of ethnic minorities. Democratic Nationalism is much less outward-looking than the New Democratic Thinking of factor A,

[11] However, Bankowicz (1994a, p. 235) exaggerates when he argues that the UDF "stands for nationalism of the authoritarian variety," though he allows that the term "fascism" might be going *too* far.

being quite suspicious of the West and its interference in Bulgarian affairs – though it is less isolationist in this regard than the Populist Isolationism of factor C. Of the three factors, Democratic Nationalism seems the one that is most happy with the political and economic status quo of post-communist Bulgaria.

Bulgaria factor C: Populist Isolationism

Bulgarian democracy is fine, if we could escape from the interventions of international financial institutions, which have only deepened our problems (1, 7, 61). Bulgaria can and must exist without foreign assistance, and be truly independent (22, 48). Democracy means tolerance, respecting the rights of others, a constitution, elections, and majority rule (8, 6, 11, 34, 58). Democracy and nationalism go together, so equal treatment of different ethnic groups is not required (49, 50). The trouble is that those who were wealthy before are wealthy now, and these former communists still exercise power (18, 29). There is much corruption at the highest levels (62). Politicians quarrel instead of solving our problems, and many nonvoters have lost faith in the parties (59, 60). So we still have to fight to show that we deserve democracy, and change our way of thinking (26, 43). We reject authoritarianism in the short and long term (30, 40, 42, 63). Young people need to know they can use their talents to get ahead, and be rewarded for the work they do, not according to their place in the hierarchy (38, 46). Democracy is not crime and anarchy (28, 36).

Our third Bulgarian discourse is populist in the classical sense of favoring the people over political elites, rather than the more pejorative sense in which the term populism is often used in an East European context – as connoting a leadership style that distributes short-term material favors to particular groups to court popularity, neglecting the public good and the long term. Still, the classical populism of this Bulgarian discourse might still worry those subscribing to a minimalist model of democracy and democratization, fearing the instability that can result from the mobilization of such sentiments by demagogues. Yet if we look at our parallel study of the United States, we find a discourse that is populist in exactly this sense, termed "disaffected populism" (Dryzek and Berejikian, 1993), which has apparently done little harm to American democratic stability.

Our third discourse's populist sentiments coexist with a critical attitude to Bulgaria's political elites, especially those former communists who enriched themselves and presided over corrupt economic deals. Populist Isolationism is the most disaffected of our three Bulgarian discourses. It shares some of the nationalism of our second discourse, but is more properly termed isolationist than nationalist. That is, it believes that Bulgaria can and should develop without interference by external powers and transnational institutions such as the European Union and the IMF, which are blamed for contributing to Bulgaria's woes.

Such isolationism is consistent with an enduring theme in Bulgarian history, which abounds in badly chosen alliances and interference by great powers. The beginning of Bulgarian statehood was marked by betrayal from the West, with Great Britain and the Austro-Hungarian Empire insisting that the San Stefano Treaty of March 1878 be abolished, and Bulgaria divided, with southern Bulgaria to be a protectorate under the Ottoman Empire. This division was confirmed by the Treaty of Berlin. More recently, the informational isolation of Bulgaria in the communist era was not overcome as rapidly as in CEE countries. In contrast to Poland, Hungary, Czechia, and Slovakia, Bulgaria did not acquire a visa-free arrangement with EU countries in the early 1990s. Finally, the IMF's refusal to renew loan arrangements for Bulgaria in the autumn of 1996 signaled the beginning of the end for the Videnov government. The IMF then became a convenient scapegoat for the BSP.

Comparisons and prospects

Our second and third discourses of democracy in Bulgaria show that disaffection, nationalism, and isolationism do exist in Bulgarian politics. These discourses have not been mobilized by political leaders in post-communist Bulgaria, despite conducive economic circumstances. Still, their presence should be noted by representatives of the transnational organizations and institutions working in and with Bulgaria, especially the EU and IMF, as well as by Bulgarian leaders working with these organizations. The potential for popular backlash against the IMF along lines seen in Indonesia and Russia in 1998 should be borne in mind. However, association with the West and its institutions has had its more positive aspects, which resonate with the outward-looking cosmopolitanism of the New Democratic Thinking discourse. The EU has provided some economic incentives unavailable to countries such as Belarus, Russia, and Ukraine. And the IMF can claim part of the credit for economic stabilization in 1997.

As we noted at the outset of this chapter, Bulgaria is often classified by external observers as backward by virtue of its Balkan location, and a laggard in political-economic reform. Our results, especially when interpreted in light of the recent history of constitutionalism and the incorporation of the main ethnic minority party into the political mainstream, suggest something quite different. The dominant discourse, New Democratic Thinking, is committed to the development of more authentic democracy in Bulgaria. Moreover, the other two factors, despite their nationalist and isolationist aspects, are otherwise highly committed to recognizably democratic and constitutional principles. Overall, the discursive map of Bulgaria is more similar to that of Poland, Czechia, and Slovakia than to Yugoslavia, Belarus, or Russia.

Our results indicate substantial consensus around the idea that democracy is "the only game in town." An inspection of table 13.1 reveals a substantial number of consensus items, many of which refer to liberal and democratic sentiments. Also striking is what these Bulgarian discourses lack: there is absolutely no nostalgia for the communist past, no longing for an authoritarian alternative, and no sense that democracy is an impossible dream. This discursive software goes a long way to explaining why Bulgaria has avoided the dire predictions of many observers, and "overperformed" as Linz and Stepan (1996, pp. 333–42) put it. All this is not to say that Bulgaria's democratic future is set fair. But Bulgarians skeptical about their own country's prospects for authentic democratic development would do well to look into a mirror, rather than listen to prophets of doom.

PART VI

Trailblazers

In this final grouping, we consider the two countries (of those we have studied; Hungary and Slovenia would belong here too) that have by most criteria traveled furthest along the path toward democratic consolidation, Poland and Czechia. As of 1999, Poland was performing better than Czechia on many counts, especially economic criteria. Poland continued to enjoy reasonably strong growth, whereas the Czech economy had been in the doldrums since 1997. Yet when it comes to politics, it could be argued that the relationship between the president and parliament has often been on a healthier footing in Prague than in Warsaw. Moreover, Czechia did not experience the "two steps forward, one step back" scenario – i.e., the coming to power, through the ballot box, of the communist successor party.

Our results largely confirm the relative democratic success of these two countries, though they also show that the discursive underpinnings or accompaniments of this success are not to be found in Western-style liberal democracy. Poland and Czechia both appear to lack nostalgic and highly nationalistic discourses of the sort we have identified in some other postcommunist countries. All this augurs well for the two countries. But inasmuch as other Central and Eastern European countries (outside the former Soviet Union) shared many of their pre-1989 experiences, there is no reason why these other countries could not one day feature a similar sort of pattern.

14

Poland

Of all the Soviet bloc countries, Poland was the most rebellious. Mass protests took place in 1956, 1968, 1970–1, 1976, and 1980–1. It was during the last of these that the most significant opposition movement in communist Eastern Europe, Solidarity, was formed. This type and scale of opposition was unique in the Soviet bloc. Indeed, Solidarity was in many ways the original source of the forces that eventually brought communism down in Europe. This heritage can give many Poles a sense of confidence, and pride in their own past, that contrasts strongly with the identity problems we have noted in several other post-communist states.

At its peak at the beginning of the 1980s, organizations associated with Solidarity mobilized up to half the Polish working population – their total membership stood at some nine and a half million (Grzybowski, 1994, p. 56), of whom around 750,000 also held Communist Party cards (Ascherson, 1982, p. 201). The declaration of martial law and banning of Solidarity in December 1981 was followed by a precipitous decline in membership, but come 1988 the leaders of Solidarity were the obvious group for the Jaruzelski regime to engage in negotiations concerning a transfer of power.

The communist regime gave way with much more grace in Poland than in almost all the other dominos of 1989 (only Hungary had as smooth a transfer of power), negotiating an agreement for competitive elections with the Solidarity leadership in April 1989. There were some significant conditions attached to this agreement, such that the elections were only "semi-free" (Frentzel-Zagorska, 1989). Just 35 percent of the seats in the Sejm (lower house) were open to genuine competition. On the Solidarity side, all candidates were selected personally by Solidarity leader Lech Wałęsa.

But the fact remains that, following the elections to the National Assembly of June 1989, Poland had a noncommunist prime minister – and had set a precedent for other countries in the Soviet bloc.

The Solidarity experience provided Poles with a heroic democratic legacy that could form the basis of the post-communist regime. But, as we shall see, there are some observers who regard this legacy as a very mixed blessing. If we look at Poland's deeper history, there is less in the way of liberal democratic experience to draw upon. Poland reemerged as a sovereign state in 1918 after at least 123 years of partition,[1] but in 1926 the lively and often chaotic multiparty democracy that began in 1918 was overthrown by the military coup of Marshal Józef Piłsudski. Piłsudski's authoritarian regime did, however, preside over a market system with a stable currency (but high unemployment), and a unified public administration, and carried out an independent foreign policy. It also stressed the importance of public morality. This emphasis had roots in a much earlier period. If we go back to the eighteenth century, we find a strong republican tradition that finds echoes in the post-communist era; we will discuss this tradition at length later.

Poland further stands out from the other post-communist countries in the enthusiasm with which its leadership adopted marketization immediately following the transfer of power. Under its radical finance minister Leszek Balcerowicz, Poland soon became recognized as the home of economic "shock therapy" marketization within Central and Eastern Europe (even though its reforms were not as radical in some areas as in others).[2] In line with the colorful – if cruel – metaphor adopted by Balcerowicz, if the cat's tail has to be cut off anyway, it is less painful to do this with one slice than little by little. Initially, the result was that unemployment and inflation climbed dramatically, while economic growth was negative, and shock therapy began to look as if it might have been a bad gamble. But the turnaround in economic performance arrived sooner in Poland than almost anywhere else in CEE, and by the late 1990s the shock therapists appeared to have been vindicated. On official statistics, Poland was the first post-communist country to see GDP per capita pass its communist-era peak (in 1996). According to the European Bank for Reconstruction and Development, as of early 1999 there were still only three CEE countries that were expected to have surpassed

[1] The reason we use the term "at least" is because there were three partitions in Poland in the late eighteenth century; we have dated the division of Poland from the most recent (1795).
[2] One of the slow areas was in permitting foreign investment; Hungary, often described as a "gradualist" in contrast to Poland, in fact liberalized on this important factor much sooner than Poland. Privatization has also been a slower and later process in Poland than is often assumed. On all this, see L. Holmes, 1996.

their 1989 GDP figures by the end of 1999, of which Poland was clearly the most successful (see *Economist*, April 24, 1999).[3]

Post-communist party politics has not been altogether salutary in Poland. Lech Wałęsa and the other leaders of Solidarity possessed great moral authority as they stepped into power in 1989, but Solidarity soon split into various parties and factions.[4] Polish parties were numerous and weak with small memberships, and it was not always clear what sort of interests they represented. The party "system" (to the extent it really was a system; a more accurate term would be configuration) in early post-communist Poland was highly polarized, making it difficult to reach stable deals that would have enabled effective and stable coalitions to form (see Korbonski, 1994, esp. pp. 225–30). The initial post-communist electoral system, which had no minimum threshold for party representation in parliament, did not help to reduce the number of parties to a manageable level. The first fully free parliamentary elections in 1991 yielded a parliament in which ten parties had at least sixteen seats apiece, with fourteen other smaller groups also gaining a toehold in the Sejm (see Lewis, 1995). Changes in the electoral law for the 1993 elections saw the number of parties in the Sejm fall to seven. However, coalitions and even individual parties sometimes subsequently collapsed or divided, so that the reduction in numbers was less marked than it initially appeared. Interventions from the Catholic Church were often unhelpful, too, in that they tended to encourage polarization rather than compromise. The success of the communist successor parties in the 1993 elections has been linked, *inter alia*, to the unbending conservative position of the church on abortion as well as its more general hostility to the left, seen as unfair in the changed circumstances (see Sabbat-Swidlicka, 1993). This conflictual approach to politics, and the apparent resistance to compromise, leads Anna Seleny (1999) to characterize Poland's post-communist democratic politics as "confrontational–pluralist," in contrast to Hungary's "compromise–corporatist" model.

The best-organized party in early post-communist Poland became the former communists, reconstituted as Social Democrats and by 1991 renamed the Democratic Left Alliance, with one of the largest memberships (150,000) of any party. (According to some sources, the Polish Peasant Party had an even larger membership, at some 200,000 – see Grzybowski, 1994, p. 59. However, this party was itself closely allied to the former communists.) The ex-communists and their allies won the parliamentary elections in

---

[3] The other two were Slovenia and Slovakia, while Hungary was expected to have reached its 1989 GDP level by the end of 1999.
[4] The Solidarity grouping in parliament split into two as early as 1990 – one faction following Lech Wałęsa, the other the prime minister at that time, Tadeusz Mazowiecki.

Table 14.1. *Statement scores on three factors for Poland*

Factor A is Civic Republicanism.
Factor B is Guided Democracy.
Factor C is Disaffected Majoritarianism.

Statement	Factor A	B	C
1 The most basic indicator of democracy is elections, when they are transparent and legal, and when they discriminate against no one.	+1	−5	+4
2 Democracy is not equal to freedom. Democracy means freedom within the limits of the law. Freedom on its own is a way to anarchy and chaos, where the strongest wins.	+5	−2	+2
3 By definition democracy cannot exclude anybody. Thus even fools, brutes, and the enemies of democracy can benefit from it.	+4	−1	+1
4 The free market is the essential feature of democracy.	+4	0	−1
5 Democracy is a system in which eligible voters in principle rule the country.	−3	−4	+2
6 Democracy stars at the local level because neighbors know best who is who.	−1	+1	+5
7 A model politician is a person who has money, and does not need to worry about his subsistence. Thus, he can get involved in politics for politics' sake, and work for the benefit of the country.	+1	−6	−2
8 Parties are necessary in a democratic society, because they are the natural source of the elites capable of governing.	−1	−2	+3
9 Free choice is not everything. The point is for this choice to have some goal.	+4	+6	−1
10 Contradictions are the engines of democracy.	+2	−4	+1
11 It is not politicians, but ordinary members who give rise to a political party. Politicians are the apparatchiks whom the party has elected.	−1	0	−4
12 Some might think that the democracy we have here and now is bad because it makes us all responsible for what is going on in the country.	−3	−1	−3
13 The minority should respect the majority's choice as well.	+1	−5	0
14 The free market and competition: this is how democracy is reflected in real life.	+1	0	0
15 When the media are financially self-supporting, they can be more objective representing and evaluating the situation in the country.	0	+1	−3
16 When there are a lot of political parties, one keeps check on another.	+1	−4	0

Table 14.1. (*cont.*)

| | | Factor | |
Statement	A	B	C
17 As a result of democracy not only slogans count. We also have the reality: the free market, competition, information, and social control over the government.	+1	−3	0
18 Democracy does not exist anywhere in the world.	−4	−5	+1
19 Real democracy exists in Switzerland. There they ask about everything in referenda.	−2	0	−1
20 In Poland we still lack such indestructible pillars as the American Constitution, the French republic, or the English queen. Here a sufficient minority can change everything on a day-to-day basis.	+1	−2	−2
21 People are not too eager to join parties or serve party offices.	−2	−4	+1
22 In Poland people are not equal. All the rights belong to the governing coalition and the church, not an average person.	0	+2	+3
23 People have not realized that their voice and their vote count.	+3	+4	0
24 We are not responsible yet at the moment. We did not have to care about anything under communism. Things were happening behind the scenes.	+2	−1	+1
25 Political games dominate over clear and sound reasoning and over political programs as well.	−3	+1	+4
26 People judge democracy through their everyday experience, and so for some democracy means unemployment.	+2	−3	+3
27 All the people who are now ruling Poland think about their career only.	−5	+1	−5
28 People do not like democracy because they have a selective memory. They do not remember how bad things were before the transition.	0	−3	−2
29 The things that take place in Poland now are the result of fifty years of centralized and socialist economy.	+1	+1	−4
30 People know political figures from television, but they do not know the parties' platforms.	−1	+2	0
31 Teenagers do not care about democracy. They do not even talk about politics.	−4	−2	−5
32 We still refer to politicians as "them" not "us."	−1	+1	+3
33 Poland is a democratic country, but only on the surface. If you looked into what is going on behind the scenes, that would not be so obvious any more.	−2	+1	+4
34 Democracy is some kind of lottery. You never know how good the elected one will be in government.	−2	+3	−1
35 Poland is still learning democracy. We resort to the Western model, but sometimes we have to fit this to our conditions, and this does not necessarily work.	+2	+4	+1

Table 14.1. (*cont.*)

	Factor		
Statement	A	B	C
36 The majority does not have to be right at all.	+6	−1	−2
37 Parliamentarians do not care about the opinion of their electorate at all.	−5	+2	−2
38 We have too many parties, especially those on the right. As a result you do not know whom to vote for.	−4	−2	−1
39 Not everybody needs democracy. If they do not want it, why force them to have it?	0	−2	−6
40 Theoretically speaking the last elections were democratic, but I think that those who won were manipulating us and our emotions.	−5	+2	−3
41 Politics starts with ideas, very enlightened and lofty ones, and everything works fine. But later on there is only money.	−4	+4	+2
42 People are ignorant about politics, and yet they vote. They do not know what they do, but they do it.	−2	+5	+2
43 I do not think that general elections are such a big deal. I vote because I hate the left, but it is not an important experience for me.	−6	−3	−5
44 Everybody votes for democratic slogans, but nobody knows exactly what they mean.	−3	+3	−1
45 It would make no sense if the minority ruled the majority.	0	0	−4
46 In democracy not everybody has equal opportunities, and that is the way it should be. People are different: some can work better, some can think better, some have more money.	+6	−3	−3
47 Majority rule generally hurts the minority.	+2	−1	−1
48 People en masse are unpredictable. It follows then that not everybody should have access to power.	+3	+3	−2
49 Maybe when Poland enters the European Union, people will see how politics is done and how it should look.	−3	−1	−3
50 We need time to learn democracy.	0	+5	+2
51 The number of parties cannot and should not be controlled.	−1	−6	−1
52 You cannot learn democracy. It has to develop by itself. You have to be on a certain intellectual level and simply attain it.	+3	+2	−4
53 Trade unions should not be politicized. They should represent employees, not politics.	−1	+1	+4
54 If the government loses the sense of its obligations toward citizens, it must be brought to account.	+3	+3	+3
55 Politicians should know when and how to reach a consensus, but this does not mean that they should sell out their voters' interests.	+4	0	+5

Table 14.1. (*cont.*)

| | Factor | | |
Statement	A	B	C
56 We should not be allowed to decide on everything because we are not specialists on everything.	+5	+6	0
57 We won the revolution. Now we have to win democracy, but we have to win it with democratic methods.	0	+3	+1
58 Politics does not have to be moral. It has to be effective.	−6	−1	−6
59 You need to know how the state works to be able to make decisions that concern it.	−2	+4	+2
60 In politics you need to know how to create propaganda.	0	−1	+1
61 People, not ideas, are the subject of democracy. This is why in a democratic state people of different religions, nationalities, and ideologies can meet and cooperate.	+5	0	+6
62 The wellbeing of the state should be the overarching value.	−1	+2	0
63 In a country in which there are democratically elected authorities and in which power can be changed through democratic procedures – and this is the situation in modern Poland – citizens should not disobey the law.	+2	0	+6
64 Law should regulate the matters of democracy.	+3	+5	+5

Poland factor A: Civic Republicanism

Democracy is the best system of government. Poland is learning to be a democracy, though the legacy of communism has yet to be completely dispelled (23, 24, 33, 35). But we should be careful not to equate democracy with majority rule or rule by ordinary voters, for sometimes the majority is wrong and the masses are unpredictable (5, 36, 47, 48). People are different and specialize in different things; some can work better, some can think better, some have more money (46). Some are best suited and most capable when it comes to politics. Thus not everyone should be allowed to decide equally on all matters (52, 56). Still, political power should be open to all kinds of people, and a democratic state should welcome people of all nationalities, religions, ideologies, and capabilities (3, 61). In this democratic state elections are important; despite the dangers of majority rule, we should not dismiss ordinary voters as ignorant, for government is in the end accountable to them (42, 43, 44, 54). Those who attain positions of power must be moral and not just effective in solving problems (58). In Poland we are lucky in that politics is not dominated by money and power games (25, 41, 55), parliamentarians do care about the opinions of their electorate rather than just their own careers (27, 37), and they do not manipulate the public (40). For politicians and ordinary voters alike, democracy means freedom – but it must be

Table 14.2. *Subject loadings on factors for Poland*

Subject	Factor		
	A	B	C
1 M, civil engineer, Harmony	−11	33*	28
2 F, interpreter, not Solidarity	64*	12	13
3 F, librarian, right-wing	52*	40*	39*
4 F, vocational teacher, apolitical	25	23	35*
5 F, secretary, Solidarity	−1	46*	−19
6 F, teacher, apolitical ex-Polish United Workers' Party (communist)	2	22	51*
7 M, law student, right-wing	46*	14	−2
8 F, real estate agent, anti-communist	18	33*	8
9 F, mathematician, Christian right	30	16	40*
10 M, student, apolitical	−33*	31	21
11 M, engineer, apolitical	0	44*	31
12 F, secretary, post-Solidarity Freedom Union (liberal)	33*	49*	16
13 F, teacher, distrust democracy	26	39*	12
14 F, pensioner, Solidarity Electoral Action/Christian right	8	25	2
15 F, sales representative, right-wing	12	45*	29
16 M, student, anti-communist	−8	50*	10
17 M, technician, right-wing	37*	54*	17
18 M, mechanical engineer, left democratic communist	49*	−1	53*
19 M, company president, conservative	27	−5	−13
20 F, nurse, pro-democracy, not political	7	36*	41*
21 M, teacher, leftist	40*	3	37*
22 F, NGO manager, apolitical	23	57*	9
23 F, marketing manager, apolitical	81*	−4	14
24 F, teacher, liberal	46*	−14	44*
25 F, librarian, rightist	25	−13	38*
26 M, businessperson, conservative	51*	9	19
27 F, teacher, neutral	61*	−7	13
28 M, retired mechanic, rightist	−3	71*	−13
29 M, lecturer, moderate conservative	46*	15	33*
30 F, pharmacist, leftist	46*	16	16
31 M, physician, rightist	42*	−8	11
32 M, lecturer, left-center	19	6	53*
33 F, teacher, center	10	45*	34*
34 F, teacher, leftist	35*	4	60*
35 F, retired, center	5	43*	39*
36 F, cook, leftist	40*	23	0
37 M, lawyer, center	−1	25	54*
38 M, retired army officer, center	−7	58*	14

*Denotes a loading significant at the .01 level.

freedom within the law (2, 63, 64), and along with freedom goes responsibility (9, 12). Free markets are an essential feature of democracy (4).

This Polish factor of Civic Republicanism represents the most direct successor to the "politics of truth" pursued by Solidarity when it constituted the civil society in opposition to the communist regime. The discourse clearly rejects the communist past, and is highly moralistic in its expectations of political figures. It defines citizenship in terms of commitment to the principles of the democratic state, not on a nationalistic or religious basis. We attach the republican label to this discourse because it is consistent with the republican political tradition, which, as we saw in chapter 1, is defined by its commitments to mixed government, the rule of law, and active public-spirited citizenship (Canovan, 1987). Active citizenship is especially emphasized in recent civic republican political thought (Sunstein, 1988; Sandel, 1996). Republicanism requires public deliberation that prompts political actors to think about their personal interests and how they connect with the interests of other individuals. Such thinking in turn requires all individuals to reflect upon the content of the public interest, as something above the pursuit of the material interest of individuals and groups.

A skeptic might ask what republican thinking in political theory has to do with Poland. In fact Poland has a long history of republican theory and practice, dating back to the eighteenth century. When we think of eighteenth-century republicanism, it is normal to invoke Jean-Jacques Rousseau and France, James Madison and the United States. But for most of the century republican ideas were more powerful in both theory and practice in Poland than in either France or the United States. Rousseau himself drew inspiration from Polish republicanism, recorded in his *Considérations sur le Gouvernement de la Pologne*. The Polish variant is sometimes referred to as "noble republicanism," because only the nobility was enfranchised. Yet nobles were about 10 percent of the population, meaning that Poland had by far the broadest franchise in eighteenth-century Europe (Walicki, 1989, p. 6). Indeed, in 1794 Tadeusz Kościuszko, leading a republican rebellion against Russian and Prussian invaders, proposed granting political rights to peasants (Stone, 1990, pp. 69–70).

Partition between Russia, Prussia, and Austria-Hungary in the 1790s ended the Polish Republic, but not Polish republican ideas. These ideas remained important throughout nineteenth- and into early twentieth-century Poland (ibid., pp. 56–7). In the West, republican ideals were abandoned, replaced by a liberalism that saw politics in terms of individuals and groups pursuing their material interests. Thus it was in Poland that the republican torch was kept alive in the nineteenth century. Observers of Poland such as Linz and Stepan who see the possibility of democratic politics only in terms

Poland factor C: Disaffected Majoritarianism

Democracy is what everyone should have (39), and we have put communism behind us (29). Democracy is first and foremost about free elections, majority rule, and political power exercised by the voters (1, 5, 43). It is about doing what is moral, as well as effective (58), and must proceed within the rule of law (63, 64). Ordinary people can and must take responsibility and power, and not leave politics to an elite (12, 46, 48). People of different religions, nationalities, and ideologies should all be welcome in this democratic state (61). Political parties play an important role in the democratic process (8, 11). Democracy starts at the local level, where people know best who is who (6). There are some problems with the way democracy works in Poland, for too much power belongs to the governing coalition and the church (22), money is influential (41), and sometimes political games dominate over good reasoning (25). So Poland often seems a democratic country only on the surface (33). This is not the politicians' fault; they generally care about the opinion of their voters, and are not just careerists who manipulate voters (27, 37, 40). Politicians must resist the temptation to sell out the voters' interests (55).

Disaffected Majoritarianism shares the rejection of the communist past with the first two discourses, and both the moralism and cosmopolitan approach to citizenship of factor A. However, it differs from these other two discourses in its complete faith in majority rule, with no need for Civic Republicanism's self-selected political elite, or Guided Democracy's political experts. This third discourse is disaffected because it highlights the problems with democracy in post-communist Poland, associated with the political influence of the Catholic Church, the power of money, and futile political game-playing. Yet its disaffection is muted compared with that found in other post-communist countries we have studied, and it does not translate into a longing for a return to the communist past or for a more authoritarian future. Like Disaffected Egalitarianism in Czechia, it seeks instead a better democracy in the future.

Prospects

Even if Grzybowski (1994, esp. p. 69) is correct in arguing that Poland has all the makings of an extreme multiparty system, this is not *per se* a cause for concern. A country such as the Netherlands has a far more fragmented party system than, for instance, the USA or the UK, and might qualify as having the "extreme multipartyism" which Sartori (1976) lamented. As we noted at the very start of this chapter, Poland had a reputation for rebelliousness even under communism, and some of this tradition has apparently been carried over into the post-communist era. Far from seeing this as a cause for concern, we would argue that, within limits (such as a shared commitment to the rule of law), such politics can be a sign of a healthy democracy. This all said, the volatility of Polish politics should not be overstated. While parties and coalitions continued to form and re-form at the time of writing, there were also signs of stabilization. Notably, Kwaśniewski easily won a second term of office in October 2000, securing some 54 percent of the vote in the first round of the presidential elections (a clear outcome many Americans might have envied a month or so later!).

Our Polish results resemble those of Czechia in that commitments to civic, republican, and democratic values are widely shared – even among those most estranged from the post-communist status quo. The social capital that Putnam (1993) believes is necessary to make democracy work effectively appears to be well-represented by the kind of civic engagement sought in these Polish discourses. Contemporary Polish discourses of democracy reveal continuity with the Polish past, in terms both of the ethical and oppositional civil society represented by Solidarity, and of the deeper tradition of Polish republicanism. There is little justification for rejecting the rich resources for democracy and democratization that these traditions and the discourses that are their legacy represent, in favor of a universal model of a liberal politics of self-interest that may make sense to some theorists of democratization, but which has little resonance in Poland's past or present. Indeed, note that Putnam based his claims about social capital on a study of another basically Catholic country with often conflictual (or "confrontational–pluralist") politics, but which is considered by most observers to be a consolidated – if lively – democracy, namely Italy. Among the post-communist states, perhaps Poland's democracy is closer to the Italian model, Hungary's "compromise–corporatist" more akin to the German. Both Italy and Germany are of course democracies (though major question marks accompany Italy's parallel "invisible government" that operated during the Cold War).

15

Czechia

In the early 1990s, Czechia was, with some justification, seen by many observers of the post-communist democratization stakes as "most likely to succeed" (see, e.g., Gati, 1990; Wightman, 1993, p. 52).[1] Although its image had been tarnished somewhat by the end of the decade in comparison with countries such as Poland, Hungary, and Slovenia, its prospects remain, on balance, among the brightest in the region.[2] Unlike almost all other post-communist countries, Czechia possessed both an industrialized capitalist economy and a flourishing liberal democracy before the communist era, more successful at that time than many West European states. This deeper historical democratic legacy and relatively high level of economic development, proximity to the West, ethnic homogeneity, and mode of extrication from communism combine in a set of truly advantageous circumstances when it comes to the prospects for both the consolidation of constitutional democracy and effective economic reform.

Czechia has perhaps the most positive historical legacies of all the countries in this study. Czechoslovakia was created at the end of the First World War by the Treaty of Versailles out of the Austro-Hungarian Empire. The interwar republic was an industrialized liberal democracy influenced strongly by the political philosophy of its first president, Tomáš G. Masaryk (president until 1935). Liberal democracy in Czechoslovakia survived even as its neighbors succumbed to fascism and authoritarianism, until the state

[1] We have already considered Poland and Czechia in a comparative article (Dryzek and Holmes, 2000), which uses the same data analysis as chapters 14 and 15 of this book.
[2] Seleny (1999, esp. p. 504) argues that Poland and Hungary were more successful in some ways than Czechoslovakia in making the transition from communism; she highlights Czechia's less impressive record on human rights and the treatment of minorities.

was dismembered by the appeasers and Nazis meeting at Munich in 1938. During the Second World War the Czech lands were ruled directly by Germany, with Slovakia a fascist puppet state. The democratic Republic of Czechoslovakia was restored briefly in 1945 until a communist seizure of power in 1948. The West allowed this seizure to happen, for Czechoslovakia had been consigned to the Soviet sphere of influence at Yalta.

The Prague Spring of 1968 was instigated by reform communists, but many Czechs invoked the memory of Masaryk and the interwar republic. Soviet tanks made sure that spring was soon followed by winter, and Czechoslovakia remained in the grip of a rigidly orthodox and anti-reformist communist regime until November 1989 when, much to the surprise of its leaders and opponents alike, this regime collapsed into nothing in the space of a few days. Between 1968 and 1989 the main opposition to the regime came in the form of the small group of intellectuals associated with Charter 77 (see Skilling, 1981), whose leaders in 1989 became the core of the Civic Forum, to which power was transferred. Czechoslovakia did not see anything like the mass movement that was Polish Solidarity, but could still lay claim to an ethical oppositional civil society.

When it became clear in 1989 that Soviet sponsorship of the communist regime had been withdrawn, mass demonstrations in Prague and elsewhere persuaded the regime to negotiate a comprehensive and immediate transfer of power to the leaders of Civic Forum. Most prominent in this group was Václav Havel, who became president first of Czechoslovakia and then of Czechia. At the moment of what Havel called the "Velvet Revolution," only power was at issue; constitutional issues were left unattended, and the communist-era constitution was kept in place (see Wheaton and Kavan, 1992). This inattention would prove significant in the subsequent "Velvet Divorce" between Czechia and Slovakia, for the old constitution was a federal one that provided for mutual veto on the part of the Czech and Slovak prime ministers (monolithic single-party control in the communist era meant this had never previously been an issue).

The Divorce that was legislated by the federal parliament at the end of 1992 was as peaceful as the revolution of 1989, partly because of a clear ethnic dividing line and the absence of any disputed territory. In addition, the two sides in the Federal Parliament readily agreed to a simple 2:1 formula for dividing state assets (Zák, 1995). Though opposed by President Václav Havel, the Divorce suited both Czech prime minister Klaus and Slovak prime minister Mečiar, because it removed their mutual veto. Klaus was a market liberal, keen on rapid privatization and marketization. Mečiar was a populist and nationalist whose commitment to constitutional politics was questionable, and who wished to move slowly when it came to privatization.

Though sometimes treated as a political failure, the Velvet Divorce in many ways smoothed the path of political and economic transformation for Czechia. The new state was ethnically homogeneous, with only a small Roma minority (the large German minority having been expelled in 1945). The democratic legacies of the interwar Republic, the Prague Spring, Charter 77, and the Civic Forum were all more clearly associated with the Czech lands than with Slovakia. The Czech lands also had a higher level of economic development than Slovakia, having industrialized earlier and emphasized less in the way of communist-era heavy industry.[3] To observers such as Vachudová and Snyder (1997), Slovakia was on the opposite side of a line running across Central and Eastern Europe, consigned to ethnic nationalism, populism, and authoritarianism. While in other chapters we have cast doubt on the solidity of any such dividing line, there were many reasons to suppose that Czechia's path to transition and consolidation was made smoother by the Divorce.

By the late 1990s Czechia's economy had a higher proportion of private ownership than any other post-communist country in CEE except Poland. Privatization in Czechia seemed to proceed with rather less in the way of favoritism toward the managers of state enterprises and corruption than that found in many other countries. The radically individualist and market-driven approach of the Klaus government appeared to set the conditions for successful capitalist growth and development,[4] though President Havel, in particular, was concerned at the loss of social capital and civil society that such an approach entailed (Elster, Offe, and Preuss, 1998, pp. 280–1).

The apparent relative lack of corruption had to be rethought in the mid-1990s, when it became clear that Czechia was not quite as clean as many had believed. By then a number of scandals involving corruption and the influence of money in politics had come to bedevil the Klaus government (see, e.g., Kettle, 1995), and these were instrumental in its defeat in the early parliamentary elections of May 1998. Our Q sort interviews were conducted in mid-1997, when public disenchantment with the Klaus government was perhaps at a peak.

Our mapping of discourses of democracy in many ways confirms the positive prognosis for Czechia. This mapping also speaks to the fears of

---

[3] Although Slovakia benefited from higher levels of investment after 1969, this was primarily in old-fashioned heavy industries, and many of the industrial complexes were redundant and even a liability by the beginning of the 1990s (see Fitzmaurice, 1998, p. 37). Czechia also had outdated plant and equipment, but to a lesser degree.

[4] Klaus was sometimes more committed to the market in theory than in practice, and low unemployment rates can be explained in part by his government's unwillingness to allow underperforming enterprises to go to the wall. Nevertheless, his rhetoric was often Thatcherite, as were many – though not all – of his economic policies.

those who see something a little peculiar and not very liberal about dominant political ideas in the country. We show that democratic discourse in Czechia is not straightforwardly liberal, but argue that there is in fact little to fear from this. Analysts influenced by liberal, polyarchal, and minimalist accounts of democracy see consolidated and stable democratic politics in terms of the interaction of parties and other organizations representing the material interests of key segments of the population, such as workers, peasants, or employers. This sort of politics does not dominate Czechia, and it is unimportant in the Czech discourses we identified. The kind of discourses we do find are mistaken by these analysts for latent anti-democratic sentiments; but in fact they prove to represent republican ideas that offer coherent and positive perspectives on democratization. These ideas can indeed contribute to a more secure basis for democratic legitimation than anything thought possible by liberal minimalists. These discourses may well be explicable in light of Czech political history; in all events, they should be treated as resources for the pursuit of more authentic democracy rather than obstacles to democratic development. Let us now turn to the content of these discourses.

Czech discourses of democracy

We conducted forty Q sort interviews, in Prague, Brno, Prostejov, Ústí nad Labem, and Jindrichuv Hradec. Analysis of them revealed two factors, which we label Civic Enthusiasm and Disaffected Egalitarianism. (In the narratives, numbers in parentheses refer to the statements from the first table.)

Czechia factor A: Civic Enthusiasm

The way to a fully developed democracy is very difficult, but it is worth fighting for because only democracy can guarantee for us freedom, human rights, and the rule of law (1, 4, 13, 59). Democracy enables us to live in a normal society, unlike the communist society we have rejected (3). While full democracy may take more than a generation to build, such that our children rather than ourselves may see the true benefits, we should not wait for either economic reform or equality to pursue democracy (4, 11, 61). There are problems such as corruption (18), but this can be corrected if political immunity is not allowed to excuse crimes (51) – for this is a real democracy, and most people now trust the state (25). Politics is not only for the rich and those with connections (15, 30). Everyone who adopts democratic rules and behaves accordingly can and should contribute to building a strong democracy, for example through participating in elections (9, 28, 38, 58). Good politicians should be responsible, honest, and loyal persons, who respect their electorate and listen to public opinion (10, 12, 27, 31, 49). Being watched closely by their electorate, those politicians who do not follow democratic rules

Table 15.1. *Statement scores on two factors for Czechia*

Factor A is Civic Enthusiasm.
Factor B is Disaffected Egalitarianism.

Statement	Factor A	B
1 Democracy is anarchy. What is not forbidden is allowed.	−6	−4
2 Democracy brings more freedom but at the same time the loss of security.	+2	+1
3 Democracy enables us to live in a normal society as opposed to a communist society.	+5	−4
4 Democratization is not an easy and straight road; it may take a couple of generations to build it.	+6	+3
5 The president is not an ordinary citizen.	−2	−3
6 The state is an organ responsible for its citizens, and is entitled to set basic rules and norms according to which people must act.	0	+1
7 Democracy needs a developed civil society and active citizens.	+4	+1
8 The senate is an important political institution which keeps a check on the activities of parliament.	0	−6
9 Every citizen has an opportunity to choose whether or not he wants to participate actively in the development of democracy.	+4	−2
10 Politicians naturally listen to the people because they have been elected by them.	−4	−6
11 If I do not stay passive and do something for democracy, I know that even though it will not affect my life it will affect the life of my children.	+2	−2
12 If politicians are able to choose what laws should be passed, and when those laws should be passed, then they will place their own interests above those of the people.	−2	+2
13 In democracy everybody has equal rights and equal duties.	+3	−1
14 Freedom is only an abstract term. People with severe problems cannot enjoy freedom.	−3	+4
15 In every democracy social differences widen and become more visible. Only those people who have money have power.	−4	+3
16 A minority always has to adapt to a majority.	−3	−1
17 People are very confused in democracy; they still do not know how to orient themselves in it.	0	0
18 Corruption is a persisting problem.	+4	+5
19 Every newly established "democratic" institution costs all of us lots of money.	−2	+2
20 There are formal conditions for democracy in Czechia, but moral conditions are lacking.	+1	+5
21 State bureaucracy has been using our money from the state budget.	−1	+2

Table 15.1. (*cont.*)

Statement	Factor A	B
22 People have power but they do not know how to use it.	−1	−1
23 The government's power is unlimited.	−5	−3
24 Foundations and other nonprofit organizations are used only for money-laundering.	−4	0
25 People do not respect laws because they do not trust the state.	−3	+1
26 People's vanity and jealousy will always be problems in our society.	+3	+5
27 Politicians want to shape public opinion for their own interests.	−3	+1
28 I do not see any reason why I should vote. The situation will not change anyway.	−6	−1
29 Even in a democracy, the preferential treatment of some persists.	+2	+4
30 Politics is only for the rich.	−5	0
31 Many politicians think that ordinary people are idiots.	−2	+2
32 The problem of ethnic hatred is created by us, the Czech majority.	−2	−4
33 If we increase the quality of civic culture, democracy will be strengthened.	+3	0
34 A strong social policy is possible only after the country reaches a certain degree of economic development.	+1	0
35 Representative democracy is much better than direct democracy, because in the latter responsibility is dispersed among too many people.	−1	−5
36 All negatives of democracy are balanced by freedom.	+1	−5
37 Everyone is able to comment on all questions concerning them and society.	0	−1
38 Everybody has a possibility to influence the result of elections.	+6	−4
39 Because of the lack of good legislation and laws people cannot effectively use them in order to exercise their rights.	+1	+3
40 NGOs' activities are very important in the spheres where the state is too weak or unwilling to operate.	+2	−1
41 Ordinary people are always uninterested in politics.	−4	−2
42 If people want to fight for truth they can. But if they accept that to prosper they must keep quiet, that is up to them to decide.	0	0
43 Every democratic state informs its citizens honestly about politics because it wants to keep their trust.	−1	−3
44 In a developed society people are concerned not only with their material needs.	0	−2
45 We all are equal, but some of us are more equal.	−1	+6
46 Ordinary people will never understand and will never have respect for the work of politicians.	−3	−5
47 It is natural that only those with a higher education and professional experience will achieve office.	−1	−1

Table 15.1. (*cont.*)

	Factor	
Statement	A	B
48 A democratic state is equally concerned with the wellbeing of the young and the old.	0	−2
49 The political elite should be created from the most honest and loyal people.	+3	+4
50 People are not obliged to seek accurate information; it should be given to them automatically.	−1	+2
51 Political immunity should not allow politicians to commit crimes easily.	+4	+6
52 A state cannot be a social custodian.	+1	−3
53 The media must be truthful about all positive and negative things in politics. There should be no censorship.	+1	+1
54 A state should delegate more power to communities. It would be mutually beneficial.	+3	0
55 The process of transformation cannot wait passively until laws and the legislature are perfect. They must be concurrent processes.	+2	−1
56 If you want a better decision, you should contact your representative.	−2	−3
57 Politicians should monitor public opinion because it reflects the opinion of their voters.	+1	+1
58 We first have to learn how to behave in, and live with, democracy.	+5	+2
59 Everybody should fight for democracy in order to live freely.	+5	0
60 People have to struggle through many obstacles if they want to effect change.	+2	+1
61 Democracy will be possible only when we are all equal.	−5	+4
62 Young people should have more of a say in politics because they were not as affected by communism.	−1	−2
63 In a democracy everybody should be able to succeed, not only those who have connections.	0	+3
64 There should be more female politicians, because our society is 50 percent female.	+1	+3

are held accountable and quickly dismissed from their posts (13, 18, 29, 41, 46, 51). So ordinary voters can make a difference. State institutions should be bound also by the same democratic rules (23). A strong democracy also needs a civic culture and an active civil society (especially nongovernmental organizations) (7, 33, 40). More power should be delegated to local communities, which can help to keep a check on the state (23, 54).

Table 15.2. *Subject loadings on factors for Czechia*

		Factor	
Subject		A	B
1	F, retired, democrat	33*	12
2	M, technician, disappointed	−8	46*
3	F, retired, democrat	55*	2
4	M, geographer, right liberal	11	48*
5	M, sociologist, liberal centrist	64*	13
6	M, student, right-centrist	67*	0
7	F, department head, conservative	65*	7
8	F, NGO officer, rightist	74*	18
9	F, office manager, apolitical	58*	27
10	F, administrator, left-center-liberal	64*	12
11	F, nurse, layman	72*	0
12	F, chemist, conservative	76*	5
13	F, administrator, right/apolitical	17	58*
14	F, laboratory assistant, neutral	1	76*
15	F, nurse, right-centrist	41*	36*
16	M, doctor, left-centrist	44*	59*
17	M, engineer, rightist	72*	24
18	F, teacher, social democrat	26	44*
19	M, state employee, centrist	53*	34*
20	M, engineer, conservative	50*	55*
21	M, state employee, left social democrat	17	49*
22	M, professor, leftist	26	29
23	M, lawyer, left/disappointed	−3	66*
24	F, librarian, centrist	22	−19
25	F, retired, right/radical/liberal	65*	−3
26	F, nurse, social democrat	65*	12
27	M, researcher, rightist	61*	20
28	M, state employee, no affiliation	68*	4
29	F, journalist, socially oriented	66*	23
30	M, journalist, indifferent	30	28
31	M, photographer, no change	−28	10
32	F, gardener, no interest	10	10
33	M, state employee, centrist	32*	56*
34	M, writer, right-centrist	61*	0
35	M, professor, right-centrist	62*	39*
36	F, blue-collar worker, centrist	18	51*
37	M, engineer, liberal democrat	73*	17
38	M, truck driver, radical right	−10	43*
39	M, office manager, radical right	−33*	63*
40	F, student, conservative-liberal	60*	30

*Denotes a loading significant at the .01 level.

As its label implies, Civic Enthusiasm's ardor for citizen participation in the post-communist polity is unbounded, though it recognizes that politicians and citizens can and should have different roles. The discourse is "civic" in its conception of what public life should entail, and it approves of the way that Czech democracy is unfolding in practice. Democracy is seen as both a condition and a project, to become more authentic and fuller with time and civic commitment. Civic Enthusiasm takes a moralistic view of politics. It is not hostile to the pursuit of material interest as such, although it recognizes vanity and jealousy as problems (26). But such pursuit is not what the core of politics is properly about. Political action is seen in terms of a collective civic project, as something inspirational rather than mundane.

It is easy to discern in Civic Enthusiasm the "politics of truth" that Václav Havel proclaimed as the hallmark of oppositional civil society in the communist era and the Velvet Revolution, and which can also be found in the political ideas of T. G. Masaryk. Masaryk opposed the unrestricted pursuit of private interests in political life, and saw in democracy objective standards of truth, not the mere reconciliation of interests. Though supportive of liberal rights and freedoms, Civic Enthusiasm is actually more of a republican discourse. As we saw in chapter 1, republicanism is normally defined in terms of mixed government, the rule of law, and active public-spirited citizenship (Canovan, 1987). It is the last of these three characteristics that is stressed in contemporary civic republican political philosophy (Sunstein, 1988; Sandel, 1996) and which also shows up in Czech Civic Enthusiasm.

This emphasis on public virtue and active citizenship makes liberals, and especially liberal minimalists, quite uneasy. Such liberals believe that stable democracy requires that the masses for the most part should not be enthusiastic about anything, on the grounds that enthusiasm can be turned to illiberal ends. In this light, democratic consolidation in Czechia and elsewhere requires that the "politics of truth" of the sort evident in Civic Enthusiasm should give way quietly to the "politics of interest," a far more mundane affair in which pragmatism and negotiated compromises between powerful interests are the order of the day.

Along these lines, Linz and Stepan (1996, p. 316) are worried that the excessive ease with which Václav Havel and his fellow dissidents committed to the "politics of truth" walked into a power vacuum in 1989 yielded a regime with "strong anti-politics tendencies." This new regime carried the *modus operandi* of uncompromising opposition from ethical civil society into government. In this light, such commitments look a lot like a mirror image of the official ideology of the communist era, where politics is seen in black-and-white terms, with clear heroes and clear villains – as opposed to the more pragmatic "politics of interest" which supposedly characterizes mature liberal democracies. Yet a closer look shows simply that republicans favor a different kind of democratic politics, indeed one that is consistent with a long tradition in political theory and practice that extends from ancient Athens and the Roman Republic through renaissance Italy, the American Founding, the French Revolution, and Polish "noble republicanism," to contemporary civic republicanism.

In believing that "truth" would conquer all, Havel saw no need to attend immediately to constitutional questions; Linz and Stepan blame this attitude for the subsequent breakup of Czechoslovakia, because it allowed the mutual veto of Czech and Slovak prime ministers to persist. They believe that if Havel had embraced the party politics of material interest then the Divorce could have been prevented. By 1991 Havel had turned his attention to constitutional restructuring, but by then it was too late.

The Linz and Stepan account here is questionable; it would have been unreasonable to expect the incoming government to start immediately on constitution-writing, given the rather pressing matters to which it had to attend. Moreover, it was the pragmatists Mečiar and Klaus who sought the breakup. The idealist Havel opposed the Divorce, and argued that it actually contravened the old constitution (see Musil, 1995). It is not clear how else President Havel and his associates should have behaved, short of entering the partisan fray themselves. Further, in those early days it remained unclear just what material interests existed and mattered, especially given the absence of a real bourgeoisie. Barrington Moore (1967, p. 418) once famously declared, "No bourgeois, no democracy." This proclamation has been falsified by the passage of time, not least in post-communist countries, but it is the sort of claim that fans of the partisan politics of material interest such as Linz and Stepan are likely to applaud.

There is no question that Havel disapproved of anything that looked like a political party, conceiving of Civic Forum as more of a movement; but this attitude is largely explicable in terms of what *the* party had done in the communist era. The squabbling between nascent party organizations that began after 1989 did little to change his mind. Havel did believe that as president he should remain aloof from party politics; but such a presidential role is not unusual in many Western countries (such as Germany).

Rather than lament the absence of a particular kind of political discourse and associated practice, we suggest that those interested in the prospects for democratic consolidation and advance in Czechia should take a closer and more positive look at the resources that the discourse of Civic Enthusiasm provides. When it comes to the legitimation of democratic institutions, it surely provides a stronger basis than the pragmatic compliance or habituation that liberal minimalists must rely upon. Moreover, its critical edge means that those interested in the pursuit of more authentic democracy can appeal to it in seeking political reform. This is especially important

to the degree that one of the hallmarks of democracy itself is the continuous exploration of the possibilities for more democracy (Dryzek, 1996a,
pp. 4–5).

Our second Czech discourse, to which we now turn, seems at first sight
very different from Civic Enthusiasm, for it condemns the post-communist
status quo that Civic Enthusiasm embraces. Closer inspection will in fact
reveal some important continuities across the two discourses in this respect,
confirming our characterization of Czech political life in republican rather
than liberal terms.

Czech factor B: Disaffected Egalitarianism

Despite the fact that the formal conditions are evident, true democracy does
not really exist in Czechia (20). Instead of the equality that democracy requires,
social differences are widening (15, 61). Life in this society is not so much better
than in a communist society (3). Yes, we have more "freedom," but only those
who have money and power can rule (14, 15, 36, 45). An ordinary citizen cannot
effectively exercise his rights, because he is struggling for economic existence,
does not know how to influence politics, and thinks it is useless anyway (11,
38, 39, 56). Politics is full of careerist and corrupted politicians, who do not
give a damn about ordinary people (10, 18, 27, 29, 31). Once they are elected,
they forget all their promises (12, 29, 51). They lie to the people and use the
taxpayers' money to create a more impenetrable bureaucracy (8, 19, 21, 43).
This hierarchical system of a representative democracy is unfortunate because it
excludes ordinary people and leaves them powerless (28, 35, 56). We need more
participation of all people in direct democracy, and an honest political elite who
will respect and listen to their electorate (35, 41, 46, 49, 63).

Our second Czech discourse is quite disillusioned with the post-
communist status quo, which is condemned for its wide and growing
social, economic, and political inequality (which Civic Enthusiasm does
not recognize as a problem), meaning that the post-communist political
economy is not a true democracy. Disaffected Egalitarianism also perceives
and condemns hierarchy, corruption, and bureaucracy. Such attitudes surely
received a boost from the money scandals and corruption that became political issues in the mid-1990s, and contributed to the downfall of the Klaus
government. More positively, Disaffected Egalitarianism sees equality as the
central characteristic of democracy, in terms of the distribution of not just
income and wealth, but also political power.

In countries such as Moldova, Russia, and Ukraine, such discontent is
translated into nostalgia for the communist era. In Russia and Romania,
it is represented by discourses that, while renouncing the past, are open to
authoritarian futures. But Czech Disaffected Egalitarianism actually looks
forward to a *more* democratic future, one in which the promise of

post-communist political and economic transformation is more authentically realized. One might perhaps explain the absence of nostalgia through reference to memories of the Soviet invasion of 1968 and the rigidly authoritarian and autarkic era that followed. Other countries with comparable experiences are just as likely to renounce in discursive terms the communist past, but as Romania and Slovakia show, this does not necessarily translate into a rejection of all kinds of authoritarianism.

The kind of democracy that Disaffected Egalitarianism seeks is participatory rather than representative, though it would contain more honest politicians who would better serve the people and the public interest, instead of themselves and their wealthy friends. Disaffected Egalitarianism is still more distant from liberal minimalism than is Civic Enthusiasm, confirming the domination of Czech political discourse by republican notions of democracy. In terms of their hopes for the long term, these two Czech discourses differ only in Civic Enthusiasm's tolerance of material inequality and a degree of hierarchy in political representation, both of which Disaffected Egalitarianism rejects. These differences render Disaffected Egalitarianism the more republican of the two discourses. But the main difference between the two discourses is in their assessment of the status quo, applauded by Civic Enthusiasm, criticized by Disaffected Egalitarianism.

Prospects

Contrary to the expectations of analysts such as Linz and Stepan, who see hostility to party politics as the direct legacy of ethical civil society (and so manifested in Civic Enthusiasm), Disaffected Egalitarianism is where one finds the real antipathy to self-interested politicians and their pragmatic politics. Thus any latent anti-democratic tendencies inherent in hostility to party politics are not associated with the Civic Enthusiasm that is the most direct discursive legacy of the ethical politics of oppositional civil society. But a closer look at both discourses indicates that a commitment to republican ideals should not be mistaken for hostility to democracy as such.

We began this chapter by noting that Czechia has been voted one of the countries "most likely to succeed" when it comes to post-communist democratization. This judgment is confirmed by the Civic Enthusiasm that approves of the way the country is developing, but still more resoundingly by the Disaffected Egalitarianism which condemns this situation. Civic, republican, and democratic commitments extend to those estranged from the status quo, and it is this which sets Czechia apart in a very positive way from most other post-communist countries we have studied (except Poland). The norms of civic engagement that Putnam (1993) would see as the social capital necessary to make both democratic politics and market economies function effectively have a strong presence in Czechia. This finding is at odds with the views of, for example, Kavan and Palouš (1999, esp. pp. 90–1), who argue that "the authoritarian culture fostered by the communist regime is too deeply ingrained in people's outlooks and behaviour to alter easily," and could take years to erase.[5] The discourses of democracy we have found reveal a strong continuity with the interwar democratic traditions of the Czech lands, and there is no need to condemn them in favor of either a one-size-fits-all minimalist model of liberal polyarchy or the supposed legacy of the authoritarian communist past.

[5] Kavan and Palouš cite as evidence for their negative outlook the fact that surveys have revealed many Czechs would trade off some democracy for a stronger state that can bring crime under control. Such an attitude is understandable, given perceptions that crime rates are high. More important is the fact that citizens in most Western democracies *also* still look to the state rather than among themselves to deal with crime – yet this is not generally cited as evidence of the decline of democracy in the West.

PART VII

Conclusions

16

Differences that matter – and those that do not

It should be abundantly clear by now that the post-communist world is home to substantial variety – and a fair degree of national idiosyncrasy – in discourses of democracy. This richness suggests immediately that applying a one-size-fits-all template of what constitutes democracy is inadvisable, still less that such a template should be applied to the evaluation of democratic development across all countries. We can talk about the way democracy works and the prospects for democratization in countries such as Yugoslavia or Belarus without assuming that democracy can only be a matter of imposition of a standard liberal constitutionalist model. What democracy means and can mean varies substantially across different countries (this is no less true for more developed countries such as Germany, Britain, France, Italy, and the United States). Of course, crossnational similarities do exist – and we shall investigate patterns of similarity and difference in this chapter. Before turning to this comparative analysis, let us summarize the light we have shed on extant accounts of political transition in the post-communist world.

East and West: matters of degree

In chapter 1 we argued against applying a universal minimalist model of democracy to assessment of the progress of and prospects for democratic transitions. Such a model assumes no consequential differences between the kinds of democracy available in the West and East, or anywhere else. But it is equally mistaken to see post-communist democratization in *sui generis* terms (as proposed, for example, by Kaldor and Vejvoda, 1999). The simultaneity of their transitions does indeed distinguish the Central and

East European states from other transition states – such as in Latin America and Southern Europe since the mid-1970s. We also accept that there is a difference between those older, more stable liberal democracies in which electoral democracy and the associated rule of law really has become the only game in town, and those in which this is much less certain. Yet we reject the notion of difference and *sui generis* as applied to CEE for two related reasons.

First, culture and political history do not permanently divide the West and CEE. There is plenty of alienation, turmoil, and repression – not to mention episodes of dictatorship – in the democratic history of the West. In the United States, civil war may be a distant memory – but intense and violent racial conflict is not, and today only around 35 percent of eligible voters (50 percent of registered voters) bother to vote in most US elections. France underwent unconstitutional regime transformation as recently as 1958. The "stateness" of many Western democracies is both recent and tenuous. Germany and Italy did not exist as nation-states until the late nineteenth century. Separatist movements, some of them violent, exist in Italy, France (Corsica), the United Kingdom, Spain (the Basque country and Catalonia), Belgium, and Canada. (On disruptive regionalism in Europe, see de Winter and Türsan, 1998.) The West should not be viewed as a stable counterpart to an unstable and conflictual East. Not all of the West's problems are processed by constitutional means.

Differences in economic development between East and West are more easily measured and more obviously pronounced. Even here, though, the margins are blurred. The differences between Slovenia and Czechia on one side, and Greece or Portugal (both European Union members) on the other, are not great. But, even if we recognize substantial differences in levels of economic development, economy is not destiny. As Przeworski, *et al.* (1997, 2000), demonstrate, the wealthier a country, the more likely that it will remain democratic. But cases such as India demonstrate that the odds can be beaten.

In short, any difference between at least the more democratized CEE states and the West look to be of degree rather than kind. (We reiterate that this recognition does not imply acceptance of a single model of democracy, such as the minimalist/electoralist one.)[1]

---

[1] We do not argue that all post-communist states are clearly on democratization paths. But we do count ourselves among the more optimistic observers. Archie Brown (2000, p. 177) *may* initially appear too negative in suggesting that less than half of the post-communist states are democratic (though not if he means that they are relatively consolidated). However, he claims that only this number are "firmly" categorized as such, while many more are "hybrid" or "mixed." Allowing that the latter are merely not very far along the democratization path produces a more positive picture.

Our second reason for not treating the East in *sui generis* terms is that *every* country is on one level *sui generis*, in the West just as much as in CEE (and this is where our differences with the minimalist model are crystallized). Indeed, this is the whole point of our analysis of what democracy and democratization *mean* in particular societies. Ranking countries on scales of democracy and freedom such as those produced by Freedom House has its uses (for an attempt at crosspolity measurement of democracy in terms of the relative power of elites and nonelites, see Bollen, 1980). But such rankings imply that there is a single scale to be ascended, and that ascent can eventually be completed. We believe that integral to democracy is the idea that it can never be completed, and that there are many ways to pursue the project. However, the observant reader will have realized that there is some implicit ranking in the sequencing of our six groups of countries.[2]

Erasing lines across the East

Our results also call into question the lines that many observers have drawn across the post-communist world. As already indicated, for example, Vachudová and Snyder (1997) put Slovakia, Bulgaria, and Romania on the wrong side of the dividing line. Huntington's (1996) line is placed slightly differently, separating Orthodox from Western civilizations. But in almost all such classifications, (most of) Romania, Yugoslavia, and Bulgaria are on the wrong, Balkan, or Orthodox side of the dividing line. In contrast, the northern part of CEE is treated as having more liberal or social democratic potential. However much Huntington's analysis is rejected by scholars familiar with the region, it remains very influential in US foreign policy-making circles, and so matters crucially when it comes to the prospects for democratization globally.

The fact that the term "Balkan" clearly has derogatory connotations is borne out by the fact that many Slovenes and even some Croats[3] balk (*sic*) at the notion that their country is part of the Balkans (Ágh, 1993, supporting this position, even refers to "Crovenia"). Perhaps even more interesting is that many Bulgarians prefer not to be seen as "Balkan" – despite the fact that the Balkan ranges are located in their country! We have no intention of denying something as undeniable as a mountain range. But we can and

---

[2] Our implicit ranking does indeed resemble that in recent Freedom House rankings. For other rankings, see the Nations in Transit table in Fish (1998, p. 217) and the World Development Report cited in Bunce (1999a, p. 764).

[3] See the letter from Darko Bubic in *Business Central Europe* (http://www.bcemag.com), September 2000, p. 10. Bubic writes that "Croatia does not belong to the Balkans – geographically, politically or historically... There is no reason to put it under the same heading as Romania, Bulgaria, Albania or the other 'stuff.'"

do challenge readymade and unquestioned assumptions about "the Balkan mentality," for various reasons.

At the most "common-sensical," it appeared to many observers, including senior officials in the European Union, throughout most of the 1990s that Slovenia was making far more progress in its transition than its northerly neighbor Slovakia. For the sake of argument, however, we shall accede to the wishes of those Slovenes who prefer not to have their country connected to the Balkans (despite the fact that it was part of pre-1991 Yugoslavia for more than seventy years). Using the method adopted in this study for assessing the commitment to – and hence prospects for – democratic discourses, Bulgaria and Romania come out ahead of Slovakia and not too far behind Poland and Czechia.

Other anomalies can be found further east. In general, it is clear that the patterns of discourses we have found in the countries of the former Soviet Union are more problematic than those present in the other countries formerly in the Soviet bloc (and Yugoslavia). But the case of Georgia is a positive anomaly in this pattern. And, without exception, in all of the countries of the former Soviet Union analyzed, we have found at least one discourse with recognizable and strong democratic commitments.

Our generally sympathetic approach to the possibilities for post-communist democratization in all parts of the region is consistent with the relatively upbeat assessments of analysts such as W. Miller, White, and Heywood (1998; based on 1993 surveys) and A. Miller, et al. (2000). Even though such surveys often reflect Western construction, and are sensitive to short-term political events, we welcome their contributions. Indeed, in an ideal world, we would like to run surveys ourselves to measure the relative proportions of the citizenry supporting each discourse. However, the collapse of communism itself demonstrates that discourses involving tiny minorities (such as Czechoslovak dissidents) that would not be picked up in surveys can eventually have substantial political effect. (Hard-line Q methodologists would also doubt that the information so generated would be worth the trouble; see chapter 2.) One advantage of an approach such as ours that can discern marginal currents is that it counters analysts who are tempted to talk prematurely of failed transitions (for example, N. Miller, 1997, on Serbia), and who fail to discern more promising possibilities beneath the discursive surface of a society.

Pasts, presents, and futures

The varied discourses and concomitant surprises we have unearthed in particular countries also indicate that it is unwise, even wrong, to categorize a country – still less predict its long-run prospects for democracy – solely on the basis of its political history and associated traditions of political culture. We have shown that culture is almost always multidimensional, and never the prisoner of any unitary history. Among discourses that can be interpreted in light of history, some can be identified with a recent past – be it opposition to a communist regime, or nostalgia for the order that such a regime provided. Others reflect a deeper history – in the Polish case, legacies from over two centuries. Still others represent a much more recent past: their values and attitudes appear to be formed in terms of positive, negative, or equivocal assessment of the performance of the post-communist regime. Then there are those discourses that make more sense in terms of comparisons with other countries and ideas, typically "the West," be these comparisons a matter of imitation, yearning, or rejection.

Thus, while we acknowledge, and indeed highlight, the influence of the past, this should be read as neither a path-dependent, nor a political-cultural, determinist interpretation of political discourses in post-communist countries, and of their influence on the way politics currently works, or on prospects for political development. Such accounts abound in the literature (see, for example, Ágh, 1993; Brzezinski, 1993); often they underpin negative evaluations and even gloomier predictions about the dire fate inevitably in store for particular countries (this is especially true of Gati, 1996). Such evaluations and predictions do, however, often have to be revised dramatically and suddenly in light of political events. For example, the defeat of Mečiar in the Slovakian elections of October 1998 suddenly made Slovakia look as though it was not confined to a version of populism verging on authoritarianism after all (events in Yugoslavia in late 2000 instigated similar reassessment). Long treated as the negative counterpart to Czechia, in terms of both economic structure and political performance, Slovakia moved ahead in the rankings. Such changes lead to a hurried rewriting of history, and this highlights what is wrong with cultural determinist accounts: they involve selective backward reading of history from present circumstances.

Among those who share our rejection of determinism are authors, such as Steven Fish (1999, especially pp. 799–811), who believe that democratization depends crucially on the contingent outcomes of elite struggles (he calls his approach "political constructivism"; see also O'Donnell and Schmitter, 1986). We differ from Fish in allowing greater scope for the influence of culture and history – but understood in multifarious terms, always providing a range of opportunities and constraints.

The influence of the past is rarely the influence of *the* past. Rather, that influence is far more complex and pluralistic than generally allowed. Particular discourses can relate positively to different pasts: the communist near past, and deeper precommunist pasts. Others will reject one or more of these pasts (perhaps all of them), or recall some aspects positively, others negatively.

Given this complexity – or, to put it in more positive terms, richness – of both legacies and reactions to them, deterministic arguments are both limiting and misleading. They are usually postulated on external observers' arbitrary selection of particular historical circumstances and symbols. Moreover, they are frequently circular, based on what appears to be happening at present in a given country, which is then explained by selective reading of the past.

To reiterate, our position, in contrast to cultural determinism, is that histories and pasts *do* matter, but that we need to be fully aware of inconsistencies and contradictions in these histories, and of varied reactions to these histories that can be found among citizens of any country. We do not deny the enormous influence of history, but simply problematize it. This enables us to view the past as providing *resources* as well as constraints. While some citizens may indeed hanker after one or more periods in the past that appear incompatible with democracy, others will reject those pasts, which is of course more conducive both to the successful operation of democracy in the present and to further democratic development. Thus resources for democracy and further democratization projects can be found not just in countries like Poland and Czechia, but also in countries like Romania, Georgia, and even Russia that have no clearly democratic episodes in their history.

Party systems and discursive fields

Having rejected determinisms based on both geography and history, let us now show how our results speak to arguments to the effect that the prospects for democratization depend crucially on party system stabilization. In line with earlier analyses of democratization that did not focus on CEE (e.g., Powell, 1982), several analysts (Shevtsova and Bruckner, 1997; Kitschelt, *et al.*, 1999; A. Miller, *et al.*, 2000) have argued that it is crucial that party systems be consolidated and stabilized in the post-communist world.[4] By the late 1990s such crystallization seemed to be occurring in some countries. In Bulgaria and Hungary, for example, the same parties were appearing election after election, with reasonably identifiable constituencies and ideologies. In other cases, such as Russia, there was partial crystallization, in that some parties had settled with identifiable ideologies and policies, and often constituencies, while each election saw too a number of new or revamped parties. The December 1999 Russian elections featured well-established parties (Communists, the Liberal Democrats, Yabloko) and a number of new ones. Over 60 percent of the party list votes (Rose, 2000a) went to these new parties, none of which was more than six months old.

---

[4] For a useful collection of classic writings on party systems since about 1960, see Wolinetz (1998).

How can more crystallized systems be facilitated? Of course, electoral systems make a difference (see Bielasiak, 1997; Isiyama and Velten, 1998). CEE countries have often adopted blends of proportional representation with simple or absolute (the latter usually allowing for French-style runoffs) majority voting.[5] The details matter: Poland's initial lack of representation thresholds led to a very large number of parties in parliament. The subsequent introduction of thresholds reduced the number of parties. Ukraine for its part had an absolute majority system with a relatively high (50 percent) minimum turnout requirement, which left many seats unfilled even after several runoffs in the 1994 elections. Ukraine then dropped this requirement and introduced elements of proportional representation in time for the March 1998 election, and reaped the benefits.[6]

The nature of executive–legislature relations also makes a difference to party systems. Stepan and Skach (1993) among others argue that parliamentarism is better than either presidentialism or a mixed system for consolidating democracy. This may be true where institutions have been reasonably well clarified, and where parties do not reflect deep social divisions. Otherwise, especially when there is both a serious identity crisis and multiple simultaneous transitions to be managed, parliamentarism may be more hazardous. But, as Hill (1994) argues, parties are unlikely to know what their roles are until there has been some clarification of the executive–legislature relationship.

Even with such clarification and the establishment of appropriate electoral rules, much still depends on the behavior of party leaders. Constitutional engineering will have limited impact if parties detach themselves from their voters (after the fashion of delegative democracy; see chapter 1), or split and re-form in short-term parliamentary games. How the presidency treats parties also matters a lot. The Russian and Polish legislatures among others have often been fragmented and irresponsible, but, like the archetypical naughty schoolboy who is disruptive partly out of frustration, might behave better if given responsibilities. In Russia, President Yeltsin after 1993 preferred punishment and rule by decree.[7]

The degree of alignment of parties with society's interests and cleavages also matters (for a classic statement of this point, see Lipset and Rokkan, 1967). Some such reflection already occurs in CEE countries, in correlations

---

[5] Hungary has a particularly complicated version of this blend, while Bulgaria's is not simple either.

[6] Following the first round of elections in 1994, only 49 of 450 seats were filled; at the end of the first round in 1998, 413 of 450 seats had been filled.

[7] Even in Russia, it is worth remembering that even the more extreme parties accept the electoral system, and engage in their disruption *within* parliament. Russia in the late 1990s did see some learning and maturing on the part of party leaders and others.

between party affiliation and cleavages such as class, gender, age, urbaniza-
tion level, religion, and ethnicity (see, e.g., Evans and Whitefield, 1996). But
support for parties does not *have* to be based on social cleavage and material
interests (A. Miller, *et al.*, 2000). Such correlations can be very fluid, just
as nowadays in the West, with many parties behaving in "catch-all" fashion
and so loosening their ties to traditional constituencies.

In the post-communist world, it has not always been clear what interests
exist that are politically salient. In other words, people have been unsure
about where they stood in the stratification of the new order, or indeed about
the key features of that stratification. If interests are unclear, then ideology
can fill the gap. At its worst, this means that authoritarian demagogues create
and then draw upon aggressive ethnic nationalism, making use of the fact
that ethnic identity may be more quickly recognizable to people than class interests. But at its best, party difference based on ideological cleavage could reflect precisely the discursive differences we have identified. To put it crudely,
one party per discourse might produce a relatively stable arrangement.

An obvious objection to this claim is that such a state of affairs would
entrench the idea that politics is mostly about constitutional arrangements
rather than within constitutional arrangements, which to Offe is the hallmark of *un*consolidated democracy. Such conflicts can be processed peacefully (Federalists versus Antifederalists in the early United States) or violently
(Free Staters versus Republicans in 1920s Ireland – a conflict that still forms
the basis of the party system in the Irish Republic). But the discourses of
democracy we identified generally do not have this all-or-nothing incompat-
ibility about them. They concern differing views about how best to organize
and operate the political economy, and in this they are not so different
from many of the discourses that one finds in association with parties in
the West. The distinction between politics about constitutions and politics
within constitutions is also in the end untenable; constitutional reform can
itself be processed by constitutional means.

In the case of Russia, in particular, we do observe between the 1995 and
1999 elections a shift in the party system that aligns it more closely with
the pattern of discourses we found in our study, carried out in late 1997.
Notably, the Russian discourse of Chastened Democracy is reasonably consistent with the platform of Yabloko; Reactionary Anti-Liberalism with the
Communist Party of the Russian Federation; and Authoritarian Development with Putin's Unity party. The first two of these conjunctions were
in place in 1995, the third occurred only in 1999. We therefore suggest,
with caution, that Russia's party system in the late 1990s crystallized further
around the discourses that pervade Russian society. And while correlation
does not imply causality, we note further that by 2000 parliamentary politics
in Russia was less irresponsible and chaotic than in most earlier years.

The Russian case shows however that the alignment of the party system in terms consistent with the popular discursive field is not sufficient to ensure (democratically) well-behaved parties and a smooth democratization path. Equally important is the content of the discourses so aligned. If a country features a party and an associated discourse that does not accept any rules of the game that do not guarantee its own domination, then democratization remains fragile, even in the presence of a crystallized party system. The three Russian discourses we identified appear to have little interest in compromise, or in recognizing one another's legitimacy. However, while seemingly unconducive to democratization, this situation does not preclude political leadership making creative use of elements of these seemingly incompatible discourses – in particular, shared commitments to honest government and enhanced state capacity to develop and implement law and policy.

Crossnational patterns

Discursive variety, richness, and complexity notwithstanding, we now attempt to summarize the crossnational patterns we have found, and draw some comparative conclusions. Inevitably, a degree of simplification and generalization accompanies this process, because in moving to this level we cannot retain in sight all the subtleties of each discourse in each country. Nevertheless, we believe that such analysis is instructive, not just in terms of what it reveals, but also in what it refutes in the way of some other generalizations about post-communist democratization that have gained currency.

We begin this summary comparative analysis with a tabular classification of the discourses we have found for each country. Table 16.1 classifies each country's discourses in terms of fourteen categories. The letters in each cell refer to the discourse in question from each country that is classified in that cell; for example, the letter D in the cell "China–participatory" refers to Chinese discourse D, Alienated Egalitarianism. Some – but not all – of the fourteen categories relate to the dimensions of models of democracy introduced in chapter 1. The reader will recall that these dimensions are:

Social democracy to libertarianism
Authoritarianism to open society
Civil society to a strong state
Pluralism to republicanism
Elitism to participation
Nationalism to cosmopolitanism.

Of these dimensions, libertarianism, open society, civil society, pluralism, and cosmopolitanism do not appear as categories in table 16.1. We

Table 16.1. *Summary of post-communist discourses*

	Liberal	Republican	Participatory	Social democratic	Moralistic	Economistic	Strong state	Elitist	Disaffected	Nationalist	Nostalgic	Communist	Presidential populist	Authoritarian
Armenia	A+			A			C	B	ABC					
Belarus	AB								A+				A−	B
Bulgaria	A		C						C	B				B
China	A		D		C				D			B		
Czechia		A	B						B					
Georgia	A						BC	B						
Moldova	B						B	B	AB		A	A		A
Poland	A	A	C				B	B	C					
Romania	A				B			C						
Russia	A					C	C		ABC		B		B	BC
Slovakia	A								A	B				B
Ukraine				A		B−C			B+C		B+	B+		
Yugoslavia	A		B						A	C			C	C

Note: A, B, C, and D refer to the discourse as defined in the country chapter. Particular discourses can appear in more than one cell. For example, Poland discourse C, Disaffected Majoritarianism, is both participatory and disaffected.

found no libertarian discourse anywhere. Emphases on open society, civil society, pluralism, and cosmopolitanism proved hard in practice to distinguish from a "liberal" classification; while there are subtle differences, in the end little is lost (at least for purposes of classification) by not distinguishing them from the liberal category – while much is gained in terms of parsimony. Though one can imagine nonliberal civil society and cosmopolitanism, in practice we found no strong representation of these possibilities.

From the general categories mentioned in chapter 1, we are, then, left with liberal, republican, participatory, social democratic, strong state, elitist, nationalistic, and authoritarian categories. To these we add – in large measure inductively, to make sense of our results – the following more specific categories of political orientation:

> Moralistic, emphasizing the need for politics to be guided by a particular morality
> Economistic, seeing the main point of politics as the promotion of wealth
> Disaffected, from the post-communist status quo
> Nostalgic, for a predemocratic past
> Communist
> Presidential populist.

Our categories are not mutually exclusive, meaning that any one discourse can appear in more than one category. For example, our Moldovan discourse A, Socialist Authoritarianism, is classified in table 16.1 as disaffected, nostalgic, communist, and authoritarian.

Let us now examine the broad patterns that the classification exercise summarized in table 16.1 reveal. First, and perhaps most importantly, we have shown that in all our countries, including those in which the post-communist road has been most troubled, at least one discourse can be found which contains resources for a democratization project. That is, all our countries have at least one discourse that is either liberal, republican, participatory, or social democratic. Even China has its Liberal Democracy discourse, and even Yugoslavia has its Democratic Future discourse. And when it comes to discourses that are ostensibly antipathetic to democracy, such antipathy *might* in some cases (even in the seemingly extreme case of Socialist Authoritarianism in Moldova, for example) be explicable in terms of perceived connections between "democracy" and the severe dislocations and disappointments that have accompanied "actually existing" post-communism. While outsiders, especially in the West, might find it hard to equate such dislocations with any accepted conception of democracy, such a link may be more plausible and apparent to the people who have had to live under such conditions.

In all cases, then, there are at least some resources for the operation of democracy, on which democratic reformers might draw. This rarely means that there is a point-by-point correspondence between a reformer's model and a discourse. Sometimes it may take considerable effort to establish connections – for example, between Romania's Civic Fundamentalism and a republican model of democracy. We have argued that democratic reform always means furthering the quest for more authentic democracy, not seeking some cutoff of acceptability – such as that specified by proponents of a minimalist approach to democracy and democratization (see chapter 1). Some discourses suggest movement beyond this particular cutoff; in some cases that cutoff itself might remain an unfulfilled aspiration, but particular discourses point toward or beyond it.

Yet we should not dwell on the positive here without also recognizing the negative – or rather negatives, because trouble assumes different forms in different cases. One source of trouble is disaffection from the post-communist political order. In Belarus, Slovakia, China, and Yugoslavia this disaffection takes the form of hostility to persistent authoritarianism, so democrats have little cause to worry. But in other cases, disaffection is more cause for concern; though, as we have noted, it may represent annoyance with the dislocations that the post-communist era has brought, rather than hostility to democracy as such. Disaffection is, however, associated with very clearly anti-democratic sentiments in Russia, Moldova, and Ukraine. In Armenia and Russia, dissatisfaction takes the form of every one of the discourses we have identified evidencing considerable disaffection from the post-communist status quo. Both countries do of course feature plenty of justifiable causes for complaint; but they are hardly unique in this respect.

The mere presence of a disaffected discourse does not of itself condemn a country to instability and anti-democratic reaction. Cynical and sometimes even overtly anti-democratic discourses can be found in the West too (for evidence on the United States and Australia, see Dryzek and Berejikian, 1993, and Dryzek, 1994). The propaganda of extreme-right groups in the United States, Western Europe, and elsewhere does meet with some discursive resonance (though also resistance).

A somewhat different kind of cause for concern from the point of view of democracy is where authoritarian post-communist regimes or governments find a supportive discourse. Belarus, China, Slovakia (under Mečiar), and Yugoslavia (under Milošević) all feature such a discourse. However, the cases of Slovakia in 1998 and Yugoslavia in 2000 show that the presence of such a discourse does not prevent a government with authoritarian leanings exiting more or less peacefully upon electoral defeat (there was some violence in Yugoslavia, though surprisingly little given Milošević's control over the police and army). The regimes in Belarus and China at the time of writing show little inclination to submit themselves to a free and fair electoral test.[8] In this reluctance they can indeed find popular discursive support – though in each case there is also a discourse that longs for such a test.

Of the countries we have examined, those with *neither* an authoritarian discourse supporting an authoritarian regime *nor* a disaffected authoritarian discourse opposing a more democratic regime are Czechia, Georgia, Poland, Romania, and Bulgaria. However, discourses we have found in Georgia, Romania, and Bulgaria present some cause for concern. In Georgia, two out of three discourses – Presidential Statism and Firm Constitutionalism – emphasize above all the need for political order accompanied by strong governmental authority, and are hostile to parliament and parties. But they could not be categorized as authoritarian because their emphasis is accompanied by support for human rights and the idea that legitimate government is founded in popular support. In our discussion of Georgia (as for Russia), we emphasized the democratic benefits of a strong and uncorrupted state that could find association with such discourses, though it is not hard to discern the authoritarian options that Presidential Statism in particular might end up supporting.

Romania too features two discourses that, while not explicitly authoritarian, appear from the outside to feature equivocal commitments to democracy. Civic Fundamentalism embodies a contradiction between strong civic commitments and support for checks and balances with a moralistic belief that in politics there are correct answers that everyone ought to recognize. While with time we can imagine such a discourse evolving in a more truly republican direction, it is also easy to imagine it becoming impatient with those who do not share its particular vision of morality (concern might be lessened here by noting that Australia has a very similar discourse of "Right-Minded Democracy" – see Dryzek, 1994). Another Romanian discourse, Deferential Collectivism, subscribes to the symbols and forms of democracy, but this commitment is very tentative, and democracy itself is treated as dispensable in the case of crisis.

This leaves Bulgaria, Czechia, and Poland as the three countries whose discursive configuration suggests the least problematic outlook for democracy. Czechia and Poland are no surprise. The inclusion of Bulgaria in this category is perhaps more surprising, especially to those who classify Bulgaria as mired in Balkan clientelism and authoritarian ethnic nationalism. There are nationalist and isolationist tendencies in two of the three Bulgarian

---

[8] On the shortcomings of the Belarusian elections in October 2000, see *International Herald Tribune*, November 1, 2000, p. 8.

discourses, but these are tempered by strong liberal and participatory commitments in the same discourses.

Four democratization roads

While we could try to squeeze more out of taxonomies of the sort developed in the previous section, and contemplate further the causes of the cross-national differences and similarities we have found, to belabor such matters would remove us further from the interpretive and possibilistic epistemological commitments we set out in chapter 1. Our basic interest is in the idea of progressively more authentic democracy in which popular control is substantive rather than symbolic, and engaged by competent citizens. In this light, a better way to distill our findings is in terms of discursive resources, opportunities, and constraints for four democratization roads: the liberal, the republican, the participatory, and the statist. Note that we do not say four roads to democracy, which could imply that democracy is a single, well-defined destination.

The first and most familiar road is *liberal*. One reason for its familiarity is that many Western analysts do not accept that any other road exists. Francis Fukuyama's "end of history" thesis may now belong to a different era of universalistic thinking about the global triumph of liberal democracy plus capitalism. But the idea that the only democracy worth talking about is liberal democracy is still widely shared among some highly influential analysts (see chapter 1).

Liberals define democracy in terms of the aggregation and reconciliation of given interests defined in the private realm and represented by parties and interest groups under a system of neutral constitutional rules that both regulate competition and specify a range of individual rights against government. The state is limited in its reach, constrained by an institutional separation of powers and the need to establish a realm for the capitalist market to regulate economic affairs. Individual pursuit of material interest is seen as the dominant fact of both economics and politics, though little is expected in the competence of ordinary citizens when it comes to politics. Liberal minimalists as introduced in chapter 1 constitute an important subset of the liberal democratic category, with the most skeptical view of citizen competence and greatest appreciation for mass apathy.

While we have found no discourse in any of our countries that is a perfect match to the liberal democratic model, we have found several that are sympathetic to its key tenets. The countries with the closest match were China (A, Radical Liberal Democracy), Belarus (A+, Liberal Democracy), Russia (A, Chastened Democracy), and Romania (A, Liberal Democracy). The relevant discourses in Belarus and Romania are very liberal in their fear of, respectively, majority rule and public opinion. The fact that China and Belarus are authoritarian systems while liberal democratic development is problematic in Romania and – still more so – Russia shows that the simple presence of a discourse does not ensure development in its direction. The discourse in question may have to contend with an overtly authoritarian regime (as in China and Belarus) as well as some vehemently anti-liberal discourses (in China, Belarus, and Russia). But at least some discursive resources for the liberal road are available.

Four countries possess a discourse that is essentially liberal democratic, but differs in one key feature. Yugoslavia's discourse A, Democratic Future, is limited in its toleration of perceived extremists, and may possibly interpret majority rule (which it favors) as Serb majority rule. Georgia's discourse A, Democratic Enthusiasm, has a more moralistic view of politics than liberals prefer (which moves it toward the republican road). Likewise, Slovakia's discourse A, Developing Pluralism, believes that political action should often be motivated by a commitment to the common good. And Bulgaria's discourse A, New Democratic Thinking, is more democratic than liberal in its denial of the need for checks on the power of an active citizenry.

Two countries have discourses that are more tenuously liberal democratic. Moldova's discourse B, Democratic Development, is somewhat statist in the kind of protection it seeks for individuals, has little interest in minority rights, and recognizes the rightful existence of a political class. Bulgaria's discourse B, Democratic Nationalism, is liberal in all respects except denial of equal rights for all ethnic groups.

Two countries have discourses that have some liberal aspects but are more social democratic in their advocacy of a relatively large and active welfare state pursuing material redistribution. Ukraine's discourse A (Social Democracy) and Armenia's discourse A (Impossible Social Democracy) fall into this category. These discourses are wary of market individualism and profit-seeking behavior and so might worry more market-oriented liberals. Still, social democracy is in the end closely related to liberal democracy.

Two seemingly surprising omissions from this list of countries with liberal democratic discourses are Poland and Czechia, which in fact highlight the possibilities for the *republican* road. In some respects this road parallels the liberal one, but differs in its identification of the essence of politics in terms of active, public-spirited citizenship, as political actors strive to discover and create common interests. This republican ideal finds clear manifestation in Poland's discourse A, Civic Republicanism, and Czechia's discourse A, Civic Enthusiasm. As we explained in the chapters on these two countries, the republican road also looms large in their history, and many of their post-communist features that alarm liberals look positive from a republican point of view. Liberals can all too easily mistake republicanism's hostility to the politics of material interest and deal-making for hostility to democracy as such.

Beyond Poland and Czechia, republican twists can also be found in the essentially liberal discourses we have noted in Georgia (discourse A, Democratic Enthusiasm) and Slovakia (Developing Pluralism) in terms of their moralistic commitment to a politics of the common good. The kind of moralism committed to clean government, social morality, collective interests, and the rule of law found in China's discourse C (Concerned Traditionalism) would have to be stretched a long way to meet republicanism, because it takes a limited view of the competence of citizens (though in this it is consistent with the Madisonian strand of republicanism), and, more seriously, wants a continued leading role for the Chinese Communist Party. Romania's discourse B, Civic Fundamentalism, shares with republicanism the idea that the common good can be defined in unitary terms, but is intolerant of the idea that people may honestly differ about what is in the common interest, and so need debate and compromise. Romania's Civic Fundamentalism treats political truth as something that exists and ought to prevail, rather than something to be discovered in dialogue.

Compared to liberal democracy, the republican path would be less interested in – indeed, would discourage – parties and interest groups representing the material interests of segments of the population. Republicanism takes a dim view of sectional interests led by careerists organizing in such terms, and so would not be especially worried by (say) a parliament that featured weakly consolidated parties. More positively, the republican path would seek both formal (state) and informal (public sphere) opportunities for the exercise and development of active citizenship. This in turn might require civic education. Networks of civic engagement are treated as more important than party systems and interest groups. When it comes to leadership, politics is conceptualized as a commitment rather than a career, and public virtue is expected of those who engage in it.

These differences notwithstanding, the republican path shares the liberal emphasis on the separation of powers and rule of law. The distinction between the two paths lies less in formal institutions than in the kinds of attitudes and motivations brought to politics, which in turn condition the nature of political interaction. For Poland and Czechia, we showed how this is manifested in the "politics of truth" associated with the legacy of pre-1989 oppositional civil society. Such politics is treated with scorn by liberal democrats such as Linz and Stepan (1996).

Liberals have even less time for the *participatory* road, given its desire to activate a citizenry liberals would consider is best left dormant. Liberals believe that this road places unrealistic demands on the political capacities of ordinary people. The participatory road has not been explored by any post-communist country, but we found participatory discourses in China (D, Alienated Egalitarianism), Yugoslavia (B, Participatory Self-Management), Bulgaria (C, Populist Isolationism), Poland (C, Disaffected Majoritarianism), and Czechia (B, Disaffected Egalitarianism). In Bulgaria, Poland, and Czechia the discourse in question appears quite alienated from the post-communist status quo. In Poland and Czechia, what the discourse seeks is in some ways a radicalization of the country's republicanism, to maximize the potential of an active citizenry, and to detach republicanism from liberalism (as represented by separation of powers and constitutional restraints). China's Alienated Egalitarianism can be interpreted as a demand for the regime actually to serve the ordinary people, rather than pretend to do so.

Aside from this discursive support, it is hard to see the participatory road as especially feasible in China, Bulgaria, Poland, and Czechia. However, Yugoslavia is different. The discourse of Participatory Self-Management is a direct heir to the self-management of economy and (later) polity practiced under Tito. That discourse and legacy constitute a viable way to think about democracy in Yugoslavia. This participatory road is especially attractive because it is not associated with a liberal model of democracy that, the demise of the Milošević regime notwithstanding, many Yugoslavs associate with the Western enemies of their country. The fact that the Participatory Self-Management discourse cuts across partisan political divisions in Yugoslavia makes it additionally promising in a deeply torn society.

When liberal (including social democratic), republican, and participatory roads are unavailable, recourse is necessary to a *statist* road. Ideally, such a road would find a supportive discourse, of the sort we have found in Armenia (C, Legalistic Paternalism), Georgia (B, Presidential Statism, and C, Firm Constitutionalism), and Poland (B, Guided Democracy). The statist road involves a strong state as introduced in chapter 1, with effective leadership committed to uncorrupted and constitutional government, making laws and guiding an administration with the capacity to implement policies, collect taxes, and resist both authoritarianism and anarchy. Such a state is especially attractive where civil society is weak, society is deeply divided, and corruption and organized crime are rampant in both polity and economy. We addressed the case for such a state at length in the chapter on Russia, more briefly in our discussions of Armenia and Georgia. Unlike Armenia, Georgia, and Poland, Russia lacks a discourse that corresponds directly to the statist democratization route. But we showed how elements even of Russia's discourses B and C, Reactionary Anti-Liberalism and Authoritarian Development, could be enlisted in support of this road – notably, in terms of their desire for an uncorrupted state, and their lamentation of alienation, loss of trust, and absence of civility and morality in government and economy.

For Russia, it is hard to see what other road is available. Georgia features an equally disastrous (perhaps even worse) set of post-communist experiences, but there the statist road can draw upon two supportive discourses – and the Shevardnadze presidency, for all its failings, has moved substantially down this route. In Armenia, the statist road is explicitly supported by one discourse, but could also make common cause with the discourse of "Impossible Social Democracy," which also advocates an interventionist, capable state (though this discourse would have to shed its pessimism).

Obviously there are dangers with the statist road (as there are with all roads). It is important not to confuse it with the liberal authoritarianism advocated by, for example, Jowitt (1992, p. 302), or the semi-authoritarianism that Gati (1996) believes represents the most likely future for most post-communist states. We have already rejected the argument that authoritarianism is conducive to – let alone necessary for – economic modernization and growth. If the strong state is to be competent, effective, constructive, and dynamic in supporting democratization, it has several tasks.

The first is to introduce a democratic constitution, though S. Holmes (1995) for one believes it is better not to do this too quickly, so as to maximize the likelihood of producing a document that better reflects a particular society's needs and discourses. Obviously, once the constitution is passed, it must be observed; a powerful constitutional court is one way of ensuring this. If transition states are to overcome the corruption and organized crime that are among the biggest threats to the rule of law and democracy's legitimacy, clear property laws must be passed and implemented. Such laws will encourage the development of legal economic activity independent of the state, which in turn will promote the organization of civil society.[9] Closely related to this is the need for effective conflict of interest laws and laws on political immunity.

A second task is to promote a division or separation of powers. At present, one of the most important ways of doing this is to promote a responsible legislature. Statist democratization would ideally involve effective executive performance facilitating norms of compromise between previously warring parliamentarians. As this happens, the executive may be confident in increasing the real powers of parliament, thus establishing rule by law instead of the rule by decree that some post-communist presidents (including Russia's Yeltsin) have practiced. A strong state, precisely because it is in important

---

[9] This is *not* to equate an independent economic sector with civil society, though as Max Weber and Barrington Moore point out, an autonomous business class can play an important civil society role in controlling and limiting the state.

respects exclusive, may even encourage (if not by design) the development of a lively oppositional civil society – though so far the democratic benefits of exclusive states for civil society can be discerned only in established Western democracies, such as Germany, where corporatist policy-making (excluding all interests except business and labor) has flourished (Dryzek, 1996b).

These four roads – liberal, republican, participatory, and statist – do not necessarily exhaust the possibilities for democratization trajectories in the post-communist world. Nor are they mutually exclusive. One can imagine, for example, a felicitous combination of statism and the social democratic variant of liberalism (appropriate, as we have noted, in Armenia). Yet reformers cannot pick and choose elements of each at will. Each road offers a relatively coherent package, a core around which democratization can be organized. And each is constrained by the discursive field we have described in each country. For any such project to be reflexively democratic requires some degree of resonance with this field. We have shown that some such project is feasible in all the post-communist countries we have studied – even Russia, which in many ways presents the least promising combination of political-economic circumstances and discourses. Situations and prospects may vary substantially across countries, but none of them should be written off. Outsiders who are genuinely committed to the democratization project can help through encouragement, keeping an open mind toward different forms of democracy, and promoting the inclusion of post-communist states in international society (e.g., through membership of the European Union). Everywhere, there are democratic projects to be pursued.

References

Ágh, Attila. 1993. The "Comparative Revolution" and the Transition in Central and Southern Europe. *Journal of Theoretical Politics,* 5 (2): 231–52.

——— 1999. Processes of Democratization in the East Central European and Balkan States: Sovereignty-Related Conflicts in the Context of Europeanization. *Communist and Post-Communist Studies,* 32 (3): 263–79.

Alker, Hayward R. Jr., and David Sylvan. 1986. Political Discourse Analysis. Paper presented at the Annual Meeting of the American Political Science Association, Washington, DC.

Anonymous. 1999. Constitution Watch: Belarus. *East European Constitutional Review Online,* 8 (4) online at http://www.law.nyu.edu/eecr/vol8num4/constitutionwatch/belarus.html.

——— 2000. Constitution Watch: Moldova. *East European Constitutional Review,* 9 (1–2) online at http://www.law.nyu.edu/eecr/vol9num_onehalf/constitutionwatch/moldova.html.

Arato, Andrew. 1993. Interpreting 1989. *Social Research,* 60: 609–46.

Arendt, Hannah. 1958. *The Human Condition.* Chicago: University of Chicago Press.

Ascherson, Neal. 1982. *The Polish August: The Self-Limiting Revolution.* New York: Viking.

Auer, Stefan. 2000. Nationalism in Central Europe: A Chance or a Threat for the Emerging Liberal Democratic Order? *East European Politics and Societies,* 14 (2): 213–45.

Avineri, Shlomo. 1997. State Weakness as an Obstacle to Democratization. *East European Constitutional Review,* 6 (1): 94–9.

Bankowicz, Marek. 1994a. Bulgaria: The Continuing Revolution. 219–37 in Berglund and Dellenbrant, 1994.
  1994b. Czechoslovakia: From Masaryk to Havel. 142–68 in Berglund and Dellenbrant, 1994.
Beck, Ulrich. 1992. *Risk Society: Towards a New Modernity*. London: Sage.
Beck, Ulrich, Anthony Giddens, and Scott Lash. 1994. *Reflexive Modernization: Politics, Tradition and Aesthetics in the Modern Social Order*. Cambridge: Polity.
Bell, John D. 1991. Modernization through Secularization in Bulgaria. 15–32 in Gerasimos Augustinos (ed.), *Diverse Paths to Modernity in Southeastern Europe*. New York: Greenwood.
Bell-Fialkoff, Andrew. 1993. A Brief History of Ethnic Cleansing. *Foreign Affairs*, 72 (3): 110–21.
Berglund, Sten, and Jan Åke Dellenbrant (eds.). 1994. *The New Democracies in Eastern Europe: Party Systems and Political Cleavages*, 2nd edn. Aldershot: Edward Elgar.
Berglund, Sten, Tomas Hellén, and Frank Aarebrot (eds.). 1998. *The Handbook of Political Change in Eastern Europe*. Cheltenham: Edward Elgar.
Bernhard, Michael. 1996. Civil Society after the First Transition: Dilemmas of Post-Communist Democratization in Poland and beyond. *Communist and Post-Communist Studies*, 29 (3): 309–30.
Bertsch, Gary. 1973. The Revival of Nationalisms. *Problems of Communism*, 22 (6): 1–15.
Bielasiak, Jack. 1997. Substance and Process in the Development of Party Systems in East Central Europe. *Communist and Post-Communist Studies*, 30 (1): 23–44.
Binder, Leonard, *et al.* 1971. *Crises and Sequences in Political Development*. Princeton, NJ: Princeton University Press.
Birch, Sarah, and Andrew Wilson. 1999. The Ukrainian Parliamentary Elections of 1998. *Electoral Studies*, 18 (2): 276–82.
Block, Fred. 1977. The Ruling Class Does Not Rule: Notes on the Marxist Theory of the State. *Socialist Revolution*, 7: 6–28.
Bollen, Kenneth. 1980. Issues in the Comparative Measurement of Political Democracy. *American Sociological Review*, 45 (3): 370–90.
Bourdieu, Pierre. 1990. *In Other Words*. Cambridge: Polity.
  1993. *The Field of Cultural Production*. New York: Columbia University Press.
Bowles, Paul, and Xiao-yuan Dong. 1994. Current Success and Future Challenge in China's Economic Reforms. *New Left Review*, 208: 49–76.
Bremmer, Ian, and Ray Taras (eds.). 1993. *Nations and Politics in the Soviet Successor States*. Cambridge: Cambridge University Press.

(eds.). 1997. *New States, New Politics: Building the Post-Soviet Nations.* Cambridge: Cambridge University Press.

Breslauer, George, Josef Brada, Clifford Gaddy, Richard Ericson, Carol Saivetz, and Victor Winston. 2000. Russia at the End of Yel'tsin's Presidency. *Post-Soviet Affairs,* 16 (1): 1–32.

Brown, Archie. 1999. Russia and Democratization. *Problems of Post-Communism,* 46 (5): 3–13.

   2000. Transnational Influences in the Transition from Communism. *Post-Soviet Affairs,* 16 (2): 177–200.

Brown, James F. 1994. *Hopes and Shadows: Eastern Europe After Communism.* Durham, NC: Duke University Press.

Brown, Steven R. 1980. *Political Subjectivity: Applications of Q Methodology in Political Science.* New Haven, CT: Yale University Press.

   1986. Q Technique and Method: Principles and Procedures. 57–76 in William D. Berry and Michael S. Lewis-Beck (eds.), *New Tools for Social Scientists.* Beverly Hills, CA: Sage.

Brubaker, Rogers. 1996. *Nationalism Reframed: Nationhood and the National Question in the New Europe.* Cambridge: Cambridge University Press.

Brucan, Silviu. 1992. Democracy at Odds with the Market in Post-Communist Societies. 19–25 in Michael Keren and Gur Ofer (eds.), *Trials of Transition: Economic Reform in the Former Soviet Bloc.* Boulder, CO: Westview.

Bryant, Christopher, and Edmund Mokrzycki. 1994. Introduction: Theorizing the Changes in East-Central Europe. 1–13 in Christopher Bryant and Edmund Mokrzycki (eds.), *The New Great Transformation? Change and Continuity in East-Central Europe.* London: Routledge.

Brzezinski, Zbigniew. 1993. The Great Transformation. *National Interest,* 33: 3–13.

Bunce, Valerie. 1995a. Paper Curtains and Paper Tigers. *Slavic Review,* 54 (4): 979–80.

   1995b. Should Transitologists be Grounded? *Slavic Review,* 54 (1): 111–27.

   1999a. The Political Economy of Postsocialism. *Slavic Review,* 58 (4): 756–93.

   1999b. *Subversive Institutions: The Design and Destruction of Socialism and the State.* Cambridge: Cambridge University Press.

Bútora, Martin. 1999. The Present State of Democracy in Slovakia. 93–104 in Kaldor and Vejvoda, 1999.

Campbell, Adrian. 1996. Local Government and the Centre in Romania and Moldova. 73–112 in Gibson and Hanson, 1996.

Canovan, Margaret E. 1987. Republicanism. 433–6 in David Miller (ed.), *The Blackwell Encyclopaedia of Political Thought.* Oxford: Basil Blackwell.

Carassava, Anthee. 2000. A Greek Tragedy. *Time Europe*. April 10.

Carpenter, Michael. 1997. Slovakia and the Triumph of Nationalistic Populism. *Communist and Post-Communist Studies*, 30: 205–20.

CCTV (China Central TV). 1988. *He shang* [River elegy]. June.

Chirot, Daniel (ed.). 1989a. Causes and Consequences of Backwardness. 1–14 in Chirot 1989b.

   1989b. *The Origins of Backwardness in Eastern Europe: Economics and Politics from the Middle Ages until the Early Twentieth Century*. Berkeley: University of California Press.

Cohen, Lenard. 1995. *Broken Bonds*. Boulder, CO: Westview.

Commisso, Ellen. 1997. Is the Glass Half Full or Half Empty? Reflections on Five Years of Competitive Politics in Eastern Europe. *Communist and Post-Communist Studies*, 30: 1–21.

Crampton, Richard. 1997. *A Concise History of Bulgaria*. Cambridge: Cambridge University Press.

Crowther, William. 1997a. Moldova: Caught between Nation and Empire. 316–49 in Bremmer and Taras, 1997.

   1997b. The Politics of Democratization in Postcommunist Moldova. 282–329 in Dawisha and Parrott, 1997b.

Cumings, Bruce. 1999. *Parallax Visions: Making Sense of American–East Asian Relations at the End of the Century*. Durham, NC: Duke University Press.

Dawisha, Karen, and Bruce Parrott (eds.). 1997a. *The Consolidation of Democracy in East-Central Europe*. Cambridge: Cambridge University Press.

   (eds.). 1997b. *Democratic Changes and Authoritarian Reactions in Russia, Ukraine, Belarus, and Moldova*. Cambridge: Cambridge University Press.

   (eds.). 1997c. *Politics, Power, and the Struggle for Democracy in South-East Europe*. Cambridge: Cambridge University Press.

de Winter, Lieven, and Huri Türsan (eds.). 1998. *Regionalist Parties in Western Europe*. London: Routledge.

Dellenbrant, Jan Åke. 1994. Romania: The Slow Revolution. 203–18 in Berglund and Dellenbrant, 1994.

Di Palma, Giuseppe. 1990. *To Craft Democracies*. Berkeley: University of California Press.

   1993. Why Democracy Can Work in Eastern Europe. 257–67 in Larry Diamond and Marc Plattner (eds.), *The Global Resurgence of Democracy*. Baltimore: Johns Hopkins University Press.

Dimitrijevic, Vojin. 1994. *The 1974 Constitution as a Factor in the Collapse of Yugoslavia or as a Sign of Decaying Totalitarianism*. Working Paper, RSC No. 94/9. Florence: European University Institute.

1996. Sukobi oko ustava iz 1974 [Conflicts over the 1974 Constitution]. 447–71 in Popov, 1996.

Dimitrov, Georgi, Petya Kabakchieva, and Zheko Kiossev. 1996. *Russia and Bulgaria: Farewell Democracy*. Sofia: LIK Publishing House.

Dinkic, Mladjen. 1995. *Ekonomija destrukcije: velika pljacka naroda* [The economy of destruction: great robbery of the nation]. Belgrade: Vin.

Dittmer, Lowell. 1987. Public and Private Interests and the Participatory Ethic in China. 18–27 in Victor C. Falkenheim (ed.), *Citizens and Groups in Contemporary China*. Ann Arbor: Center for Chinese Studies, University of Michigan.

Djordjevich, Dusan. 1999. Report on South-Eastern Europe: Concepts, Histories, Boundaries. Report on a conference held at the School of Slavonic and East European Studies, University of London, June 19. Online at http://www.ssees.ac.uk/concrept.htm.

Dryzek, John S. 1994. Australian Discourses of Democracy. *Australian Journal of Political Science*, 29: 221–39.

1996a. *Democracy in Capitalist Times: Ideals, Limits and Struggles*. New York: Oxford University Press.

1996b. Political Inclusion and the Dynamics of Democratization. *American Political Science Review*, 90 (3): 475–87.

Dryzek, John S., and Jeffrey Berejikian. 1993. Reconstructive Democratic Theory. *American Political Science Review*, 87 (1): 48–60.

Dryzek, John S., and Leslie Holmes. 2000. The Real World of Civic Republicanism: Making Democracy Work in Poland and the Czech Republic. *Europe–Asia Studies*, 52 (6): 1043–68.

Dudwick, Nora. 1997. Armenia: Paradise Lost? 471–504 in Bremmer and Taras, 1997.

Dunlop, John. 1993. Russia: Confronting a Loss of Empire. 43–72 in Bremmer and Taras, 1993.

Elster, Jon, Claus Offe, and Ulrich Preuss (with others). 1998. *Institutional Design in Post-Communist Societies: Rebuilding the Ship at Sea*. Cambridge: Cambridge University Press.

Encarnación, Omar. 2000. Beyond Transition: The Politics of Democratic Consolidation. *Comparative Politics*, 32 (4): 479–98.

European Commission. 1997. *Agenda 2000: Commission Opinion on Slovakia's Application for Membership of the European Union*. Brussels: European Union.

Evans, Geoffrey, and Stephen Whitefield. 1996. Cleavage Formation in Transitional Societies: Russia, Ukraine and Estonia. Unpublished paper presented at the 1996 Annual Conference of the American Political Science Association, San Francisco.

Fischer-Galati, Stephen. 1991. *Twentieth-Century Romania.* New York: Columbia University Press.

Fish, M. Steven. 1998. Democratization's Requisites: The Postcommunist Experience. *Post-Soviet Affairs,* 14 (3): 212–47.

1999. Postcommunist Subversion: Social Science and Democratization in East Europe and Eurasia. *Slavic Review,* 58 (4): 794–823.

Fitzmaurice, John. 1998. *Politics and Government in the Visegrad Countries.* London: Macmillan.

Flers, René de. 1984. Socialism in One Family. *Survey,* 28 (4): 165–75.

Frentzel-Zagorska, Janina. 1989. Semi-Free Elections in Poland. Unpublished paper presented at the Australasian Political Studies Association Annual Conference, Sydney.

Fukuyama, Francis. 1989. The End of History? *National Interest,* Summer: 3–18.

1992. *The End of History and the Last Man.* New York: Free Press.

Gallagher, Tom. 1995a. Democratization in the Balkans: Challenges and Prospects. *Democratization,* 2 (3): 337–61.

1995b. *Romania after Ceauşescu: The Politics of Intolerance.* Edinburgh: Edinburgh University Press.

Ganev, Venelin I. 1997. Bulgaria's Symphony of Hope. *Journal of Democracy,* 8 (4): 125–40.

Garnett, Sherman, and Rachel Lebenson. 1998. Ukraine Joins the Fray: Will Peace Come to Trans-Dniestria? *Problems of Post-Communism,* 45 (6): 22–32.

Gasiorowski, Mark J. 2000. Democracy and Macroeconomic Performance in Underdeveloped Countries. *Comparative Political Studies,* 33 (3): 319–49.

Gati, Charles. 1990. East-Central Europe: The Morning After. *Foreign Affairs,* 69 (5): 129–45.

1996. If Not Democracy, What? Leaders, Laggards and Losers in the Post-Communist World. 168–98 in Mandelbaum, 1996.

Gibson, John, and Philip Hanson (eds.). 1996. *Transformation from Below: Local Power and the Political Economy of Post-Communist Transition.* Cheltenham: Edward Elgar.

Gilberg, Trond. 1990. *Nationalism and Communism in Romania: The Rise and Fall of Ceauşescu's Personal Dictatorship.* Boulder, CO: Westview.

Gitelman, Zvi. 1994. Nationality and Ethnicity in Russia and the Post-Soviet Republics. 237–65 in White, Pravda, and Gitelman, 1994.

Glenny, Misha. 1993. *The Fall of Yugoslavia.* London: Penguin.

Green, A. T., and C. Skalnik Leff. 1997. The Quality of Democracy: Mass–Elite Linkages in the Czech Republic. *Democratization,* 4: 63–87.

Grzybowski, Marian. 1994. Poland: Towards Overdeveloped Pluralism. 36–73 in Berglund and Dellenbrant, 1994.

Habermas, Jürgen. 1979. *Communication and the Evolution of Society.* Boston: Beacon Press.

Hadzhiiski, Ivan. 1997. *Optimistichna teoria za nashya narod.* Sofia: Otechestvo.

Halbach, Uwe. 1997. Präkare Transformation: Reform und Stabilitätswahrung in Kaukasien und Zentralasien. 105–15 in Höhmann, 1997.

Havel, Václav, et al. 1985. *The Power of the Powerless: Citizens against the State.* Armonk, NY: Sharpe.

Held, Joseph (ed.). 1992. *Columbia History of Eastern Europe in the Twentieth Century.* New York: Columbia University Press.

Hellén, Tomas, Berglund, Sten, and Aarebrot, Frank. 1998. From Transition to Consolidation. 365–77 in Berglund, Hellén, and Aarebrot, 1998.

Hill, Ronald J. 1994. Parties and the Party System. 88–108 in White, Pravda, and Gitelman, 1994.

Hindess, Barry. 2000. Representation Ingrafted upon Democracy. *Democratization,* 7 (2): 1–18.

Höhmann, Hans-Hermann (chief ed.). 1997. *Der Osten Europas im Prozeß der Differenzierung: Fortschritte und Mißerfolge der Transformation.* Munich: Carl Hanser Verlag.

Holmes, Leslie. 1993. *The End of Communist Power: Anti-Corruption Campaigns and Legitimation Crisis.* New York: Oxford University Press.

——— 1996. Poland and Hungary: Two Approaches to Post-Communist Transition? *Russia and Euro-Asia Bulletin,* 5 (12): 1–8.

——— 1998. The Democratic State or State Democracy? Problems of Post-Communist Transition. Jean Monnet Chair Papers, no. 48. Florence: European University Institute.

Holmes, Stephen. 1995. Conceptions of Democracy in the Draft Constitutions of Post-Communist Countries. 71–81 in Beverly Crawford (ed.), *Markets, States and Democracy.* Boulder, CO: Westview.

——— 1996. Cultural Legacies or State Collapse? 22–76 in Mandelbaum, 1996.

——— 1997. What Russia Teaches Us Now: How Weak States Threaten Freedom. *American Prospect,* 33: 30–9.

Holtbrügge, Dirk. 1996. *Weißrußland.* Munich: Beck.

Hua, Shiping. 1992. All Roads Lead to Democracy: A Critical Analysis of the Writings of Three Chinese Reformist Intellectuals. *Bulletin of Concerned Asian Scholars,* 24: 43–58.

Hughes, J. 2000. Transition Models and Democratisation in Russia. 21–49 in M. Bowker and C. Ross (eds.), *Russia after the Cold War.* London: Longman.

Hunter, Shireen. 1993. Azerbaijan: Search for Identity and New Partners. 225–60 in Bremmer and Taras, 1993.

Huntington, Samuel. 1991. *The Third Wave*. Norman: University of Oklahoma Press.

1996. *The Clash of Civilizations and the Remaking of World Order*. New York: Simon and Schuster.

Huskey, Eugene. 1999. *Presidential Power in Russia*. Armonk, NY: M. E. Sharpe.

Ionescu, Ghita. 1964. *Communism in Romania: 1944–1962*. Oxford: Oxford University Press.

Isaac, Jeffrey. 1994. Oases in the Desert: Hannah Arendt on Democratic Politics. *American Political Science Review*, 88 (1): 156–68.

Isiyama, John T., and Matthew Velten. 1998. Presidential Power and Democratic Development in Post-Communist Politics. *Communist and Post-Communist Studies*, 31: 217–33.

Janos, Andrew C. 1995. Europe, East Central. 442–51 in Seymour Martin Lipset (ed.), *Encyclopedia of Democracy*, vol. II. London: Routledge.

Jenner, William J. F. 1992. *The Tyranny of History: The Roots of China's Crisis*. Harmondsworth: Penguin.

Johnson, James. 1991. Rational Choice as a Reconstructive Theory. 113–42 in Kristin Monroe (ed.), *The Economic Approach to Politics*. New York: HarperCollins.

Jones, Stephen F. 1993. Georgia: A Failed Democratic Transition. 288–310 in Bremmer and Taras, 1993.

1997. Georgia: The Trauma of Statehood. 505–43 in Bremmer and Taras, 1997.

2000. Democracy from below: Interest Groups in Georgian Society. *Slavic Review*, 59 (1): 42–73.

Jowitt, Ken. 1992. *New World Disorder: The Leninist Extinction*. Berkeley: University of California Press.

Kaldor, Mary, and Ivan Vejvoda. 1997. Democratization in Central and East European Countries. *International Affairs*, 73: 59–82.

(eds.). 1999. *Democratization in Central and Eastern Europe*. London: Frances Pinter.

Karasimeonov, Georgi. 1998. Bulgaria. 335–64 in Berglund, Hellén, and Aarebrot, 1998.

Karatnycky, Adrian. 1995. Ukraine at the Crossroads. *Journal of Democracy*, 6 (1): 117–30.

Karl, Terry Lynn, and Philippe Schmitter. 1995. From an Iron Curtain to a Paper Curtain: Grounding Transitologists or Students of Postcommunism? *Slavic Review*, 54 (4): 965–78.

Kavan, Zdeněk and Martin Palouš. 1999. Democracy in the Czech Republic. 78–92 in Kaldor and Vejvoda, 1999.

Kettle, Steve. 1995. Of Money and Morality. *Transition*, 1 (3): 36–9.

King, Charles. 2000. *The Moldovans: Romania, Russia and the Politics of Culture*. Stanford, CA: Hoover Institution Press.

Kirschbaum, Stanislav. 1995. *A History of Slovakia: The Struggle for Survival*. London: Macmillan.

Kitschelt, Herbert, Zdenka Mansfeldova, Radslaw Markowski, and Gábor Tóka. 1999. *Post-Communist Party Systems: Competition, Representation and Inter-Party Cooperation*. Cambridge: Cambridge University Press.

Kitzinger, Celia. 1986. Introducing and Developing Q as a Feminist Methodology. 151–72 in Sue Wilkinson (ed.), *Feminist Social Psychology*. Milton Keynes: Open University Press.

Kolarova, Rumyana. 1999. Democratization in Bulgaria: Recent Trends. 150–61 in Kaldor and Vejvoda, 1999.

Konrád, George [György]. 1984. *Antipolitics*. Boca Raton, FL: CRC.

Kopecky, Petr, and Cas Mudde. 2000. What Has Eastern Europe Taught Us about the Democratisation Literature (and Vice Versa)? *European Journal of Political Research*, 37: 517–39.

Korbonski, Andrzej. 1994. From Annus Mirabilis to Annus Horribilis? Poland 1989–1993. 219–33 in Joan Serafin (ed.), *East-Central Europe in the 1990s*. Boulder, CO: Westview.

Krawchenko, Bohdan. 1993. Ukraine: The Politics of Independence. 75–98 in Bremmer and Taras, 1993.

Król, Marcin. 1999. Democracy in Poland. 67–77 in Kaldor and Vejvoda, 1999.

Kuzio, Taras, and Andrew Wilson. 1994. *Ukraine: Perestroika to Independence*. London: Macmillan.

Lang, David. 1962. *A Modern History of Georgia*. London: Weidenfeld and Nicolson.

1970. *Armenia: Cradle of Civilisation*. London: Allen and Unwin.

Lei, Guang. 1996. Elusive Democracy: Conceptual Change and the Chinese Democracy Movement, 1978–9 to 1989. *Modern China*, 22 (4): 417–47.

Lewis, Paul G. 1995. Poland's New Parties in the Post-Communist Political System. 29–47 in Gordon Wightman (ed.), *Party Formation in East-Central Europe: Post-Communist Politics in Czechoslovakia, Hungary, Poland and Bulgaria*. Cheltenham: Edward Elgar.

Lijphart, Arend. 1984. *Democracies: Patterns of Majoritarian and Consensus Government in Twenty-One Countries*. New Haven, CT: Yale University Press.

Linz, Juan J., and Alfred E. Stepan. 1996. *Problems of Democratic Transition and Consolidation: Southern Europe, South America, and Post-Communist Europe.* Baltimore: Johns Hopkins University Press.

Lipset, Seymour Martin. 1959. Some Social Requisites of Democracy: Economic Development and Political Legitimacy. *American Political Science Review,* 53 (1): 69–105.

Lipset, Seymour Martin, and Stein Rokkan. 1967. Cleavage Structures, Party Systems and Voter Alignments: An Introduction. 1–64 in Seymour Martin Lipset and Stein Rokkan (eds.), *Party Systems and Voter Alignments.* New York: Free Press.

Lydall, Harold. 1986. *Yugoslav Socialism.* Oxford: Oxford University Press.

Macintyre, Alasdair. 1973. Is a Science of Comparative Politics Possible? 171–88 in A. Ryan (ed.), *The Philosophy of Social Explanation.* Oxford: Oxford University Press.

Mandelbaum, Michael (ed.). 1996. *Post-Communism: Four Perspectives.* New York: Council on Foreign Relations.

Markus, Ustina. 1995a. Heading off an Energy Disaster. *Transition,* 1 (5): 10–13.

1995b. Still Coming to Terms with Independence. *Transition,* 1 (2): 47–52.

Marples, David. 1993. Belarus: The Illusion of Stability. *Post-Soviet Affairs,* 9 (3): 253–77.

1999. *Belarus: A Denationalized Nation.* Amsterdam: Horwood.

Marsh, Christopher. 2000. Social Capital and Democracy in Russia. *Communist and Post-Communist Studies,* 33 (2): 183–99.

Mihajlovic, Srecko, *et al.* 1991. *Od izbornih rituala do slobodnih izbora* [From election rituals to free elections]. Belgrade: Univerzitet u Beogradu IDN.

Miháliková, Silvia. 1996. The Painful Birth of Slovak Democratic Political Culture. *Slovak Sociological Review,* 1: 51–68.

Mihalisko, Kathleen J. 1997. Belarus: Retreat to Authoritarianism. 223–81 in Dawisha and Parrott, 1997b.

Mihut, Liliana. 1994. The Emergence of Political Pluralism in Romania. *Communist and Post-Communist Studies,* 27 (4): 411–22.

Miklos, Ivan, 1998. Privatization. 117–26 in Martin Bútora and Thomas W. Skladony (eds.), *Slovakia 1996–1997: A Global Report on the State of Society.* Bratislava: Institute for Public Affairs.

Miller, Arthur H., Gwyn Erb, William M. Reisinger, and Vicki L. Hesli. 2000. Emerging Party Systems in Post-Soviet Societies: Fact or Fiction? *Journal of Politics,* 62 (2): 455–90.

Miller, Nicholas J. 1997. A Failed Transition: The Case of Serbia. 146–88 in Dawisha and Parrott, 1997a.

Miller, William, Stephen White, and Paul Heywood. 1998. *Values and Political Change in Postcommunist Europe.* New York: St. Martin's Press.

Mitev, Petar-Emil. 1997. Party Manifestos for the Bulgarian 1994 Elections. *Journal of Communist Studies and Transition Politics,* 13 (1): 64–90.

Moore, Barrington. 1967. *Social Origins of Dictatorship and Democracy.* Harmondsworth: Penguin.

Mueller, John. 1996. Democracy, Capitalism, and the End of Transition. 102–67 in Mandelbaum, 1996.

Munck, Geraldo L., and Carol Skalnik Leff. 1997. Modes of Transition and Democratization: South America and Eastern Europe in Comparative Perspective. *Comparative Politics,* 29: 343–63.

Murrell, Peter. 1993. What Is Shock Therapy? What Did It Do in Poland and Russia? *Post-Soviet Affairs,* 9 (2): 111–40.

Musil, Jiří (ed.). 1995. *The End of Czechoslovakia.* Budapest: Central European University Press.

Nagy-Talavera, Nicolas. 1967. *The Green Shirts and Others: A History of Fascism in Hungary and Romania.* Berkeley: University of California Press.

Nathan, Andrew. 1985. *Chinese Democracy.* New York: Knopf.

Nathan, Andrew, and Tianjian Shi. 1993. Cultural Requisites for Democracy in China: Findings from a Survey. *Daedalus,* 122: 95–123.

Nelson, Lynn, and Paata Amonashvili. 1992. Voting and Political Attitudes in Soviet Georgia. *Soviet Studies,* 44 (4): 687–97.

Nodia, Ghia. 1995. Georgia's Identity Crisis. *Journal of Democracy,* 6 (1): 104–16.

O'Donnell, Guillermo. 1994. Delegative Democracy. *Journal of Democracy,* 5 (1): 55–69.

O'Donnell, Guillermo, and Philippe Schmitter. 1986. *Transitions from Authoritarian Rule: Tentative Conclusions about Uncertain Democracies.* Baltimore: Johns Hopkins University Press.

Offe, Claus. 1991. Capitalism by Democratic Design: Democratic Theory Facing the Triple Transition in East Central Europe. *Social Research,* 58: 865–92.

Oi, Jean. 1992. Fiscal Reform and the Economic Foundations of Local State Corporatism in China. *World Politics,* 45 (1): 99–126.

OSCE. 1997. Human Rights and Democratization in Slovakia. Organization for Security and Cooperation in Europe, September.

Ost, David. 1993. The Politics of Interest in Post-Communist Eastern Europe. *Theory and Society,* 22: 453–86.

Pateman, Carole. 1970. *Participation and Democratic Theory.* Cambridge: Cambridge University Press.

Peng, Yali. 1996. The Politics of Tobacco: Relations between Farmers and Local Governments in China's Southwest. *China Journal*, 36: 67–82.

1998. Democracy and Chinese Political Discourses. *Modern China*, 24: 408–44.

Pesic, Vesna. 1996. The War for Nation States. 3–59 in Popov, 1996.

Pickel, Andreas. 1993. Authoritarianism or Democracy? Marketization as a Political Problem. *Policy Sciences*, 26: 139–63.

Pickvance, Chris. 1999. Democratisation and the Decline of Social Movements: The Effects of Regime Change on Collective Action in Eastern Europe, Southern Europe and Latin America. *Sociology*, 33 (2): 353–72.

Pippidi, Alina Mungiu. 1999. Romania: From Procedural Democracy to European Integration. 135–49 in Kaldor and Vejvoda, 1999.

Plasser, Fritz, Peter A. Ulram, and Harald Waldrauch. 1998. *Democratic Consolidation in East-Central Europe*. Houndmills: Macmillan.

Plichtová, Jana, and Ferenc Erös. 1997. Meaning of Some Political and Economic Terms in Relation to Experience of Two Slovak and Hungarian Generations. *Sociológica*, 29: 723–37.

Popov, Nebojsa (ed.). 1996. *Srpska strana rata*. [The Serbian side of the war]. Belgrade: Republika.

Powell, G. Bingham. 1982. *Contemporary Democracies: Participation, Stability, and Violence*. Cambridge, MA: Harvard University Press.

Powers, Denise. 1998. Authenticating Democratic Transitions: Bringing the Demos (back) in. Unpublished typescript, University of Iowa.

Prizel, Ilya. 1997. Ukraine between Proto-Democracy and "Soft" Authoritarianism. 330–69 in Dawisha and Parrott, 1997b.

Prybyla, Jan S. 1989. Why China's Economic Reforms Fail. *Asian Survey*, 29: 1017–32.

Przeworski, Adam. 1991. *Democracy and the Market: Political and Economic Reforms in Eastern Europe and Latin America*. Cambridge: Cambridge University Press.

Przeworski, Adam, Michael E. Alvarez, Jose Antonio Cheibub, and Fernando Limongi. 2000. *Democracy and Development: Political Institutions and Well-Being in the World, 1950–1990*. Cambridge: Cambridge University Press.

Przeworski, Adam, and Fernando Limongi. 1997. Modernization: Theories and Facts. *World Politics*, 49 (2): 155–83.

Putnam, Robert D. 1993. *Making Democracy Work: Civic Traditions in Modern Italy*. Princeton, NJ: Princeton University Press.

Pye, Lucian. 1966. *Aspects of Political Development*. Boston, MA: Little Brown.

1985. *Asian Power and Politics: The Cultural Dimensions of Authority.* Cambridge, MA: Harvard University Press.

Rady, Martyn. 1992. *Romania in Turmoil.* London: Tauris.

Ramet, Sabrina. 1997. Democratization in Slovenia: The Second Stage. 189–225 in Dawisha and Parrott, 1997c.

Ratesh, Nestor. 1991. *Romania: The Entangled Revolution.* New York: Praeger.

Remington, Thomas F. 1997. Democratization and the New Political Order in Russia. 69–129 in Dawisha and Parrott, 1997b.

2000. Putin's Third Way: Russia and the "Strong State" Ideal. *East European Constitutional Review,* 9 (1–2), online at http://www.law.nyu.edu/eecr/vol9num_onehalf/feature/strongstate.html.

Renmin ribao [People's Daily], September 7, 1994.

Renmin ribao, haiwai ban [People's Daily, overseas edition], October 5, 1995.

Rose, Richard. 2000a. How Floating Parties Frustrate Democratic Accountability: A Supply-Side View of Russia's Elections. *East European Constitutional Review,* 9 (1–2), online at http://www.law.nyu.edu/eecr/vol9num_onehalf/feature/supplyside.html.

2000b. Uses of Social Capital in Russia: Modern, Pre-Modern, and Anti-Modern. *Post-Soviet Affairs,* 16 (1): 33–57.

Rose, Richard, and William Mishler. 1993. *Reacting to Regime Change in Eastern Europe.* Glasgow: University of Strathclyde Studies in Public Policy, No. 210.

Rose, Richard, William Mishler, and Christian Haerpfer. 1998. *Democracy and Its Alternatives: Understanding Post-Communist Societies.* Cambridge: Polity.

Rostow, Walter. 1971. *Politics and the Stages of Growth.* Cambridge: Cambridge University Press.

Rueschemeyer, Dietrich, Evelyn Huber Stephens, and John D. Stephens. 1992. *Capitalist Development and Democracy.* Chicago: University of Chicago Press.

Rupnik, Jacques. 1981. The Restoration of the Party-State in Czechoslovakia since 1968. 105–24 in Leslie Holmes (ed.), *The Withering Away of the State: Party and State under Communism.* London: Sage.

Rusinow, Dennison. 1977. *The Yugoslav Experiment 1948–1974.* London: Hurst.

Rutland, Peter. 1994. Democracy and Nationalism in Armenia. *Europe–Asia Studies,* 46 (5): 839–61.

Sabbat-Swidlicka, Anna. 1993. The Polish Elections: The Church, the Right and the Left. *RFE/RL Research Report,* 2 (40): 24–30.

Sakwa, Richard. 1999. *Postcommunism.* Buckingham: Open University Press.

Sakwa, Richard, and Mark Webber. 1999. The Commonwealth of Independent States, 1991–1998: Stagnation and Survival. *Europe–Asia Studies*, 51 (3): 379–415.

Sandel, Michael J. 1996. *Democracy's Discontent: America in Search of a Public Philosophy*. Cambridge, MA: Harvard University Press.

Sartori, Giovanni. 1976. *Parties and Party Systems: A Framework for Analysis*. Cambridge: Cambridge University Press.

1991. Rethinking Democracy: Bad Polity and Bad Politics. *International Social Science Journal*, 129: 437–50.

Schedler, A. 1998. What Is Democratic Consolidation? *Journal of Democracy*, 9: 91–107.

Schmitter, Philippe, and Terry Lynn Karl. 1994. The Conceptual Travels of Transitologists and Consolidologists: How Far to the East Should They Attempt to Go? *Slavic Review*, 53 (1): 173–85.

Schneider, Eberhard. 1997. Begriffe und theoretische Konzepte zur politischen Transformation. 17–25 in Höhmann, 1997.

Schöpflin, George. 1993. *Politics in Eastern Europe*. Oxford: Blackwell.

Schumpeter, Joseph A. 1942. *Capitalism, Socialism, and Democracy*. New York: Harper.

Schwartz, Karl-Peter. 1993. *Tschechen und Slowaken: Der lange Weg zur friedlichen Trennung*. Vienna: Europaverlag.

Seidel, Gill. 1985. Political Discourse Analysis. 43–60 in Teun A. van Dijk (ed.), *Handbook of Discourse Analysis*, vol. IV. London: Academic.

Seleny, Anna. 1999. Old Political Rationalities and New Democracies: Compromise and Confrontation in Hungary and Poland. *World Politics*, 51 (4): 484–519.

Sher, G. 1977. *Praxis*. Bloomington: Indiana University Press.

Shevtsova, Lilia, and Scott Bruckner. 1997. Where Is Russia Headed? Toward Stability or Crisis? *Journal of Democracy*, 8 (1): 12–26.

Shue, Vivienne. 1992. China: Transition Postponed? *Problems of Communism*, 41: 157–65.

Shulhyn, A. 1963. The Period of the Central Rada (Council). 725–46 in Volodymyr Kubijovič (ed.), *Ukraine: A Concise Encyclopedia*, vol. I. Toronto: University of Toronto Press.

Šimečka, Martin. 1997. Slovakia's Lonely Independence. *Transitions*, 4 (3): 14–21.

Šimečka, Martin, and Stefan Hríb. 1999. Slovensko nie je dierou na mape Európy [Slovakia is not a hole on the map of Europe; an interview with Madeleine Albright]. *Domino Fórum*, January 20–27, 1999.

Skilling, H. Gordon. 1976. *Czechoslovakia's Interrupted Revolution*. Princeton, NJ: Princeton University Press.

1981. *Charter 77 and Human Rights in Czechoslovakia.* London: George Allen and Unwin.

Skocpol, Theda. 1979. *States and Social Revolutions.* Cambridge: Cambridge University Press.

Sowards, Steven. 1996. Lecture 12: Bosnia-Hercegovina and the Failure of Reform in Austria-Hungary. On-line at http://www.lib.msu.edu/sowards/balkan/lect12htm.

Stepan, Alfred, and Cindy Skach. 1993. Constitutional Frameworks and Democratic Consolidation: Parliamentarism vs. Presidentialism. *World Politics,* 46 (1): 1–22.

Stephenson, William. 1953. *The Study of Behavior: Q Technique and Its Methodology.* Chicago: University of Chicago Press.

Stokes, Gail. 1989. The Social Origins of East European Politics. 210–51 in Chirot, 1989b.

Stone, Daniel Z. 1990. Democratic Thought in Eighteenth-Century Poland. 55–72 in M. B. Biskupski and James S. Pula (eds.), *Polish Democratic Thought from the Renaissance to the Great Emigration.* New York: Columbia University Press.

Subtelny, Orest. 1998. *Ukraine: A History.* 2nd edn. Toronto: University of Toronto Press.

Sunstein, Cass R. 1988. Beyond the Republican Revival. *Yale Law Journal,* 97 (8): 1539–90.

Suny, Ronald. 1989. *The Making of the Georgian Nation.* London: Tauris.

   1993. *Looking toward Ararat: Armenia in Modern History.* Bloomington: Indiana University Press.

   2000. Review of Joseph R. Masih and Robert O. Krikorian, *Armenia: At the Crossroads. Europe–Asia Studies,* 52: 726–7.

Suster, Zeljan E. 1998. Development of Political Democracy and Political Party Pluralism in Serbia 1903–1914. *East European Quarterly,* 31 (4): 435–48.

Szomolányi, Sona. 1997. *Slovakia: Problems of Democratic Consolidation and the Struggle for the Rules of the Game.* Bratislava: Slovak Political Science Association and Friedrich Ebert Foundation.

Tétrault, Mary Ann, and Robin L. Teske. 1997. The Struggle to Democratize the Slovak Republic. *Current History,* March: 135–9.

Tigrid, Pavel. 1975. The Prague Coup of 1948: The Elegant Takeover. 399–432 in Thomas Hammond (ed.), *The Anatomy of Communist Takeovers.* New Haven, CT: Yale University Press.

Tilly, Charles. 1993. *European Revolutions, 1492–1992.* Oxford: Basil Blackwell.

Timmermann, Heinz, and Alexander Ott. 1997. Restauration und Reaktion in Belarus. 94–105 in Höhmann, 1997.

Tismaneanu, Vladimir. 1998. *Fantasies of Salvation: Democracy, Nationalism, and Myth in Post-Communist Europe.* Princeton, NJ: Princeton University Press.

  1999. Understanding National Stalinism: Reflections on Ceauşescu's Socialism. *Communist and Post-Communist Studies,* 32 (2): 155–73.

Todorova, Maria. 1997. *Imagining the Balkans.* New York: Oxford University Press.

Tolz, Vera. 1998. Forging the Nation: National Identity and Nation Building in Post-Communist Russia. *Europe–Asia Studies,* 50 (6): 993–1022.

Tolz, Vera, and Irina Busygina. 1997. Regional Governors and the Kremlin: The Ongoing Battle for Power. *Communist and Post-Communist Studies,* 30 (4): 401–26.

Tompson, W. 2000. Putin's Power Plays. *World Today,* 56 (7): 14–16.

Toulmin, Stephen. 1958. *The Uses of Argument.* Cambridge: Cambridge University Press.

Unger, Roberto M., and Zhiyuan Cui. 1994. China in the Russian Mirror. *New Left Review,* 208: 78–87.

Urban, Michael, with Vyacheslav Igrunov and Sergei Mitrokhin. 1997. *The Rebirth of Politics in Russia.* Cambridge: Cambridge University Press.

Urban, Michael, and Jan Zaprudnik. 1993. Belarus: A Long Road to Nationhood. 99–120 in Bremmer and Taras, 1993.

Utechin, Sergei. 1964. *Russian Political Thought: A Concise History.* New York: Praeger.

Vachudová, Milada, and Tim Snyder. 1997. Are Transitions Transitory? Two Types of Political Change in Eastern Europe since 1989. *East European Politics and Societies,* 11: 1–35.

Verdery, Katherine. 1991. *National Ideology under Socialism: Identity and Cultural Politics in Ceauşescu's Romania.* Berkeley: University of California Press.

Verheijen, Tony. 1995. *Constitutional Pillars for New Democracies: The Cases of Bulgaria and Romania.* Leiden: DSWO Press.

Walicki, Andrzej. 1989. *The Enlightenment and the Birth of Modern Nationhood: Polish Political Thought from Noble Republicanism to Tadeusz Kościuszko.* Notre Dame, IN: University of Notre Dame Press.

Wallerstein, Immanuel. 1974. *The Modern World System.* New York: Academic Press.

Wheaton, Bernard, and Zdeněk Kavan. 1992. *The Velvet Revolution.* Boulder, CO: Westview.

White, Gordon. 1994. Democratization and Economic Reform in China. *Australian Journal of Chinese Affairs,* 31: 73–92.

White, Stephen, Judy Batt, and Paul Lewis (eds.). 1993. *Developments in East European Politics.* London: Macmillan.

White, Stephen, Alex Pravda, and Zvi Gitelman (eds.). 1994. *Developments in Russian and Post-Soviet Politics*. London: Macmillan.

Wightman, Gordon. 1993. The Czech and Slovak Republics. 51–65 in White, Batt and Lewis, 1993.

Wilson, Andrew. 1997. Ukraine: Two Presidents and Their Powers. 67–105 in Ray Taras (ed.), *Postcommunist Presidents*. Cambridge: Cambridge University Press.

Wilson, Andrew, and Artur Bilous. 1993. Political Parties in Ukraine. *Europe–Asia Studies*, 45 (4): 693–703.

Wise, Charles R., and Trevor L. Brown. 1999. The Separation of Powers in Ukraine. *Communist and Post-Communist Studies*, 32 (1): 23–44.

Wolchik, Sharon. 1992. Czechoslovakia. 119–63 in Held, 1992.

    1995. The Politics of Transition and the Break-Up of Czechoslovakia. 225–44 in Musil, 1995.

Wolinetz, Steven B. (ed.). 1998. *Party Systems*. Aldershot: Ashgate.

Yenal, Oktay. 1990. Chinese Reforms, Inflation and the Allocation of Investment in a Socialist Economy. *World Development*, 18: 707–21.

Žák, Václav. 1995. The Velvet Divorce: Institutional Foundations. 245–68 in Musil, 1995.

Zakaria, Fareed. 1997. The Rise of Illiberal Democracy. *Foreign Affairs*, 76 (6): 22–43.

Zaprudnik, Jan. 1993. *Belarus: At a Crossroads in History*. Boulder, CO: Westview.

Zhang, Mingshu. 1994. *Zhongguo "zhengzhi ren"* (The Chinese "political man"). Beijing: Zhongguo shehui kexue chubanshe.

Zhu, Jianhua, Xinshu Zhao, and Hairong Li. 1990. Public Political Consciousness in China: An Empirical Profile. *Asian Survey*, 30: 992–1006.

Index

Aarebrot, Frank, 15–16, 206–7
Abkhazia, 134, 147–8, 157
Africa, 4, 108
agency, 25, 27
Ágh, Attila, 192, 257
Albania, 110, 177, 257
Albanians, 62, 69
Albright, Madeleine, 178
Alexander, King, 57
Americas, 108
    Latin, 256
    see also United States of America
Anatolia, 133
Angola, 108
anti-politics, 228–9, 237,
    248
Arendt, Hannah, 236
Armenia, 24–5, 131, 133–46, 156, 168,
    273
    authoritarianism, 145
    clanism, 137, 138
    constitution, 136
    diaspora, 134, 135
    discourses in, 137–46, 266, 269, 271,
    272
    elections, 135–6
    identity problems, 133, 146
    nationalism, 135, 136, 145
    parliamentary assassinations, 135, 136,
    137

pre-communist history, 133
prospects, 146
war with Azerbaijan, 134,
    136
Armenians, 147
Asia, 108
    Central, 80
    East, 53, 54
Ataturk, Mustapha Kemal, 133
Auer, Stefan, 12
Australia, 108, 267
authoritarianism, 10, 11, 16, 111, 114,
    154, 171, 206, 237, 240, 263–5, 271,
    272; see also individual country
    entries
'Autumn of the People', 3, 31, 59, 60,
    236
Azerbaijan, 133, 134, 135
Azeris, 147

Balcerowicz, Leszek, 226
Balkans, 16, 171, 192, 206, 257; see also
    Europe, Southeastern
    backwardness, 206–7
    mentality, 215, 257–8, 267
Baltic states, 15–16, 109, 110, 147, 158,
    206
Bankowicz, Marek, 218
Basque country, 256
Beck, Ulrich, 18